THE NURSE & THE POSTMASTER

DAVID & ZENI TARLING

POST OFFICE

venue~

Order this book online at www.trafford.com/07-0450
or email orders@trafford.com

Most Trafford titles are also available at major online book retailers.

Note for Librarians: A cataloguing record for this book is available from Library
and Archives Canada at www.collectionscanada.ca/amicus/index-e.html

Printed in Victoria, BC, Canada.

ISBN: 978-1-4251-2046-7

*We at Trafford believe that it is the responsibility of us all, as both individuals
and corporations, to make choices that are environmentally and socially sound.
You, in turn, are supporting this responsible conduct each time you purchase a
Trafford book, or make use of our publishing services. To find out how you are
helping, please visit www.trafford.com/responsiblepublishing.html*

*Our mission is to efficiently provide the world's finest, most comprehensive
book publishing service, enabling every author to experience success.
To find out how to publish your book, your way, and have it available
worldwide, visit us online at www.trafford.com/10510*

 www.trafford.com

North America & international
toll-free: 1 888 232 4444 (USA & Canada)
phone: 250 383 6864 ♦ fax: 250 383 6804 ♦ email: info@trafford.com

The United Kingdom & Europe
phone: +44 (0)1865 722 113 ♦ local rate: 0845 230 9601
facsimile: +44 (0)1865 722 868 ♦ email: info.uk@trafford.com

10 9 8 7 6 5 4 3

FIRST AND FOREMOST

A SPECIAL thanks to Andrew Tzionis of AM Venue Ltd. in Limassol Cyprus, for his friendship and assistance with designing the cover and graphics of this book.

A brief outline of two people's lives, how we met and the travels we are fortunate to have been on. We live our lives to the full and hope to continue travelling.

I would like to express my warmest thanks, to my loving husband, my soul mate, best friend and co-author.

This book is dedicated to our children. Giles, Craig and Sarah who have supported and encouraged both of us, since we have been living together. We have now left them to seek their own independence. This is the hardest decision we both had to make, but they have managed admirably.

A special thanks also to my mother, sisters, brothers and their families and friends; also David's other child, John as well as his sister and family.

It is also in memory of my sister Sonia, who died in Dubai, on 13th January 2006.

I would like to extend my appreciation to the Churchill Hospital Oxford for giving me the opportunity to take up my career in nursing. I am very proud to have been a nurse, especially carrying out my training in England. The modern day home of nursing, that was started by Florence Nightingale in 1853. I believe;

NURSING IS ONE OF THE BEST VOCATIONS IN THE WORLD.

nurse *n.*
a person formally educated
and trained in the care of the
sick or infirm

postmaster *n.*
the official in charge
of a post office

David & Zeni Tarling

venue

Book 1

Philippines

1

TRUST me, I am a nurse. My name is Zenaida Tarling (nee Ledesma) or Zeni for short.

I was born in the Philippines, known as the Pearl of the Orient Sea, which has the following South East Asian countries as neighbours: China and Hong Kong, Malaysia, Indonesia, Borneo, Thailand, and Japan. The Philippine archipelago consists of 7,107 islands and 200 volcanoes, a number of these are still active and there is frequent seismic activity, the majority being insignificant. The last major earthquake was in 2004 in Mindanao which measured 6.5.

Typhoons are experienced on the islands every year.

There are three main seasons. The hot and dry season, which is from March to May, the wet season runs from June to October and the cool dry season is from November to February.

Three seas surround the islands, the Pacific Ocean, the South China Sea and the Celebes Sea, giving 17,500 km of coastline. It has a population of almost 88 million and is the largest Christian country in Asia. 80% are Catholic, 15%

Muslims, the majority of whom are based in Mindanao, and the remaining 5% are of various denominations.

The country is divided into three regions of islands.

Luzon, where the Nation's capital, Manila, is situated. Metropolitan Manila is the 11th most populous metropolitan area in the world. Quezon City which is part of Metropolitan Manila has the largest population of the Philippines.

The Visayas Islands has western, central and eastern districts. Cebu City being the main tourist resort, Mindanao in the south has 6 districts including the Autonomous Region in Muslim Mindanao.

The country is rich in natural beauty, having many different types of plants. Exotic orchids thrive well here and there are around 900 different species.

Filipino culture is a mixture of Malay, Chinese, Spanish and American influences. Independence was declared from the Spanish in 1898 and was gained from the United States of America on 4th July 1946.

The Spanish legacies survive in the ceremonies and street parties as well as the catholic religion and the major introduction of modern education. The American influence is all around with the English language widely spoken and almost all schools teach in English. The Philippines is the 3rd largest English speaking country in the world. Other American influences include fast food, music and a great knowledge of films and the Hollywood scene.

The largest U.S.Air Force Base outside the mainland of the United States was in Pampanga, which is in the Central Luzon region. At its peak it had around 15,000 people living there. In 1942 it was taken over by the Japanese in World War II and it was finally regained in 1945. The nearby volcano of Mount Pinatubo erupted in 1991.It was 490 years since its last eruption and the Americans decided to pull out of the area and the base was handed over to the Philippine Government.

Since leaving my native land 34 years ago, it has changed dramatically. It has become more cosmopolitan, and is one of the world's fastest growing regions. Commercial and residential areas have increased with large shopping malls, with boutiques selling designer clothes, electrical appliance shops, bookshops, internet cafes. In fact everything you see in all other countries of the world. There are also international hotels, restaurants, and new high tech hospitals; tall skyscrapers which house large banks and commercial offices. New road systems contribute to the development of the country, winding their way in and around Manila and other regions are developing the same as Luzon.

This modern, thriving country, with many schools and universities, was known as one of the best seats of learning in South East Asia. There are around 8 million Filipinos working overseas and it has emerged as the largest provider of health care personnel. In every hospital in the USA, UK, and Saudi Arabia, you will find a Filipino doctor, nurse, medical technologist, physiotherapist or maybe all of the above. Despite the astronomical cost of education in the Philippines, the school of nursing is booming. As the salary for nurses is not as attractive at home, many seek fame and fortune overseas. Often, parents have to sell their property to subsidise the training cost. I was fortunate to train as a nurse in Oxford, England.

My youngest sister, Mary Jane, graduated from the University of the East, in Manila and is now, a practicing nurse in the USA. Her son Mark, who is only 10, says he would like to become a nurse. Another sister, Belinda trained in Kansas, USA and currently works there as a nurse. Her daughter Katy is currently studying nursing, as is another of my nieces, Hannah. Her sister Michi however, worked in the school of nursing and was responsible for the enrolment of students into the nursing programme in California. Two other sisters, Lourdes and Cora, are both in the healthcare business. My sister-in-law, babes, who is also a nurse is married to my brother Maurice. They live in Minnesota along with their daughter Nina. Another sister Sonia lived in the Philippines and owned a laundry business. However, she was chronically ill and unfortunately fully aware of the inside of hospitals. She died in January 2006. My brother Junior, lived in America, but is now back home in the Philippines. Another brother, Julio, died of cancer at 40. My sister, Rosemarie, lives in Brescia, Italy with her husband Fabri and their children. She works in the family business. I am the second child of the ten siblings. Both parents being devout Catholics, did not agree with family planning. My father, Leonardo, but known as Leo, died on 20th of August 2001. My mother, Rebecca, is an active 78 year old, and lives with my sister Mary Jane and her two sons, Mark and Timothy (also known as TJ).

I grew up and was raised in the city of Manila during the time of Elvis Presley, the Beatles, Elizabeth Taylor, John F. Kennedy, and his wife Jackie. Like everyone else who lived during that time, I will always remember the assassination of President Kennedy. When I was 6, there was an eclipse of the sun, which Mother made us look at through a bowl of water.

The Beatles landed in the country on 3rd of July 1966, after a 2 week tour of Germany and Japan. They performed two concerts at the Rizal Memorial Football Stadium and attracted an audience of 80,000 people. There was a mix up over an invitation from the then President Marcos and his wife Imelda, to meet them. Imelda Marcos became famous for her huge shoe collection.

We lived on 5th Avenue, Grace Park, a suburb of Manila. We, at that time being my parents, Sonia, my older sister, who was born 5th of January 1947 and my late brother, Julio, born 19th of July 1951 and myself. The five bedroom house also had a living room, dinning room, a kitchen and a balcony. There were two staircases, one leading to the entrance of the house, the other towards the outside bathroom and toilet. The downstairs area was converted into flats for our relatives. The neighbourhood was near the riverbank and there were tropical trees such as guava, mango, cashew nuts, jack fruit, papaya, as well as banana growing everywhere. Beautiful scented flowers of all colours bloomed throughout the year. Sampaguita is the national flower, but other common flowers such as the hibiscus, bougainvillea, gardenia, dahlias, and jasmine, make the rainbow of colours very appealing. Within walking distance from home was a large Chinese community. Every year they had festivals and organized events depicting their culture and traditions and Sonia and I would go and watch. We would also play around the house with our cousins. Hopscotch, tug of war, and hide and seek being the favourites. We really enjoyed playing in the safe environment that I often explored before starting school.

When my father returned from his journeys he would always bring us toys. Sonia and I shared the miniature iron and ironing board and the doll's house, with its small, well crafted furniture. Julio, played with his cars and train set, or even dressed up in his cowboy suit. My mother's sisters would often come and stay. Auntie Miling, made Sonia and I beautiful dresses, and Auntie Virgie took care of us when my parents went out. The love and care in a happy environment gave me a good foundation for my future life, and I would like to think that it made me a better person.

The first memory I have of my journey through life, was when I was about 5 and being held in the arms of my late father, who was trying to console me, whilst I was crying. I don't know why I was so upset though. I started my schooling in Kindergarten before attending the local school. One day, my father parked his black Buick car outside the nursery. When my cousin and Julio got inside, it rolled into the street. Luckily no one was hurt. The school was walking distance from home, and as mother walked us to school, I clearly remember the beautiful blue bells. The early morning mist would glisten on them as the sun rose higher in the sky. This made me appreciate nature more and observe all the different species of plant life, surrounding us.

In school all of our classes were taught in English. The Pilipino language is used throughout and is also a core subject. Good manners and right conduct were taught. I will never forget when I had learnt to count. I would go around the house counting the number of wooden strips that made up the hardwood floor. As soon as I was able to read, I would buy comics and magazines. Mickey Mouse and Goofy were my favourite cartoon characters, whilst in the magazines I would read about the lives of personalities in the news. After leaving school, we would go to the local market. There would be people examining the varieties of fresh fruits, vegetables, fish, and meat, available from the numerous stalls before making a purchase. Chickens were sold live and were slaughtered immediately before cooking. I never liked going to the kitchen when chicken was on the menu. On returning home, I would often sit by the window sill and draw pictures of the house and garden, whilst also looking at the cashew nut tree, as over the weeks it became heavy with its fruit.

My parents employed a 30 year old, single mother as a maid. She brought along her 3 year old daughter, and when Sonia and I were off school we would play with her. The daughter could only have liquid food, as she could not chew anything solid.

The clothes hung on the washing line at the side of the house, and turned very crisp, as they dried in the blistering sun. On Friday, my father would often meet us at the end of the road. He would buy us treats of chocolate, sweets, or grapes. If he had been to the summer capital Baguio, we would get a large basket of succulent, sweet and lovely, red strawberries that grew there abundantly because of the cooler climate. The local corner shop was owned by two Chinese brothers and if mother needed anything, I would be sent to get it. I didn't mind, as I could also buy some sweets, bubble gum or fresh pork scratching for myself. Weekends would find us driving around different areas. It was really enjoyable, as we stopped and watched the big ships in the harbour, or went to Luneta Park, now Rizal Park. The sea wall faced the palm tree lined bay, with wonderful sunsets that seemed to set the sea on fire. Occasionally we would have a picnic.

Every year, between June and October, there are monsoons. Flooding is normal. We would stay indoors and look at the river, which was only 100 yards away. Fortunately our house was on a hill, so we could see the river, as it widened, taking all the green/brown water, at a head long speed to its outlet. Surplus water spilled over and flooded the surrounding areas, before gradually receding, leaving a wet, brown quagmire of land in its wake. When the rain was not torrential, Sonia and I used to go outside and play. It was a lovely feeling, as the cool, heavy drops of water vibrated on our bodies before it fell to the ground, disappearing quickly in the searing heat.

One day, Julio went missing. The whole neighbourhood helped the family to search of him. My father went down to the river, walking backwards and forwards in the water, which was just above his knee, whilst checking both banks. The search lasted the whole day. Late in the afternoon, Julio turned up with one of our neighbours. She had evidently taken him for a walk. Poor Julio looked really bewildered and frightened. We were all delighted to have him back.

I will always remember the woman who took Julio for the walk. She was in her fifties and an alcoholic. She looked dreadful, with her uncombed, frizzy hair. Her deep red mouth indicated that she had been chewing, beetle nut. The habit of chewing beetle nut is used as substitute for cigarettes, although it is a mild hallucinogen. The nut is used, not only in the Philippines, but also in surrounding countries. It produces a red juice, when chewed, which should be spat out. It makes the mouth look very red and in the long run, stains the teeth and can cause oral cancer. Her sunken eyes glared into nothing. Her incoherent speech and alcoholic breath were proof of her disabling habit. Her unsteady gait always made us wonder if she was about to fall.

2

CHRISTMAS, is the most celebrated festival in the Philippines, as in most Christian countries. The cool breeze of the December weather felt lovely upon opening my window in the morning. Like towns throughout the world, decorations are being sold and adorn most areas. The most creative are the lanterns, which are hung and displayed in most houses. They are very colourful and the motifs are all different shapes and sizes. People bustle around preparing for the event, buying presents and all types of delicacies. How I love the magical atmosphere! People seem friendlier. Friends and relatives, gather together along with the neighbours at social gatherings. Carol singers add that little extra bit to the celebrations. These start on the 16th of December with pre dawn masses. The stalls outside the church sell various sweet and savoury dishes, such as steamed rice cake with a grated coconut topping and steamed yam. The celebrations culminate with a midnight mass on the 24th. Families then go home for a post midnight feast. Some of the dishes that would be served at this feast are succulent pig roasting on the spit, the leg of sweet cured ham, arroz valenciana (sticky rice, with saffron, along with chicken , pork, peas, and raisins) Quezo de Bola (cheese), pansit(noodles), chestnuts, apples, grapes, cakes, mashed sweet yam, fruit salad, and other delicacies.

The opening of Christmas gifts on the 25th is quite exciting. We also get to visit relatives and godparents who give us more gifts. One Christmas season, my parents went to a staff Christmas party held by the Shell Oil Company. Their picture ended up in the company's magazine. I felt really proud.

Just after my tenth birthday, I was admitted with a bad chest infection to the old St. Luke's Hospital, in the centre of Manila. This was where I met my first nurse. She was looking very smart in her white, pressed uniform, white stockings and shoes, and the white cap covering the top of her black hair. She was so gentle and reassuring, that I decided there and then that I would become a nurse. This was also the first time I tasted peaches. As I don't think they are grown on the island, I assumed they were canned. I also suffered badly with nose bleeds. On many occasions, I remember mother taking me to the local clinic, which was well equipped and spotlessly clean. I would be given, an intramuscular injection of vitamin k, as I would bleed profusely. I will always remember, how clean the clinics and hospitals were, especially the San Lazaro Hospital which specialises in skin disorders. I had a bad wound on my leg, which would not heal, until they gave me the correct medical treatment. I certainly appreciated all the help given to me and it made me more resolute to pursue a career in nursing.

One summer holiday, was spent in the province of Negros Occidental. Both my parents were born there and my two grandmothers lived there. The island of Negros is part of the group of the Visayas islands. The island is divided into Negros Oriental, the South Eastern part and the Occidental section, which is the North West. We went by ferry and had to spend a night at sea. The sleeping area had numerous folding canvas beds, which were surrounded by luggage and varying sizes of boxes brought by travellers. As Julio was too young, it was only Sonia and I that wandered around the ship. I remember, watching the ropes being cast off, before we slowly pulled away, from Pier 2 in Manila. It was lovely looking over the rail at the water below. The waves rolled gently by, until I saw the sun set below the watery horizon. As dawn approached so did the island. We could see the house lights on the distant shore, as we edged closer to the harbour of the capital city Bacolod. The city grew with the sugar industry. Victoria Milling reputedly had the world's largest sugar refinery here. As soon as the ferry docked, passengers started unloading their goods and disembarking. We used the local public transport to get to my mother's mother home. She lived 30 miles to the north of Bacolod, in the coastal town of Manapla. When we arrived, she was standing in the doorway of her shop. She was a slim lady, in her late fifties, with slightly greying hair, which was combed back into a bun. Her black sarong and clean, white, embroidered blouse, made the rosary beads around her neck more noticeable. This religious lady would go to church every day before opening her shop. She offered prayers for us and we were blessed. I believe she was blessed also, as she brought up 8 children and lived until nearly 100 years.

We stayed in the house for a few days. The large wooden home had no rear garden. The front area had plenty of beautiful, sweet scented flowers. From the side of the house, you could see the area used for cock fighting. As soon as the sun rose, we would head towards the beach, going by fruit trees and coconut palms with the green fruits hanging from the tree. Upon arrival at Balulan beach, we would climb down the rocks, and run around on the pebbles which lay in front of the very pale, crystal blue water. The gentle waves would come on shore and disappear into the crevices of the rocks and then retreat into the Visayan Sea. As we couldn't swim, we ran through the shallow water, throwing stones at the waves. We would collect different types of empty shells and play various games with them. Sonia and I would also go down to the river on occasion with our cousins. The area was so green and picturesque.

After our time in Manapla, we travelled by jeep to the small village of Guicay. This was the home of my father's mother. The village was so small and very few people lived there. The jeep was unable to make it to our final destination. This meant we had to walk the last few miles. The blistering sun shone through the palm trees. It was so peaceful, like paradise. The silence was only broken by a flock of birds taking flight from the greenery nearby. Local children walked barefoot along the paddy fields. I felt grateful for my shoes, as the penetrating heat made the ground very hot. In the distance, a farmer could be seen, ploughing his field with a water buffalo pulling the plough. The farmer was trying so hard to guide it. When we were tired of walking, we sat in the shade of a coconut palm. Someone my father knew was passing by, and he asked if we would like a drink.

He saw the smile on our faces and quickly climbed the tree, brought down a coconut and broke open the shell. It was so refreshing. Soon after we came across a few houses; some were no more than huts. One had a herd of goats in the garden. Finally we arrived at our destination. I recognised my grandmother right away as she had visited us in Manila. Her stoop and grey hair made you think she was older than 60 years, even though she was dressed in a colourful striped sarong and thin white blouse. Her house was built in the traditional way. It had a raised bamboo floor, bamboo walls and a thatched roof made from palm tree leaves. There was no electricity and the cooking was carried out on an open fire. Cold, crystal clear water was drawn from a well nearby. To take a shower one would use water from a large, elevated drum, which stored rain water. If there was no rain, one had to go down to the river to fetch some water. Paraffin lamps were used to light the houses at night. If you didn't want to sleep on the bamboo bed, you could always sleep on a mat, which was made of woven palm tree leaves.

The chickens outside would act as an alarm clock, waking us up at the crack of dawn. The large garden was home to coconut, banana and various other fruit trees. The enormous vegetable patch was the source of the daily food requirements. It was also a source of food for many birds, as they pecked at the vegetables. I'm sure Grandma didn't mind. There was no stress in the village. No bills and all the food was natural and organic. That may have helped her live till the age of 98. My cousins, Sonia and I would explore the huge sugar plantations nearby. I really enjoyed the holiday. It gave me an insight into how the village people lived and the absolute beauty of the place. I now realise how fortunate I was to have seen, lived, and experienced the natural beauty and goodness of the Island. One day, I hope to return to the Province of Negros Occidental and the small village of Guicay.

3

MY final year in elementary school saw me leaving St Joseph Academy. It has now been renamed La Consolacion College. It was the end of me catching the school bus and having to recite the rosary until we got off. Discipline played an important role in the school, run by the Mother Superior, who was also the Headmistress. No more exercises on the balancing beam and I had to say goodbye, to the white, long sleeved blouse and blue pinafore dress, which was the school uniform. Just memories remain of school Field Day when our class performed a Mexican dance, dressed in a Mexican costume made of taffeta. I would no longer be attending the private school run by the Augustinian Order in Grace Park, Caloocan City. We had lived in Grace Park for nearly 11 years, during which time the family had increased. Maurice was born on 22nd September 1953 and Lourdes my second sister joined us on 7th May 1955. I clearly remember her being born, at home behind a makeshift room. Blankets hung around the bed so we couldn't see what was happening. Cora my third sister was born almost 2 years later in the hospital. Junior on the 22 November 1959 was my youngest brother. Belinda emerged into the world on 16 July 1961 to complete the Grace Park family.

My father was asked to relocate to the Province of Batangas, to work at the Shell refinery in Tabangao, which was about a 2 hour drive from Manila. Moving day was quite eventful. The younger members of the family sat in the cab of the flat bed lorry. The older ones sat on the back with the furniture, along with the neighbours who helped us move. I clearly remember wearing a straw hat, whilst relaxing on the sofa with the sun shinning on me. The bumpy road and swinging vehicle, made me realise how lucky I was to be sitting there, as we drove along to the brand new, rented bungalow.

Sonia and I helped unload the furniture. There was a cananga tree, which is known as ylang-ylang. The lovely fragrance of the plant lingered in the air. The extract of the plants are used in perfumes around the world. Tropical trees abound in this sleepy village. Walking down the road you would come across mango, orange, lemon, satsuma and avocado trees. We had only been in the place for a few months when Maurice fell off the fence and onto the vegetable patch which was father's pride and joy. The rows of cabbage, onions and carrots looked a sorry sight.

Sonia, Julio, Lourdes, and I attended St. Bridget's College. This private school had an excellent reputation and had an immaculately manicured garden, with sweet scented flowers. It was started in 1913, as a girls'school. The Bishop of the diocese, the very reverend Joseph Petrelli, asked for help from Sisters of The Order of the Good Shepherd who were working in Rangoon, Burma, at the time. Later Irish and

American Sisters came over from the main house in France. Boys were excluded until 1953. Maurice went to a different nearby school, as his class at St. Bridget's College was full.

One of the pupils was an American girl who was the same age as myself, but in a different class, and was pretty and smart. She never mingled with us, and travelled to and from school in a horse drawn carriage. I was told her parents owned an ice plant, which seemed a pretty cool occupation.

Lourdes, attended kindergarten in the school and looked very cute, in her white short sleeved blouse and blue pinafore dress. She would always cling to me and I would hold her hand whenever possible. We never went away, as our relatives usually came to visit us. I remember feeling very lonely, leaving my friends and relatives back in Manila. Our most important visitor visited daily, delivering warm, fresh bread, which we would eat at the big kitchen table. The bread was buttered and then topped with thickly spread strawberry or coconut jam. We often strolled to the nearby creek and dipped our feet in the cool, shallow, flowing water. I remember perspiration trickling down my forehead, as the warm sun penetrated my skin.

Opposite our house was some vacant land. My parents decided to buy it and within a few months our new home was built. The large acacia tree next to the house would now be across the road. I wondered if another of our regular visitors would come and see us in our new place. He would always be in his green leather suit and greet us with his favourite saying. "Tok-Eh" It would always be in the early hours, when he appeared, walking along the ceiling! We would usually call our mother and the 14", flat looking lizard, the Tokay Gecko, would be dispatched through the window. Fortunately, he didn't like the road and stayed in his home in the acacia tree.

The new, wooden house was built on stilts. It had three bedrooms, a living room, kitchen and bathroom. What I liked most of all was the balcony. I would sit there for hours, until the sun sank below the horizon. Although the house was bigger, the garden was smaller, and surrounded by bushes. One of which was coffee. The region was known as a coffee growing area. One day mother came home with a pig. My parents, Sonia and I looked after it, as everyone else was too young. Mother decided to start a small laundry business for the Shell oil refinery club house, and hired a lady to help. You should have seen the garden. It was usually adorned with white table cloths, sheets and towels.

My father, proved to be very popular at work and people would often turn up at the house with fresh fruit and other delicacies. This was in appreciation for his help in finding them work, usually at the refinery. His bosses who were mainly British, Dutch, American and Filipino would always blow their horns as they drove by. That kept the Gecko away.

A wife of one of the managers went home to Holland and returned with some souvenirs and clothes, her children had grown out of and gave them to our family. Wasn't that kind?

The neighbour's immaculate garden was full of bougainvilleas, hibiscus, poinsettias and dahlias. They looked lovely with their vibrant colours.

We only stayed in the region for a couple of years, as Cora was knocked down by a passenger jeep, in front of our house and was rushed to hospital with severe facial injuries. My father took the driver to court, but dropped the case when he found out that his lawyer was also defending the driver! In fact he was a close relative.

My father was furious and decided to get a transfer back to Manila, which the company approved. We found a home for our pet pig, and said goodbye to our friends and neighbours.

Once in the Coloocan district of Manila, we found temporary accommodation with my Auntie Milling and Uncle Carling and their three children, Vangie, Alex and Julius. As their wooden house was built on my parents land, it was decided to physically move it to vacant land nearby. Four long, strong pieces of wood were placed under the front, back and the sides of the house. It was then carried by a large number of people, to the new site, about 20 metres away. After being set down on the base it was then secured. Our new house, which was colossal and built of concrete blocks, was then built on the now vacant site.

It was here that Rosemarie was born on 5th May 1963. I went back to St. Joseph Academy, whilst Sonia studied commerce at University of the East in Manila.

One of my biology projects was about centipedes. The project required drawing a centipede, illustrating its various parts, and it would be presented on open day. My father asked a graphic designer friend to help out. He did. It was a brilliant oil painting, on a 2ft square piece of plywood. Every weekend, I would help my mother with the household chores and looking after the children. On the way back from the market, I would stop and buy some treats, with my pocket money. Usually a magazine with stories and facts about film stars. An occasional treat, would be when we went to the cinema. We saw a lot of Elvis Presley films, as well as "The Ten Commandments", "How the West was Won", "The Sound of Music", and other family films. We didn't have a television, just an old Philips radio. Look at what the youngsters today have: T.V., DVD, MP3, radio, computer, digital camera, and not forgetting the mobile phone. Even so I am sure I was a lot happier than most of them are today.

Sweet sixteen and my final year at high school. Hurray!! I had graduated. Wearing my cap and gown, I waited with the others until my name was called, then walked up and collected my certificate. I am sure our parents were proud of us all. We said our goodbyes, but unfortunately never kept in touch with each other. I often wonder what has happened to everyone! My father took voluntary redundancy and decided to go into business. We moved to another area of Coloocan City. A new house, with a small grocery store attached.

During this time I enrolled at the Far Eastern University, in a Pre-Nursing course. It was a two year course, leading to a two year nursing internship programme, including practical work at the hospital. There were now two of us at University and money was a bit tight. After a few years we moved to Quezon City, another area of metropolitan Manila. It is a very popular area and in the commercial district with plenty of shops, supermarkets and large buildings. Araneta Stadium was the local landmark and in 1960, was the world's largest domed coliseum. My parents rented a house, as they couldn't find anywhere big enough for our large family. After several years, they moved to Antipolo which is just outside Manila. My father was offered a job by the Secretary of State for Social Services. As one of his former bosses from the Shell Company in Manila, he knew my father was a good driver and confidante. At that time, my parents were operating a fruit and vegetable stall in Cubao, an area within the city. They would drive to the nearby province and buy all the fruit and vegetables, which at times I used to help sell.

Sonia became a working student and got a job as a secretary in one of the law offices. She was offered a job in the Social Services Department a few years later. All children in the family, except Rosemarie, were now in school. I finished my Pre-Nursing course and intended to enter the internship programme at the Ortanez General Hospital School of Nursing. . One of the headlines at the time was the massacre of several Filipino nurses in Chicago. An intruder got into the nurses quarters and started shooting. This didn't deter me and one of the questions on the entrance exam, referred to this incident. Sixty people were chosen out of the 1,000 applicants. I wasn't one of them! Better luck next time.

During that time, we had some good news within the family. On 19th September 1967, the final member of our family arrived. Mary Jane. Praise the lord, another girl, another mouth to feed and another candidate for nursing. If there is a world shortage of nurses don't blame my mother. She has tried really hard!!

One morning, I received a letter from a gentleman I had met a year earlier. He wanted us to meet before proposing marriage. He advised me that he had joined the U.S. navy and was serving aboard the U.S.S.S. Enterprise. The worlds first nuclear powered aircraft carrier and the longest ship in the world. Naturally my heart gave a flutter, but as I was only 18. I would wait and see how I felt when he returned the following year. When he arrived, he told me that he had met someone else. Such is life.

I had decided to wait a year before attempting the internship programme again. My father asked about my future plans and said had met a distant relative the last time he was in Negros. He was the local Mayor and his mother was in Manila recovering from brain surgery. He was looking for a companion for her whilst she recovered. We went to see the tiny, frail, yet elegant lady, who told me to call her Auntie. If I accepted the job, I would be treated as one of the family. I accepted the offer and moved into my own room in her apartment in Quezon City. I missed the family, but my father had promised to take me back home on the week ends, which he did.

Auntie told me how she had become paralysed and unable to walk after her surgery. One day she could not find the bell to summon for assistance, but somehow managed to get up and go to her bathroom. From that moment she became a Christian. It was strange, but enjoyable looking after her. One day with my humble family, the next with a member of one of the sugar plantation owners and also having the use of a maid! During the months that followed, Auntie continued with her hospital treatment, until she was well enough to go back home. It was agreed that I would go and visit her. Events however prevented this.

Instead of doing the nursing internship I decided to enrol at the De Ocampo Memorial School and study Medical Technology. This is the study relating to the analysis of blood, urine and faeces. I got talking to one of the students about going abroad, and she gave me the address of the Churchill Hospital in Oxford, England. The employment was for nursing assistants, as there had been an influx of nurse training applicants. My parents were a bit wary and against the idea. The next day in chemistry class, I was talking to Linda Diaz, (later to become Dardeau). She had applied for nursing training and was waiting for a reply. After telling her about the nursing assistant post, she asked for the address. We agreed that if she was successful, then I would also apply. She was and I did apply after my family agreed to the idea.

Linda and her sister Nori, who applied at the same time, left for the U.K.. That was the start of our life long friendship. A few weeks later, I was accepted at the same hospital, along with a classmate from university. A work permit was granted and after going to a local seminar about Britain, preparations got under way. Linda had written, saying that she and Nori were fine and enjoying their life and work in Oxford. I had the necessary vaccinations, whilst my father, kindly booked the air ticket and gave me $500 to start my new life. Sonia bought me a huge suitcase and some thick clothes to keep me warm in the British climate. The wife of my father's boss, who was a doctor in charge of family planning for the Philippines, gave me a lovely cream mohair coat, with a 'Made in England' label. I believed she had been to Oxford and she passed on some information about traditions and customs in Britain. I saw as many relatives as possible before my send off party. It was 8th February 1971. I was just twenty one years old and leaving my homeland. My family, relatives and friends took me to the airport. The time for goodbyes had come. Everyone was upset, but also pleased for me. I waved as we went through immigration to the departure lounge. As we boarded the Cathay Pacific Airways for my first flight abroad, I wiped away the tears. That was it. This was the point of no return. There was no going back.

4

WE had an 8 hour stop over in Hong Kong, before carrying on with our flight to England. We were taken to the Miramar Hotel in Kowloon. It was a new experience for me to stay in a hotel. I was amazed at the size and beauty of the place. The service was marvellous. My friend and I had a lovely meal brought to our room. I ordered a steak, but didn't tell them how I wanted it cooked! It was delicious, even though the blood started to appear on the plate as I cut into it, and the pale pink liquid, started to gather around the freshly cooked vegetables. Afterwards we went out into the hustle and bustle of the city. There were shopping centres everywhere. I bought a nurse's watch, ready for my new career. We really enjoyed ourselves. It was a strange feeling. Only a short flight from home, yet the country was so different. I must admit, I did spare just a brief moment to wonder if I had done the right thing. A taxi took us to the airport to catch our B.O.A.C. (now British Airways) flight to London, England. It was a long smooth flight, and I had no fear of flying. We were served various meals, one being an English breakfast, with bread, marmalade, and various cheeses.

Waking up after a short sleep, I looked out of the window and saw some mountains covered with snow. The first snow I had ever seen. The pilot read my thoughts, and told us they where the Swiss Alps. A few hours later we landed in London's Heathrow Airport.

It was the 9th February and winter in England. I thought "This is it. We are in England". It was to be my homeland for 34 years.

We exchanged our dollars for sterling, the local currency, and followed our travel instructions to Oxford. An hour or so later, we got into a taxi for our last lap of the journey.

We were going to the Churchill Hospital in Headington, Oxford. The hospital opened in 1940, for emergency and medical services for casualties following local air raids. Fortunately it was found to be unnecessary and it was leased to the Americans for their medical needs. The official opening of the hospital, (named after the war time Prime Minister), was carried out by the Duchess of Kent in January 1942. It reverted to a civilian hospital with the first patients taken in during January 1946.

It was two very nervous, very tired and very cold, young ladies that walked up to the porter's desk and introduced ourselves. A slim, middle aged lady, in a dark blue suit walked towards us. The Nursing Officer, spoke quietly and politely, by introducing herself, then asked if we came from Africa. We advised her, as we walked to the canteen that we were Filipinos. The salad meal we had was so different to the food back home. With the ham, we had lettuce, cucumber and tomatoes. At 7.30pm a taxi arrived and took us to the

Slade Hospital, where Linda and Nori were staying. Both hospitals, as well as the Radcliffe Infirmary, were part of the United Oxford Hospitals Group.

The taxi driver dropped us off in front of a dark red brick building on a dark night, with the cold air blowing on my face. Another nursing officer introduced herself and gave us a guided tour of both the inside and outside of the nurses' home. I was so grateful for the warm, mohair coat that kept out the bitter cold air. We then received the keys to our rooms. The room had a wash basin, chest of drawers for my clothes, and Oh Yes, a bed. How I longed to snuggle up in it. Linda and Nori came to visit us. It was great to see them. A part of home! Then it was time for bed, after a long, exciting, interesting and safe journey to our new country.

Fortunately, the next day, all we had to do was sign our contract, get the doctor to check our immunizations, and collect our white uniforms and dark brown capes. This would keep us warm and dry, during the English winter, (and summer!). We bought our brown lace-up shoes during the afternoon. The old hospital buildings were partly brick and wood and surrounded by trees, bushes and a well cared garden. The hospital looked after infectious diseases, with one ward for convalescence. On the third day, I tried a meal in the canteen, for which we received free tickets. It was on the ground floor, along with the kitchen, sitting room and administration section. I ordered mutton as I had never tried it before. In fact the smell and taste of most of the meals were strange to me.

Fortunately, Nori and Linda had found a shop selling oriental food and Nori cooked us some Filipino dishes. One day, a member of the staff passed by and commented about us cooking our food again.

My first duty was in a convalescence ward. Here, I was introduced to the members of staff, who were British, Spanish and Swedish. Everything was so clean. For that we had to thank a short middle aged lady with a North of England accent. Whenever I met her, she would always greet me with "Hello Ducky".

One of my ward duties was to serve tea and cake around 3.00p.m.. I soon became proficient in the English art of tea making. On our days off, we would go into Oxford with Linda and Nori. My first journey into the city centre on a red double decker bus was eye opening. The old buildings, colleges, banks, shops and restaurants were of stunning architecture. No wonder it is a major tourist attraction, known as the City of Dreaming Spires. It must be one of the most beautiful old cities in the world. The University has been a seat of learning since 1096. In 1190, it took in its first overseas pupil. The oldest colleges of Balliol and Merton were established between 1249 and 1264. Around 40 colleges now make up the University, which sets and marks exams and award degrees. Many famous politicians attended the University among them are Margaret Thatcher, Tony Blair, Bill Clinton and now his daughter Chelsea. Britain's oldest museum, the Ashmolean, was started in May 1683 by Elias Ashmole. The Bodleian Library has been collecting manuscripts and books since 1602.

I am so delighted to have chosen Oxford as the place for my permanent abode. I have now spent more time in England than in my homeland. It has given me many happy memories, but as with everyone, there have also been bad times. My next area of work was the infection ward, where all patients are barrier nursed. Before entering, we had to wash our hands and wear a gown, mask and gloves. Outside each room there was a sink and rubbish bin. There was a lady in her seventies, who after ringing her bell to use her commode, would start singing, "Show me the way to go home, I'm tired and I want to go to bed".

While cleaning the bed pan in the sluice one day, I miss directed the water in the sterilizing unit and got soaked. Fortunately the water was clean, I think!

From this ward I moved on to the chest infection ward, where a religious, Irish gentleman gave me a 10"high wooden crucifix when I left. I still have it, after all these years and I believe it has helped me with my journey through life.

We took a lot of photographs and sent them home. I still felt homesick at times and took a decision not to get in touch for a while, to help me settle down as I always felt terrible when I wrote to them.

We were joined by Mariet and Nimfa, they are Linda and Nori's sisters. The Slade Hospital has since closed.

Six months later Nori, myself and my other friend were offered and took up the opportunity for nurse training. Linda started first, about 6 months before we did. In September1971, I started together with Nori and my friend. The State Enrolled Nurse course was held at the John Radcliffe School of Nursing, located at the Radcliffe Infirmary which was at the end of Woodstock Road, close to the city centre. The hospital was opened on 18th October 1770 and is where penicillin was first used intravenously on a man in 1941. I am proud of the history of my training school. In 2000 the building was bought by Oxford

University. On 27th January 2007 it closed and all services were transferred to The John Radcliffe and Churchill Hospital. Nursing studies are carried out at Oxford Brookes University.

The course was a two year programme, but was abolished in the late 80's. The nurses who attained the qualifications are known as Registered Nurse level 2. We all had a practice training session in the classroom, where we had dummies. Oranges were used for our injection techniques. When re- located to new living quarters in the Arthur Sanctuary House in Headington, I was on the third floor and my friends on the first. One night, Linda called me and asked if she could stay with me over night, as the autumn leaves and the shadow of the tree gave her an eerie feeling.

Nori carried on cooking her good meals. Mariet and Nimfa joined us after a few months and we had good evenings, as they both played the piano.

Our studies were carried out by having several weeks of study periods, followed by weeks of practical work experience in the wards. Discipline was the keyword, not only on the ward, but also in Miss Flower's class. Working as a nursing assistant prior to studying certainly helped. One day whilst working on my first ward, my clinical instructor came over and told me I was having an assessment the following day. It happened when the staff nurse and I were giving a bed bath to a lady who had a stroke and was unconscious. Even though I was unsure if the patient could hear me, I kept telling her what I was going to do. I passed my assessment, but another student failed as she didn't communicate with the patient. My allocation to a surgical ward was my first introduction to someone who had passed away and I had to prepare the body. I got a bowl of warm water, flannel and towel and then froze. I had to see the nurse in charge who went back with me and showed me the correct way of laying out a body. Even so, that night I didn't sleep very well.

My third training ward was gynaecology. It was busy, with a lot of emergencies.

Here I carried out my first injection, on a frail old lady with very thin skin. I asked the staff nurse if I could change the needle for a smaller one. She agreed and that was the first of many injections I carried out.

I didn't really like my first night on duty. One night sister would walk round the ward with a large torch and shine it straight in the patient's face, to see if they were awake.

If they weren't there was certainly a chance they would be after the round. My training in the children's ward was really enjoyable, but I felt sorry for them and also their parents, who suffered with them. I felt nervous weighing the babies in the old fashioned scales, similar to the ones used for weighing vegetables. I don't know how many bottles I sterilized, or the number of feeds made, but there were a lot. Early one morning the staff nurse made some toast. It was lovely, but as soon as the nursing officer appeared the toast disappeared! No one was allowed to eat in the wards. Nowadays there is a room set aside for staff breaks. Staff contributions are made for the coffee, toast etc.

I spent a long time in my fifth ward, the Geriatric Unit. Three months. It was two miles from the city centre, along the Cowley Road in east Oxford and has since been demolished. I was allocated to the Rehabilitation Unit. One of my night duties had me working with a male staff nurse from

Mauritius. He was young, kind and very good looking, as well as a hard working nurse. He often burst into song, his favourite being "Rose Garden". He didn't do requests! He had never been off sick, thoroughly enjoyed his job and was completely dedicated. Another male staff nurse I worked with studied Theology in his spare time.

At the end of every practical session, we would have exams to see if we could carry on with the training. One morning, I had terrible back pain and struggled to get out of bed. The staff doctor told me I had strained my back. There was no lifting equipment available in those days.

It was holiday time. My Filipino friend and I went with a shy Malaysian girl in the same class to Estoril in Portugal, 15 kilometres from the capital Lisbon. We visited the Church of Our Lady of Fatima. On May 13 1917, Our Lady appeared for the first time and said "I come from Heaven". In all there were 6 apparitions, the last being on the 6th June1929.

We thoroughly enjoyed our holiday. The only upset was when we were given a complimentary sherry with our evening meal. At 04.00 in the morning, I woke up itching all over my body, but mainly across the back. I had been scratching for a while when I decided to look in the mirror. My back was full of red lumps. I had a cool shower which helped a bit. I think it was an allergic reaction to the sherry. The holiday came to an end and the studying started again.

My next area of work was the operating theatre. The surgeon on duty was a tall dark, handsome Filipino, performing a total hip replacement on that day. We became friendly and Linda, Nori, Mariet, Nimfa, and I were invited to his flat and introduced to his wife and young daughter. That was the start of some really good parties. At the parties, were American Air Force personnel, from Upper Heyford in Oxfordshire and trainee Japanese pilots from Kidlington, (Oxford) Air Training School. We met more Filipino doctors and nurses, as well as Government officials from the Philippines doing master degrees at Oxford University.

Meeting all the Filipinos made us feel less homesick. On their return to the Philippines, most became Directors of Hospitals, others consultants, and Philippine government officials who worked in Consulates around the world. We knew three doctors that did their post graduate course at the Nuffield Orthopaedic Centre in Oxford which is world renowned for Orthopaedic treatment.

One doctor was very kind to my family, as he helped my brother Maurice. He had an industrial accident and was unable to walk, as he was in constant pain. As soon as the doctor knew he was my brother, he took on the responsibility of his treatment.

We were all so grateful for his help.

The female accident service ward was mainly for patients with falls, road traffic accidents, fractures and some minor injuries. When doing a night duty, I had to go round with the night sister and give her the patients name and diagnosis. That wasn't easy, as there was a large change around in the ward every day. The Irish agency nurse working with me was off on holiday in Ireland. On her return she brought me back a beautiful plaque. It was a leprechaun on a piece of shamrock. I thought that was really kind of her. My Filipino friend worked in the male accident service ward, across from mine and we would meet during coffee and lunch breaks.

In the Neurology ward it was hectic. Brain surgery meant that total nursing care was required. With observations being taken every quarter of an hour, it was non stop checking. The Radcliffe Infirmary is renowned for the treatment of neurological problems. The surgical ward had a lot of patients, with colostomy operations and numerous colostomy bags needed emptying. In the Female Medical ward, I was performing my final practical exam and finishing the aseptic dressing technique, when I realized I had to cut the gauze. Unfortunately, I didn't have a pair of scissors. I had to apologize to the nursing assessor, who was examining me at the time! I ran to the next ward and borrowed a pair of sterile scissors. I can't explain how anxious I was over the next few months as I waited for my results.

The final ward, after two exhausting, gratifying, interesting and enjoyable years, was the male medical ward. I was in charge of the night duty. I was supposed to be helped by a nursing assistant, but she never turned up! The night sister did the medicine rounds with me. After that I was left alone with a 1st year student with instructions to contact the night sister if any problems occurred. During that night, I had to call her when I had to change a bag of an intravenous infusion. A patient suffered chest pains and the night sister called the doctor. The student nurse was great and I thanked her and the night sister for their help and support, after I handed over to the morning staff. The patient who suffered chest pain during the night, felt better after the treatment given by the doctor, and observations were carried out throughout the night.

That was it. Now for the final theory exam. Whilst awaiting the results, we decided to have another party. This time it was a costume affair. A few weeks previous, I was given an Arab style, green velvet dress, decorated with gold coloured sequins. On the night, at the Churchill Nurses Home sitting room, I had my hair Cleopatra's style and was adorned in jewellery. My friend introduced me to a friend of her American boyfriend. Not Julius Caesar! We became friends and 4 years later got married.

I had applied and was accepted in the Plastic Surgery Unit. A week later, the exam results came through. I PASSED! In fact we all did. It was December 1973. I was 24 years old and my future lay ahead of me. This called for a party.

Upon qualifying, we moved into new quarters at 9 Ivy Lane, near the John Radcliffe maternity hospital in Headington. We had a home warden and a couple to look after us, by providing clean linen etc. To my surprise, 24 years later, the home warden became a resident in the Nursing Home where I worked. She would tell her visitors how she looked after me. What a small world and what a circle of life.

5

LINDA started her training ahead of us, and had already qualified. She was working in the operating theatre at the Churchill Hospital. She met Ed Dardeau, an American stationed in Oxford and working as an electrical engineer for an American company after graduating as a validictorian.

After a year, Linda did her State Registered Nurse training at the Princess Margaret Hospital in Swindon, a town near Oxford. After passing her exams with the best marks ever achieved by a nurse, she joined Ed in Germany, where he was working at the time. Linda worked in a German Hospital. They then went to America, where they got married. She is currently working in a Kaiser Hospital, in California, as an operating theatre nurse. Mariet also trained in Swindon like Linda and after qualifying went to America along with Nori. They recently finished their nursing career at the City of Hope Medical Center in California. Nimfa met Brian, an American stationed at the U.S. Base in Upper Heyford. After getting a Best Nurse award in the School of Nursing, they moved to California following their marriage in Oxford. She works as a Registered Nurse at the City of Hope Medical Center. They have three girls, one of them, Cheryl, is a Registered Nurse. My Filipino friend, also met an American from the U.S. Base, got married and moved to America where she did further nursing studies. The last time I heard from her, she was a Nurse Manager, in an Intensive Care Unit in Colorado.

During my years of nursing, I have worked with nurses from over 35 countries and from all continents. I greatly admire all these nurses, as well as nurses throughout the world, especially in war torn countries and countries that have natural disasters. Let me assure them all how greatly they are thought of by everybody, irrespective of nationality, creed, colour or religion. To them all a sincere thanks from the world.

The Plastic Surgery ward was small consisting of only 20 beds. It was very busy on operation days and Sundays, the admission day. I opted for the 6 months Plastic Surgery course. There were two consultant surgeons. One for private patients, the other looked after those covered by the National Health Service. The main proportion of cases were for the repair or rebuilding of deformed or missing parts of the body. There was also an oral surgery unit within the section. Coinciding with one of my lectures, a patient was admitted for a Mandibulectomy, an operation on part of the jaw to remove a growth.

Another patient was admitted with enormous thighs and had trouble walking, as the excess fat wobbled around. A bilateral reduction from both thighs resulted in a few pounds of fat being taken from either side. With breast reductions or enlargements, the surgeon on duty often asked that the correct bra size be taken into the operating theatre for use after the operation. In January, the course involved skin flaps. Another excellent lecture in the same month was on nose injuries and deformities. This was very helpful, as we had a number of Rhinoplasty operations. This is the repair or forming of a new nose following the removal of a growth, or to improve the appearance or function of the nose, with cosmetic surgery. In February of the same year, I experienced the only sex change operation in my career. This operation was only carried out under referral from the psychiatrist. Various skin grafts are performed for severe burns, after excision of birth marks, growths, or ulcers.

A patient had come over to England to have a facial scar revision, following a road traffic accident. He couldn't speak any English and everything was said through an interpreter.

Stoke Mandeville Hospital is in Aylesbury, a town about 20 miles from Oxford. I went there with another nurse as part of our 6 months Plastic Surgery course, and we stayed for 3 weeks to learn about the management and treatment of burns, for which the hospital is famous, as well as the treatment of spinal injuries. One patient had such severe burns, that a painkiller had to be given before fresh dressings were applied. In order to remove dry bandages, the patient had to be submerged in a bath of warm water.

You could see the relief when it was all finished. Unfortunately, I left before finding out what happened to the patient.

On returning to Oxford I was assigned to the children's Plastic Surgery ward for a few weeks. The ward sister showed me around. She was a quiet, conscientious lady. Children were admitted with Cleft Palates. This congenital defect of the mouth's roof is caused by failure of the medial plates of the palate meeting. A hair lip often accompanies this condition, causing indistinct and blurred speech due to a defect of the cleft. It is usually repaired when the child is 3 months old. The palate repaired around 9-12 months. Before the child starts talking all revision of nasal deformity is complete before the child starts school. I felt really sorry as I spoon fed them. There were cases involving prominent ears. This surgery was usually carried out on young children, after they had been teased at school.

At the end of my course I had to do a case study and I chose the nose reconstruction. I passed the course and was presented with a certificate.

Soon after, I was approached by the Nursing Officer and asked if I would go to the Renal unit for a day, due to staff shortages. I agreed. I never returned to the Plastic Surgery ward and months later, became a permanent member of the Kidney Transplant team.

I am proud to have been on Sir Peter Morris's team that performed the first kidney transplantation in Oxfordshire. We reverse barrier nursed the patients in isolation rooms, to make sure no infection was transferred to them. On entering the room, we would don a mask, gown, gloves, cap and plastic overshoes, all of which had been sterilized. Hands would be washed upon entry and exit. I got pretty warm in the summer wearing the protective clothing. On admission and discharge, we would disinfect the patient's room. This involved all items, including the pens used for writing up the notes. The walls, floors and surfaces were washed by the domestic cleaner. The beds, bedside tables, lockers and all equipment used were cleaned by nurses. No reported M R S A (Methicillin Resistant Staphylococcus Aureus), was detected then. Bed linen, blankets and the patients clothing were changed daily. The family and friends that visited were required to wear the same type of protective clothing as the staff. The ward sister was well organized and ensured the highest standard of care was always carried out. A clinic was set up for the patients to have follow ups, after their discharge from hospital.

I thoroughly enjoyed working in the unit. The staff was tremendously kind, hardworking and very professional, within the team and with the patients. A new unit was to be built, but I decided to stay and the old unit became that for Urology and Chest Surgery. Before the change over, I went on holiday with a friend from the Dermatology ward. We visited France, Belgium, Austria, Switzerland and Germany. We had a wonderful time, touring and finding good cheap campsites. In Belgium though, when we filled up the car with petrol there was a discrepancy with the payment. The lady who served us demanded more money. When we declined, she took the car keys and only gave them back after we had given her the amount she wanted.

6

ONE Saturday morning before Easter, the weather changed from drizzling rain to a chilly, spring day with the sun shining. A black Rolls Royce arrived from a small village adjoining Oxford. Out I stepped in a beautiful, white satin gown, the long veil covering my face and holding a bouquet of pink roses. I was to marry my first husband. The wedding dress made by my Malaysian flatmate, (who was a trainee midwife and studied textile design), made me feel like a million dollar bride.

The honeymoon was spent in Hammamet, which was the first tourist destination in Tunisia. It is 64 km south of Tunis and famous for its miles of sandy beaches.

On our return we boarded our mid morning flight back to Gatwick. Halfway through the flight, the captain announced that we would experience turbulence and to make sure we had our seat belts on. It was when the oxygen masks came down, that the pilot announced, we were flying at maximum height. I looked out of the window and it was pitch black. The plane was flying as if it was a piece of paper in the wind. I started reading a prayer for travellers that was in my bag. After a few minutes, the flight smoothed out and the inside pressure reduced. The captain announced he would make an emergency landing in Scotland, but in fact landed in Manchester. After landing, one passenger got very agitated and hysterical and demanded to be let off the flight as she wouldn't fly anymore. The pilot advised that her luggage could not be unloaded. She was undeterred and got off leaving her luggage to finish the journey, with the rest of us, to Gatwick. What a traumatic flight! I always carry my prayer book, rosary and small icon with me now and it has made me more nervous of flying.

I went back to work in the Urology and Chest surgery ward. There was no oxygen mask dropping from the ceiling, but a few patients had them! The Chest Surgery ward dealt with a lot of cancer patients having Lobectomy, the surgical treatment involved the removal of one of the affected lobes of the lung. It was the same for Brochiectasis and Pneumonectomy. We also looked after patients undergoing Pleurectomy, the surgical removal of the membrane that covers the lung (Pleura). Patients were admitted for a Bronchoscopy. This is when the bronchi is examined with a bronchoscope.

We had cases of Gastrectomy, when surgical excision of part of the stomach is performed.

There was a staff nurse, who was very regimental and strict, but she was very caring and attentive to the patients. Fortunately, she liked working with me and I would usually end up in Urology on operation day. This was always a hectic day after Prostatectomy operations. This operation on the prostate gland was carried out to assist the patient with passing urine, which had become difficult due to the enlargement of the prostate. We also had minor cases of Cystoscopy, an examination of the interior of the bladder, as well as Cystectomy a major operation for cancer of the bladder. It is a removal of the urinary bladder. I met the staff nurse from the ward 27 years later. She was admitted to the hospital for the Care of Elderly where I was working. Unfortunately, it was no use introducing myself as she was rather confused and didn't recognise me.

Two years later and I was really looking forward to my 3 weeks holiday. We were going to the Philippines. Our flight was delayed for 12 hours. So we had to stop over in Bangkok, Thailand. It was terrible weather and the city centre was flooded.

It was 8 years since I had last seen my family. As you can imagine emotions ran really high as we greeted each other. There had been tremendous changes since I had left. I couldn't recognise some of the streets and places. New buildings and shopping centres had been built in so many different areas.

We stayed in a holiday house in Baguio. From here we went to see the famous rice terraces. Baguio is a market town, which sells a huge variety of fruit and vegetables. We enjoyed our holiday and it was lovely to see my family again. When we left I was wondering how long it would be, before I would see them again.

One afternoon whilst shopping, I was stopped by the Director of Nursing. I was reprimanded for wearing my uniform out of the hospital grounds, which was not allowed. I had recognised her, as she was a friend of my mother-in-law.

Three years after getting married, I became pregnant. Before the birth we had a visitor from Ventura, California. She was a friend of my ex-husband's family. It was the start of my friendship with Jean Apple and her now late husband, Sam. Jean knew I was pregnant and she brought some beautiful silk nighties for me to wear, when I had to go to hospital for the birth.

7

NINE years after landing in England, our first child, Giles, was born. Jean and Sam Apple came over again with their friends .She brought me some bed linen and a bed cover, also towels in various colours. This is typical of Jean. She is generous, kind and caring. She returned twice the following year, first with her son Michael then again with a friend.

When Giles was 2, my parents visited us and brought my niece, Hannah, (Lourdes daughter), who was 7 years old that time.

Her father owned a travel agency, specialising in tourism between Japan and the Philippines. Unfortunately her parent's marriage had failed before her visit. It was lovely to see them and it made me feel as if I was still an integral part of the family. I was sorry to see my parents and Hannah go home, as I did not know when I would see them again. However, the following month my sister, Cora, came to stay. Whilst with us we had our family holiday and all went to Malta. This small archipelago of seven islands, five of which are inhabited, lies halfway between Sicily and North Africa.

The main island of Malta is only 264 sq. kilometres and houses the capital, Valetta and its harbour. We also visited Gozo, which is only 67 sq. kilometers, and accessible only by ferry. It is reputed to be more picturesque than the larger island of Malta. After 2 weeks in the Mediterranean, we went back home. Giles was christened and Cora became his godmother, before returning home.

Three years later, our second child, Craig, was born. Belinda came over from the Philippines and helped out with the children. It was very kind of her. She also stayed for 3 months, becoming Craig's godmother, before going home and getting married to Cliff, an American who was working in Saudi Arabia at the time. They returned to America soon after.

It was in 1983 when we moved to another house in our home town of Kidlington. You approached the detached house, which is located on a large plot, down a long driveway. It is secluded and the nearest neighbours are 100 yards away.

One summer holiday, we went to the Greek island of Crete and stayed in the small village of Malia. We toured around the island saw the ruins of Konosos, which was discovered in 1878. The palace of Konosos dating back to 2000-1350 B.C. had been restored.

We decided to go for a holiday to America and visit my friends from the nurse training days. Linda, Nori, Mariet and Nimfa as well as their sister Belen. It was great to see them again. It was 8 years since they had left England. We stayed with Nori and Mariet in Duarte, California. Their beautiful house has a lovely swimming pool, so we could keep cool. Belen paid for us all to visit Las Vegas and treated us to a show. We met Jean Apple and her family and stayed with them in Ventura. Jean took us to Disneyland, San Diego Zoo and Sea World. We also went to Tijuana in Mexico. Jean treated us to everything and we were so grateful. Mariet and Nori took us to the airport after saying our goodbyes. Linda and Nimfa were working. We walked through the airport to catch our flight back home. As we entered the plane, the song "You've Got a Friend" was playing. I was upset, thinking of the friends I was leaving behind.

At home, we decided to extend the house, making into a 10 bedroom residence. My in-laws agreed to come and live with us. Unfortunately my father-in-law was diagnosed with cancer before they could move in. The huge house was for just the four of us. I was in favour of opening a residential home for the care of the elderly, but this never materialised.

We had booked a holiday, to visit my sister, Rosemarie, in Italy, when my father-in-law died. We went ahead with the holiday, as this is what my ex-husband wanted. He went home for the funeral.

Reggio Emilia is a Northern Italian town and inhabited since the 2nd century. We stayed with Rosemarie in her flat. Rosemarie took us to the sleepy part of Montacatini Terme. It is a beautiful place and has four different types of spa water. It is known as the City of Spas. Although its history dates back to the 14th century, it was in 1733, that the spa water became famous worldwide. The house of Rosemarie's friend was about 100 years old and a large number of big oil paintings hung on the walls.

The children and I slept on a mattress, whilst Rosemarie slept in the bed, with another of her friends. I heard them whispering and Rosemarie told her friend not to tell me, as I might be scared. After my insistence I was eventually told, that there was a ghost in the house.

Perhaps I shouldn't have insisted on knowing what they were talking about! I curled up under the sheets and started praying.

On a previous week end, when Rosemarie was visiting and watching television whilst lying on the sofa, the light was off. At about 4.00 o'clock in the morning, she noticed the shadow of a woman with long black hair. She called her friend but of course at that time, she was asleep. Rosemarie covered herself with a blanket and waited till the morning. Just like me! The following day, Rosemarie related what had happened. Her friend confessed, there was a friendly ghost in the house and felt its presence whilst cooking in the kitchen. Her daughter also felt the presence whilst in her bedroom. That was where we slept! Fortunately we were not staying another night otherwise I don't know what I would have done.

When we left, I thanked Rosemarie's friend and her husband for their hospitality and also for looking after the ghost. We left at 8.00 o'clock in the evening, there were no street lights. It was pitch black except for the car lights. I kept thinking about the friendly ghost. On our return to Reggio Emilia, my ex-husband arrived back from England.

Rosemarie took us to Pisa, better known for its Cathedral's bell tower. The Leaning Tower of Pisa. The building started in 1173 took 200 years to complete and has 294 steps. We had also been to Verona, the place made famous for the story of Romeo and Juliet. The city, founded in the 1st century is famous for its culture and arts. The cathedral, which was started to be constructed in 1187 was only completed many centuries later. The house where Juliet lived dates back to the 13th century. Romeo didn't have far to walk, as his house, Casa Montecchi was only two minutes away. The Madonna fountain was built in 1368, whilst the roman theatre still has opera performances in the summer. Not for the 22,000 people that it used to seat, as part is not used, due to wear and tear over the years.

A month after arriving back home, Ed and Linda came over from Duarte, California for a holiday. I really enjoyed having them and we took them around the area.

I had to attend events with my ex-husband. One product launch was in the Royal Plaza Hotel, Montreux, Switzerland, which lies on the shores of Lake Geneva. It was a formal dress affair which required dinner jackets and evening gowns. I wore a backless black velvet evening dress. I felt embarrassed when entering the forum. Someone came to me and said I looked stunning! Another person approached me and wanted to know, who I was and where I came from. It turned out to be the chairman of the company. Another launch was held in Palma Mallorca, the capital of the Spanish Balearic Islands. It is a beautiful place and recently voted the best place to live in Spain. At all the events, I felt as if I was under the microscope, including the one at Blenheim Palace, the ancestral home of Sir Winston Churchill, the war time Prime Minister. The Duke of Marlborough and his family still live there. It was also a lovely formal dress affair. The highlight being when, men dressed as Beefeaters, (retired soldiers that guard the Tower of London), called the gathering to order, rang a bell and announced that "Dinner is Served". Years later, I was talking to a lady, who was one of the staff at the same establishment where I worked. It turned out that she was at the same party, with her ex-husband.

At one Christmas party I attended, I was introduced to the Honourable Douglas Hurd, our local Member of Parliament, whom at that time was Britain's Foreign Secretary. He is a very pleasant and polite man and became Baron Hurd of Westwell in 1997. There are very few politicians as nice as he.

Our holiday at the La Manga Club on the Costa Calida, on the warm coast of Spain, turned out to be the our last family holiday. The sporting club is set in 1,400 acres of land. It has 20 restaurants and bars, 3 golf courses, 28 tennis courts, 8 football pitches and 2 cricket grounds. It is said to be one of the top resorts in the world. We had a fantastic time.

After our holiday, I decided to quit night duty, which I was doing, so I could still see the children in the day. I worked as a casual nurse, only during term time.

A year later Lourdes and her daughters, Hannah and Michi along with Mary Jane came to visit us. It was so nice having the family again. Mary Jane extended her stay, but after 3 months the others had to return home. Mary Jane went to see Rosemarie in Italy after leaving England.

Two years later Mary Jane married a Filipino seaman, who worked aboard a cargo ship. She had already petitioned to live in America with our parents. Unfortunately the marriage did not work out.

Nori, Mariet and Andrea came over to see us. Nori had decided to treat them all to a holiday. I was told Ed, Linda's husband, had been made redundant from his job and they intended to live in Hawaii.

It was Christmas 1994 and my marriage had failed. I decided to take the children to Kansas City, to see Belinda and her family. We had a good Christmas, even though the boys were missing their father. All the houses were decorated with lights and other decorations, all except Belinda's house. Unfortunately the lights had been lost and only turned up late on Christmas Eve. The beautifully decorated Christmas tree certainly made up for it. Belinda cooked a turkey and trimmings, as well as other delicacies. The boys had their minds taken off the situation by playing with Katy and Tyler, Belinda's children. On our return home, early in the New Year, we found out that the house had been broken into and my concern for our future returned. I was very fortunate to be able to call upon the family friend, George Kruzewski, for any jobs needed around the house. He never charged me for doing anything and I will always remember his kindness.

I continued working as a casual nurse, so I could look after and give support to my children.

A gentleman approached me whilst I was working in the out patients clinic of the Plastic Surgery unit. He asked if I recognised him. I told him I did. The patient had undergone a kidney transplant when I was working in the unit. We had a chat and I was so pleased to see him fit and well, after almost 10 years.

I always felt lonely towards Christmas, as I had no adult to share it with. I decided we would go to see Rosemarie in Italy. Her Italian husband, Fabri and 6 months old daughter Venessa made up the family then.

Their house is located at the outskirts of the town of Brescia. They have a beautiful villa, on 3 floors, with a basement. Fabri built a magnificent stone fireplace here. Also he crafted a huge table made of very thick natural wood which could seat up to 12 people. What impressed me the most was the electronic gate. The newly built Italian house has a terracotta tiled floor. Wood and glazed tiles feature strongly. The Christmas tree in the living room decorated with lights, tinsel and other decorations stood near the fireplace. The log fire with its yellow flames, cast its heat into the large room.

Three days before Christmas and the snow arrived in Brescia. The thick snow lying on the road also covered the paths around the house and garage. So we helped Fabri clear it away. We celebrated with the Christmas meal on the 25th December, after opening the presents. Fabri's grandmother had made some ravioli soup. It was really nice! The main Christmas day meal was pasta with meat. Fabri's parents are very kind and hospitable. We thoroughly enjoyed spending Christmas with them. I always tried to give the children nice presents, which meant I would go without a lot of things during the year.

The boys never mentioned the family situation. All I could give them was my love and support. This I willingly did. They reciprocated by spoiling me on Mother's day, with a huge breakfast in bed. I am so grateful for their support and kindness. Thank you both very much.

8

OCCASIONALLY, I had to work on a Sunday morning and I would cook the boys a full English breakfast before leaving. They only had to put it in the microwave to heat it up. I was always back home for lunch. The contact telephone number was always by the phone. One morning I was in the kitchen, not knowing how I could carry on and what awaited us, my sons came in and we talked about our future. I told them that my father had petitioned for the family to live in America, but I was unable to take it up, as I wanted to give them both stability, until they finished school.

The next year, we visited Cora who was now living in Switzerland. Bern, the capital of the country was quiet. The snow covered the roads, but the trams ran frequently into the city centre. On Christmas Eve, we went shopping for a turkey and other seasonal food. Cora's friend from Daly City, on the outskirts of San Francisco, arrived. It was the first time I had met Boots and her sons, Jason and Alex who were the same age as my own sons. The children played happily, as I cooked the Christmas dinner. I had brought a Christmas pudding and cake from Oxford, so we could have a traditional English Christmas lunch. We opened our presents after the meal. My niece, Hannah, joined us for the New Year at a pub in Bern. There was a karaoke contest. Hannah came second and Boots third. Didn't they do well? The remainder of the holiday was spent shopping. Boots, loves buying, not only for herself but also others. She bought me a lovely Bally wallet.

Cora and Boots went to Milan on a shopping expedition and stayed overnight.

After 2 weeks, Cora was left by herself, as we went back to England and Boots, Jason and Alex returned to San Francisco. This was our last Christmas away from home as the old family. The next one we spent at home and my mother-in-law came to stay with us. Everyone enjoyed themselves. Sadly she passed away in 2001. She was a good mother and grandmother.

On one of the summer holidays we managed to visit the Philippines. It was the first time that my children had been to the land of my birth. We stayed with Lourdes in an area of Metropolitan Manila. It was lovely to be back in my homeland.

During our stay, there was a monsoon and we were unable to get out for 3 days, because of the flooding in the area and along the streets.

One night the boys along with Hannah, and Michi went out for the evening. Although very worried, I waited until 2.o'clock in the morning before asking Lourdes to find out what was happening. They had been for a meal and then decided to go for a show. It was finally 4.o'clock when they got back. It had taken them a long time trying to get home because of the traffic.

We visited several places, our family friend, was kind enough to take us around.

Whilst there, my sister Sonia, who was then 50 years old, looked like a lady who was at least 70. She could hardly walk and looked so thin. She was diagnosed with a collapsed lung and Chronic Obstructive Pulmonary Disease. It was really hard for me to see her in such poor health. About twice a week, we would have to take her to hospital, for consultation, or if she was short of breathe. Lourdes and I, on one occasion, ended going around all the pharmacies in Quezon City between 11.00pm and 1.00am, in order to find some medicine for her. One day she was admitted to the hospital, after waiting for a bed to become available. Her maid stayed with her all the time. I felt really sorry for Ulysses, her son, as he was very close to her. He has since become a steward, for one of the world's top airlines. Fortunately Sonia improved, and was allowed home before the end of our holiday.

Due to Sonia's illness, she was not able to join her husband in Saudi Arabia and stayed in the Philippines.

We spent one month in the Philippines and thoroughly enjoyed our stay, despite the bad weather. I was just so grateful that Sonia had improved so much before we left for home.

We stopped over in Kuwait, where we caught our onward flight to England.

Whilst the children attended secondary school, I worked full time in a nursing home and when possible also worked as a casual nurse, in the Oxford Centre for Enablement, which is sited in the Nuffield Orthopaedic Centre in Oxford. The unit is split in two. One side looks after the rehabilitation for head injuries, whilst the other side was respite care for those with multiple sclerosis. I was pleased to work with the staff here, as they worked well together as a team, ensuring the highest standard of care was delivered.

We managed to get through life with its ups and downs.

We thoroughly appreciated the help and support given to me and my family, by my son's friends Llewelyn, Raymond, John Paul, their mum Esther and dad Roland. Esther and Roland are both qualified nurses and now own a Nursing Home in Southport.

I thoroughly enjoyed working in the Nursing Home as a staff nurse. I got great satisfaction, working in areas for the Care of the Elderly, looking after those who are suffering from dementia, as well as frail. I listened to them tell stories of the strange events that had beset them during their life. I also comforted them when they became depressed. I liked this part of my profession so much.

A 21 year old male care assistant from Burundi, Africa, told me he got solace from reading his Bible.

I decide to do the same and was drawn to the Psalm of David.

9

IN the year 2001, Belinda telephoned to say that our father was very poorly. I decided to go to America and visit them all.

The Sunday morning flight, from Heathrow, London to Kansas, gave me time to think about his past, and how both my parents had helped me through my earlier years and how my future would evolve.

My father had a good command of English, and was employed by the Shell Oil Company after serving in the United States Armed Forces. He was one of the unwilling participants of the 1942 Death March in the province of Bataan, when the Japanese occupied the Philippines during World War II. Although he didn't like to remember it; we were told, how they were forced to march for a distance of about 90 miles in the blistering sun. They were all weak as they didn't have enough food, and a lot of them were also sick. There was no shade from the relentless April sun. If anyone fell or dropped back, they were executed by any means. Even though they passed by fresh water, they were not allowed to drink. Instead, they would stop at a badly polluted stream. Here the guards allowed them to quench their thirst. He had nothing to eat, except grass and other edible things which they picked up along the way.

On one occasion, a Japanese guard tried to chop off the head of the person walking next to him. This time the guard failed. My father was made to carry the soldier, and was told later that despite the soldier's head being nearly severed, he had somehow survived. Blood had been running out of the open wound and in no time the flies began to settle on the blood that had dried. The head moved uncontrollably, and my father was unsure of the situation. It is not known how long my father carried him after he died. He was only allowed to put him down when they stopped for the night.

This episode made my father weaker than some of the other prisoners, and when passing over a canal he fell in. Fortunately the guards left him for dead as he floated in the water. Somehow he survived and was found by the Filipino resistance the next day. He weighed only 5 stone and had malaria, but thank God he lived.

During the six day march, about 10,000 American and Filipino prisoners out of 70,000 died.

On arrival, as I couldn't see Belinda, who was picking me up, I started phoning her. A tap on the shoulder, made me turn to see my smiling sister. When we reached Mary Jane's apartment, I was greeted with delight by everyone. I hadn't seen them for 5 or 6 years. It was a lovely reunion, and despite my father looking grey, you could see his sunken eyes showed the happiness within. He was sitting on the sofa. A weak and exhausted gentleman. His portable nasal oxygen, which he couldn't manage without was always running at the prescribed rate from the cylinder. I leaned forward, gave him a big hug and a kiss. I was so delighted, when he responded by passing his hand, gently across my hair. He always dressed well and liked to wear the Bally shoes that Rosemarie had brought over from Italy. He told everyone where they had come from. How he loved his strong black coffee. Until his health deteriorated, he had travelled back to the Philippines every year. My visit lasted for 3 weeks, during which time I helped my sisters look after him. One morning, Lourdes and I took him to the bathroom in his wheelchair along with his oxygen. He thoroughly enjoyed the quick shower, instead of a bed bath. After drying him off and dressing him, we checked his fingers and toe nails. After getting him back into a nice clean bed, I started with his mouth care, which I did frequently.

The medical and personal care was a full time job and I was pleased to help. One day, I picked up a book, by the side of his bed. It was "Corrigedor" .One I had bought in Oxford, relating to the arena of war in the Philippines. As I started reading it to him, he dropped off to sleep. Mary Jane was responsible for his medication and Lourdes was responsible for his personal hygiene. Belinda, made doctors appointments and decisions for my parents, if they were unsure of anything. Mother always prepared his liquid food and drink supplements, as well as anything else required. My father had come up with a way of summoning his care givers. He used his walking stick to knock on the wall. One knock was for Lourdes, two for my mother, and three, or continuous knocking for Mary Jane. The system worked very well. After 3 weeks, I was ready for my weekend flight back to London. I had a long talk with my father, and ended by saying that next time, I hope he would feel better and brighter. I gave him a hug and kiss before saying goodbye.

Rosemarie had phoned us and wanted mother to go to Italy for a break, as she realized how exhausted she was. It was arranged for her to fly with me and stay in England, before flying on to Italy. Following all our farewells, Belinda drove us to the airport.

Mother stayed for 2 weeks with us at our home in Kidlington. My sons were delighted to see her and prepared her room, ready for when she arrived, and gave her a beautiful flowering plant as a welcome present. After her stay it was Italy bound. We were collected from the airport in Brescia by Rosemarie and taken to her house, a few minutes drive away. We were greeted by Vanessa, her 7 year old daughter and Gabrielle, her son, only a few months old. Her mother -in law was looking after them, as Fabri her husband was working. Rosemarie knew how much our mother wanted to see the Pope. So after 2 days, we both set off to Rome, courtesy of Rosemarie and Fabri. We took the Eurostar and as we sat in the train I saw how exhausted and drawn my mother was, looking so much older. I assumed, she was starting to feel more relaxed, from looking after my father and our trip across the Atlantic. Regardless of how tired she must have been, she looked very smart, in an elegant cream suit, with a pale brown top. I had started to doze off, when mother woke me up to say, that a man was collecting the rubbish, as I grabbed the empty coca cola can, I realized, he was in fact the ticket collector. After he had seen our tickets, we looked at each other and burst out laughing.

Rosemarie's Filipino friend was waiting to meet us. We stayed in their studio flat which is attached to their house.

We were very grateful for their hospitality. It was the typical Italian style house, with a grape vine in the front abundant in lovely, dark red, mouth watering, grapes, it had marble floors and a beautiful iron staircase. Her husband and daughter greeted us, but, they could only speak Italian, so we were unable to carry on any conversation.

We were taken to the city centre and told about the public transport, before being dropped off at the Vatican. After many hours of waiting in a queue, to go through the security checking procedures, we entered the quadrangle, where the Pope was giving his daily service. Mother had taken a small hand bell in to be blessed. She had bought it earlier for my father to use instead of his stick. Whilst the service was in progress, mother started ringing the bell. As the lady next to us was praying, I advised her to stop. She apologized, and you could see on her face how happy she was to be seeing Pope John Paul II. We felt it as a great privilege being blessed by his Holiness. As I am a strong Roman Catholic, religion has revolved around my life. The blessing gave me satisfaction and gratitude. After the service we visited the Coliseum. The huge area, held 50,000 spectators when it was in use between 20-82 A.D.

Every 25 years, there is an opening of the Holy doors, in the four Basilicas of St. Peters, St. Mary Major, St. Paul and St. John Lateran. On this occasion, they were opened by the Pope. We were very fortunate to visit all four churches. The focus on the door is to remind every believer that crosses its threshold to confess that Jesus Christ is Lord. We were so grateful to perform this act whilst there. It was a beautiful and magnificent experience to be part of the religious festivities.

After thanking Rosemarie's friend and her family for their hospitality, we went to the station for our return journey to Brescia. We were waiting for the train to come, when I suddenly noticed the name Brescia on the board. The Eurostar, was just starting to leave, the platform! Fortunately, we caught it and Fabri picked us up from the station in his luxurious BMW. His car phone rang. He started talking to Rosemarie. Evidently, he had jokingly told her that we had missed the train. The next day, I went back to England, leaving mother in Italy, for another week before she returned to Kansas.

After three months, father's health had deteriorated, so I decided I would go and see him again. My parents had moved into Belinda's house since my last visit, as Mary Jane had problems negotiating his wheelchair out of the house for his doctor's visits. My father was now bedridden and the doctor had made the decision that he would not benefit from any further treatment. We could only give him tender, loving care and keep him comfortable. By the time my mother had returned from Italy, he had deteriorated so much, he was unable to use the bell she had bought and got blessed for him. All his feeding was by a tube as he was unable to swallow. Maurice came over from the Philippines where he was living at the time. Together, we would try and take care of him and we stayed awake at night to look after him. Maurice would massage his legs, whilst I frequently changed his position to prevent bed sores. We ensured his oxygen and feeding tubes were working correctly. My father was still conscious and lucid whilst I was there. His bedroom resembled a hospital, with all the apparatus, tubes, and medications. We managed to get a photograph together.

It is a lovely reminder of him, as I see it each day when at home. He was a wonderful loving father, who worked hard in his life, to support us and provide a better future. We did our best to give him the care he deserved during the final days in his life. After two weeks, I had to return home. It was heart rending leaving as I knew I would never see him alive again.

Two months later, Belinda phoned to tell me he had passed away. I felt upset, that I wasn't with him during his final moments. My father died at the age of 82, after spending his last 13 years as an American citizen. He was diagnosed with Chronic Obstructive Pulmonary Disease. Twenty years previously, he was advised to stop smoking, as he had developed, Emphysema. He battled with his illness for many years. My Mother and Mary Jane took care of him. They were then living in Kansas, close to Belinda who also helped.

The Home Manager of the Nursing Home where I was working granted me compassionate leave. Once more l had to cross the Atlantic. Cora came over from Switzerland where she was then living. Rosemarie and her baby son arrived from Italy. My father had told Belinda he would like a 21 Gun Salute at his funeral, and before he died she told him that his wish was granted. His body was laid in the Chapel of Rest in Kansas, in a copper casket. Beautiful, fresh, long stem red roses, arranged in a sheath were set on a tall stand near the casket. This was the family's tribute. Wreaths were given by the other mourners and my nursing friends from England, now living in California, sent a condolence card and a generous contribution towards the funeral costs. At the grave yard, was a big blue marquee, with matching colour chairs which were laid out in rows for the mourners.

It was very moving and poignant, when the Veterans delivered the 21 Gun Salute and gave the folded American flag to my mother. As the priest delivered the Eulogy for my father, we felt proud of the things he had done. When the pianist played Amazing Grace, tears flowed down my cheeks. I noticed that Belinda's son, Tyler and his sister Katy were also very upset. My parents had looked after them when they were young. Belinda and her husband Cliff did a marvellous job organizing everything. After the funeral we all gathered at Belinda's house, where her friends had prepared a lot of food. After a while people began to leave. Now was the time my mother needed comfort and support.

10

DURING 2001, my life changed. I arrived home to find a letter from a gentleman called David. He will tell you how this came about later. What a co-incidence! The name reminded me of the Psalm of David that I read daily. I replied to him and gave my phone number, so he could contact me. I am pleased to say he did and we arranged to meet in Oxford. We sat and had a drink in the Randolf Hotel, in the city centre. We talked about our past and what was happening with us now. I really enjoyed the evening and looked forward to our next meeting. Unfortunately he was very busy and only rang once a week. I found out that he was a Postmaster and also ran a store in the same premises. That could explain why he was so busy.

One afternoon I came home very upset, because of the animosity shown to me by a co-worker. I cooked the evening meal for the boys and then went to my bedroom. Craig gave me a call and told me David was on the phone. I was so pleased. As I picked up the phone, I burst into tears. I apologised and told him I had been upset by someone at work. He told me he would pick me up in an hour and we would go for a drink and a talk. I dashed around getting ready. When he arrived, he took me to the "Bear" at Woodstock. I told him my problem and we talked it through. I decided to ask my manager for a change in duties. This worked for a while, until the other nurse had a shift change.

When I met David my life changed. I am now happy and content with life. After 6 months of being together, David sold his house and moved in with me. His daughter, Sarah, came with him. I get on very well with her, treated her like my own daughter and enjoyed looking after her. She gets on very well with the boys and they think of her as their sister.

Yes, life has worked out very well. David's son John lived with his mother and I see him a lot less.

Just after David and Sarah moved in, I went on a trip, which I had booked weeks earlier, with my friend Esther and her husband Roland, to Lourdes in France. We went on a pilgrimage to the Pyrenees area in the South West of the country. It was in the village of Lourdes where Marie-Bernarde Soubirous was born, in 1844. In 1858, she had an encounter with The Blessed Virgin Mary. This turned out to be the first of eighteen apparitions. After the first one or two apparitions, people began to visit the site, where she had her encounters. The water at Lourdes is said to have healing properties. This resulted when the Virgin Mary asked Marie Bernarde to drink the muddy water. As she started to drink it, the water turned clear. It is now revered by people the world over. Esther and I went to one of the baths. We had to wait 4 hours before being given a robe to change into. A white towel was wrapped around me and I said my prayers after being held by two ladies, who immersed me up to my neck in the water. Although I was told the water was cold, I did not feel it at all and it was a strange sensation, as when I got out, there were no footprints left behind me as I took the robe offered and went to dry myself. People from all different walks of life come to Lourdes. Some were in wheelchairs and on stretchers. A number of miracle cures are said to have occurred, to people who have bathed in the water. During the evening a procession was held which ended with prayers in different languages.

We saw the house where Marie Bernarde lived. The village has become one of the most visited religious, Christian sites in the world and was visited by Pope John Paul II in August 1983. Marie-Bernarde Soubirous, known as Bernadette, died in 1879. She was only 35 years of age, but her mission in life had been fulfilled. Her body lies in a glass case, in the Convent of Gidard at Nevers and is on view to the public. It is as if she had just closed her eyes. All her skin and every other feature remains as if in life.

In 1933 Bernadette was canonized. Saint Bernadette is the patron saint of sick persons and of Lourdes.

Whilst in the area, we also visited Le Puy En Velay, a small sleepy village, famous for its lentils. On the summit of Mount Comeille, a huge cathedral, the Notre Dame, was constructed between the 5th and 12th centuries AD.

The area is very scenic and I returned feeling much better, both in body and soul.

Three months later, we all celebrated Christmas at home. It was the start of my new family life. Soon after David proposed marriage. I heartily accepted. We left our address at No. 222 to be at the Bicester registry office at 2 o'clock in the afternoon on the 22.02.02, to be joined together as man and wife. It was just a small gathering. All the children and David's sister, Janet, attended the service. I felt so elegant in my cream organza embroidered dress that was given to me by my friend Irma. Irma, another Filipino, and I, worked together in the nursing home. We became friends and when she knew I was getting married, she offered the dress, which was made in the Philippines. I was so grateful for her kindness.

We had a small family meal, before going for our reception later. This was held at the Holiday Inn in Oxford. I changed into my blue chiffon dress and went down to the reception room, to meet our guest, friends, relatives and co-workers. As I entered, the matching colour motif of the tables really impressed me and the flowers adorning the tables smiled their greeting. The long buffet table was beautifully arranged with appetising, delicious and mouth watering food. The two tier cake proved to be just as good. There was a champagne toast to wish us well in our future life together. When the disc jockey started playing, "Wonderful Tonight", David swept me to the dance floor. The dancing went on till late at night. It was such a lovely and memorable evening. The following morning we were up early and left for our honeymoon in Paris.

This is it, the start of our new life together. Let me say how much I enjoy my life with David and I look forward to many more years together.

As to my career in nursing; I left full time employment, as a casual nurse, in different hospitals and nursing homes. After 34 years, I decided to retire early and give a chance and all the worries, to the younger ones. When I met my first nurse in the Philippines and decided to enter the nursing profession I had no idea of what demands lay ahead of me. I can only say, as I look back, that I have found it the most rewarding career and I have experienced great satisfaction in giving care to the suffering, comfort to the sick and infirm as well as those with terminal conditions. Above all I found it necessary to treat everyone with respect and dignity. I hope I succeeded with all my goals.

I now enjoy my life as a housewife and traveller. I also like to recall the happy memories of my life as a child, a mother, as David's wife and of my career, of which I have briefly written about above.

Book 2

Oxford

1

AS I walked through the side door, I turned left at the fence facing me. Looking to the left, across the immaculately manicured lawn, I noticed a round wooden summerhouse. That's all I remember of my first home in Windle, which is near St. Helens, in England. Years later when going past the end of the lane, along the East Lancashire Road, which runs from Manchester to Liverpool, I remember my Mum and Dad pointing out the bungalow, as we went to visit grandma at the weekend.

Forgive me, let me introduce myself. My name is David Neale Tarling. I was born on the 4th September 1946. My parents, Walter George and Janet Emma also had a daughter.

My sister Janet was born two years before me, in the same month. We have always been very close.

123 Ashton Road, in Newton- Le-Willows, was our next house and about 8 miles from Windle, down the East Lancs. Road towards Manchester.

It was on the right hand side of the road, leading into the town centre, which was another mile away. We would pull into the large drive, which had two sets of double gates.

One was at the front of the driveway and another closing off the rear of the property. The drive also swept in front of the large detached house and stopped in front of the main front door. This area made a lovely skating rink in the winter. At least that's what Janet and I thought, but Mum and Dad had other ideas, as it would never last more than a couple of days!

In the house near the kitchen, there was a set of bells, which showed a marker, each time a bell was pushed in the room described. That was fine if you had maids, but I don't think Mum would have been very pleased if Janet or I tried to call her on them. We just wouldn't dare.

It was from this house that my sister and I started school. It was a private school owned by a friend of our parents. We had to walk to the centre of the town, to attend "Green Bank", which was on the left hand side about half a mile from the railway station.

My parents owned a bakers and confectioners in nearby Earlestown, so I started school the same time as my sister. That must have been bad news for me, as I was only 3 and Janet was 5.

The school was an old converted bank, previously a private home, with a lovely large playground at the back. After the cemented area, which was large enough for all the pupils to play on, there was a big rough garden which we could use in the dry weather.

Discipline was strong and if you weren't paying attention in class there was a strong possibility that either a piece of chalk, or the board duster, which was wooden on one side would be thrown at you to wake you up. What a shot the teacher was. You could guarantee that 9 times out of 10 the missile would find its mark. If you misbehaved, then it would be the cane. A nice long thin green one! The cane never actually hit you to start with, as it was stopped just before your hand or knuckles. The problem was that the cane was so willowy, the whiplash from the cane, meant you were hit at least twice due to the vibration. Yes I did receive it. However if I had told my parents I would have either been smacked again or sent to bed. Discipline is right and necessary and I would never complain about being punished, as it made me respect my elders and do as I was told by those older than I. Even animals in the wild are chastised by their parents if they do anything wrong.

Both my sister and I stayed at the school until we had taken our eleven plus. This was a nationwide test, which was sat by all pupils, to see if they were able to qualify for entry into the local grammar school. If you didn't succeed you went to the secondary modern. Unfortunately, academic standards seem to have eroded since State Grammar Schools were replaced by Comprehensives.

During the school holidays we would spend most of the time at home. Mum would look after us in the morning and Dad in the afternoon. This was because my father started work around 05.00 in the morning, in order to light the ovens so they reached the right temperature. After baking all the bread and cakes he would come home and my mother would go and decorate the cakes, or serve in the shop in the afternoon. Dad would go back to work again between 8.00pm or 9.00pm every night and make the dough for the bread so it could rise by the next morning.

We were fortunate to have pets. The cat or kittens used to be dressed up by Janet in dolls clothes, after which they would go outside and usually sit on top of the gate posts. As you can imagine the passers by used to stop and stare. When the cat got fed up with the attention, it would come back in and Janet would take off the clothes and it would wonder off and do the normal things cats do.

When I was a bit older I was allowed to have a guinea pig. It was called 'squeeky' and more or less had a run comprising of the garage and garden. This was because somehow or the other he always got out of his cage. When dad came in some nights and it was dark, he would see the guinea pig in the light from the headlights, as he scrambled back to his 'cage'.

On one occasion my sister was looking out through the back window, when a cow stared at her from the garden. It had managed to break the fence down at the back and walk through a small hedge. It really enjoyed the flowers and bushes. Dad wasn't as keen on the idea as the cow was, so it was quickly returned to where it had come from. We patched the hole up until the farmer repaired it.

One morning in late April, it had snowed so much overnight that the snow was as high as the 6 foot back gates. Naturally, Janet and I thought it was great, as we could have the day off school. No! The thought never even went through Dad's mind. I was given a spade and told to dig the snow away. That's a point. Where did Janet get to whilst I was doing this? I remember she turned up when it was all clear and we set out for school. The roads were pretty bad, but with a lot of care and sliding we got to school ready for lunch hour. No, a bit of snow wasn't going to stop us. All the other parents had reacted the same way and most pupils had turned up eager to learn. Well, eager to go home at night and have snow ball fights and build snowmen.

Coronation Day, 2nd June 1953, saw the crowning of Queen Elizabeth II. in Westminster Abbey, attended by 8,000 guests. Dad had bought a television so we could watch the events. In fact there was a nationwide increase in television sales for the event. It was a national holiday and the crowds filled the streets with their patriotic flags.

We spent all day watching the new television. Our only break was when Janet and I dashed down the road to get some sweets from the shop! It was a marvelous event to watch.

Royalty from around the world, along with Heads of States, all assembled in the Abbey to hear Her Majesty swearing her allegiance to the country and church, and to watch the placing of the crown on the Queen's head. The musical fanfare proclaimed the highlight of the proceedings.

It was British pomp in all its glory, done in a spectacular fashion. Of all events staged, nothing is done better anywhere in the world, than those national occasions carried out by the British. Royal weddings and funerals, as well as the funeral of Sir Winston Churchill, were all carried out with such precision, pomp and feeling, that all those who viewed the events are bound to remember, especially watching all the cranes bow their long metal necks, bending at the waist to pay homage to this special 'commoner'.

Some Sundays, Dad would take us down to the roundabout at the end of the road. This is where the East Lancashire Road ran, and near to where the new M6 motorway was being built. Often, when we sat down on the grassy bank, we would look down and see an accident, caused almost every time due to speed.

A lot of weekends however would see us travelling from Newton-Le-Willows to Southport or Halsall. My father's mother lived in Southport and my mother's mother who lived on a farm in Halsall, a small village between Ormskirk and Southport, in Lancashire. Janet and I always enjoyed going there. There were so many things to do and see.

Travelling along Carr Moss Lane we turned right, into the narrow driveway, with ditches on either side that would only permit one vehicle at a time to use it. At the end of the drive, we would turn right by the living room window into the farmyard. On the left was a large Dutch barn, which held the hay and straw for the cattle in the winter. There was also space for the thrashing machine, binder, potato planter and a manure spreader. Whenever possible there would also be a four wheeled trailer. The tractor shed was behind us as the car was parked in front of the back door. We would walk into a large conservatory. On the left was the kitchen and dining area. In the comer of the large room, steps led up to an equally large loft area. We would spend hours up there, going through all the knick - knacks.

The kitchen/dining area had a huge Aga cooker along the centre of one wall. Next to it, was a recess that held the telephone, with a window looking over a square area, which was filled on three sides with animal sheds and a large brick built barn. As you entered the barn there was a vertical ladder going up to the loft. It was great going up there. It was very steep and awkward to get onto the loft floor when you reached the top. It was usually filled with hay and straw and was always very hot.

On one of our visits, I can remember my Uncle Tom lifting me onto the top of a huge shire horse called Bess. As I was only young it seemed a long way down to the ground.

The toilet was outside. There was no such thing as an indoor water closet. Turning right on entering the house, you would find the living room. I seldom went in there as I was usually outside. However, I remember the room well with its lovely sideboard along one wall. Adorning the walls were pictures and various items, with a lovely big mirror over the fireplace. One of the items was a silver sword in its scabbard. Grandma always said that it would be mine eventually. However, it disappeared after the farm was sold, never to be seen again! Well, not by me anyway.

As you went through the door at the corner of the room, there was a small cupboard on the right. This was where Gran and the dog, 'Birdie', a large Pyrenean Mountain dog, would go in the event of a thunderstorm. Both were scared when the claps of thunder and fierce lightning would surround the farm, before moving on along the coast. Passing the cupboard would lead upstairs. I remember that all the bedrooms where on the right and the driveway ran alongside the house. If Janet or I stayed, ours was the third bedroom along.

We spent many happy days at the farm, walking all around the farmyard, across the fields, playing tennis on the tennis court. We would sometimes stack up the sheaths of corn, go fishing for tadpoles in the ditches nearby, play with the cats, feed the cows, or ride on the tractor or trailer.

On our way home we would usually stop in Ormskirk and Dad would buy some fish and chips wrapped up in newspaper. These we would eat either in the lay-by outside the teaching college, as it was then, or as a special treat we would go along the 'rabbit run' and have them there. The 'rabbit run', was just a quiet lane outside Ormskirk, that always appeared to have rabbits running along or across it. There were also lovely rhododendron bushes. In the summer they had masses of red or white flowers and looked very colourful as we passed by and joined the main road further along. I imagine the lane has long since gone along with all the bushes.

One evening Dad came into the living room and said that the sky down the road was red and it could be that the Woodlands Garage was on fire. Janet and I went with him to see what was happening. Sure enough, the garage was one huge blaze. Firemen were trying to put out the flames, which were engulfing all the buildings. Men were unlocking and running into the garages, trying to get out the lorries used in the haulage business. Firemen were foaming down all round the petrol pumps in case they blew up. We watched from the other side of the road, but the police asked us to go home as the area was unsafe. When we went back the following day to survey the scene, the building was but just a shell. The petrol pumps, petrol tanks and most of the lorries had been saved. This chapter of my life made me realise what fire can do and to take care at all times when fire is involved.

When I was 10, I got impetigo. This was caused by scratching a spot and getting infection in it. It got pretty bad and every night I had to have silk gloves tied to my hands and feet, to try and stop the infection, as I would scratch all the spots at night whilst asleep. I remember the itching was terrible and I had calamine lotion covering the spots, which where over most of my body, to try and ease the irritation. This didn't work, so the doctor gave me penicillin. That turned out to be a bit of a bad move as it was discovered I was allergic to the penicillin. Just my luck! I can remember the worst day. Mum was at my bedside with my Auntie Gladys, the wife of my Uncle Stanley, whom was my father's brother and lived just down the road. When the doctor arrived, I heard them talking as if it was in the far distance, yet they were all looking at me over the bed. The doctor explained that he had got this special cream, it was new and made in France. He didn't know what the reaction would be, as it still hadn't had proper trials. He looked at me and said, 'Well this is it, we can't do any more, it is up to him whether he lives or dies'. Suddenly I was looking down on myself, with the doctor, my aunt, and Mum staring at me. Looking down at them I started to think about what he had said. Then, looking to my right I saw a tunnel, with a massive light at the end. As I started to go down the tunnel, I remembered what the doctor had said, and realised that I was still young, and with any luck, I had a long life ahead of me.

I decided that I wanted to live. Immediately I was back in my body, with the doctor saying, ' He seems to have passed the worst and with luck he should be alright now'. I didn't realise at the time and I told no one, but I had an out of body experience. It is something I will never forget and still remember it as if it was yesterday. It gave me faith, made me appreciate life and not to fear death. This must have made a big influence during my life. It taught me to be tolerant, have faith in myself, in others and in the Lord and to enjoy life. We are here for a short time, and must make the most of all things, even those that appear detrimental to you.

Dentists aren't the most favourite people to visit in their professional capacity. I agree with that sentiment; especially when I was young. I used to go to a dental surgeon and I found out why he was a surgeon. He told Mum that I needed some teeth taken out to make more room for the new ones coming through. She thought that made sense. What a pity. I had thirteen teeth extracted, all at the same time. I was given gas, before my mouth was emptied of my treasured eating tools. I dreamt of a large wide rushing stream, with lots of flowers, mainly daffodils, standing upright by the running water and in the green banks and field nearby. After my dream it was back to reality. A thick woollen scarf, wrapped twice around my face and mouth, as we headed back home for a nice few days of liquid food. So many teeth never disappeared from my mouth again. Thank goodness. In fact, I wonder if I have even got 13 teeth left in my mouth now!!

On Saturdays, when we got older, Janet and I would walk to the shop from home. It was a few miles, but we walked through the new houses into Earlestown. Occasionally we would get 6d (old pence) in pocket money and I would walk down to the market, get a second hand comic and an ice-cream.

As you turned right outside the shop, at the corner of Market Street, there was a lamppost. We were always told, that this is the place that George Formby wrote his song, 'Leaning on the Lamppost', whilst waiting to meet someone. Above the shop, just a couple of years before we left the business, Mum and Dad decided to convert a room into a café. Eddie Calvert, 'The man with the Golden Trumpet', had something to eat there whilst in town.

Some Saturday afternoons, Dad and I would join Uncle George Littler, a friend of my Father's and go to support St. Helens rugby league team. We really enjoyed ourselves and dad would take his hip flask when it was very cold, in order to warm us up inside. We went to watch them at Wembley Stadium a couple of times. On both occasions, the game was against arch rivals Wigan. Our team won once and so did Wigan.

When we were small, Janet and I tried to help in the bake house, by making the holes in the mince pies and other little jobs. When the cake mixture had been put in the cases, Janet and I would scrape out the bowls with our fingers and eat the mixture that was left. It was lovely and very sweet.

My father was not enrolled into the military as he was advised by the War Office that he had to bake for the armed forces whenever they told him to. This involved working whilst bombs dropped all around. The nearest, exploded just outside the back yard and devastated the back street and threw debris on the bake house roof. Fortunately Dad wasn't hurt and he continued to get the bread ready for the troops. To this day, I love eating the crust of a freshly baked loaf, with lots of butter and some jam. Perhaps not the healthiest thing to eat, well not with the amount of butter and jam I use, but it tastes fantastic.

After sitting my 11 plus, the exam to get into the Grammar School, Mum and Dad decided to move south to the county of Surrey. This was because I suffered terribly with a bad chest and the doctor advised my parents, that I would be a lot better if I moved nearer to some pine trees.

We consequently moved to Elstead, a village half way between Farnham and Godalming. The main road runs at the edge of the village and the village green. Just after the village green and going towards Farnham, the road goes over a bridge which spans the river Wey. This is the area where we would go down to the river edge and jump into the clear water and play around during the summer period.

Our family moved into "Sunrise Stores", a small general store, which was almost opposite the recreational ground. Unfortunately, the store has now been closed and another house built on the side garden. When we moved in, it was a large 3 bed roomed house, with the shop area at the front. Behind the detached garage, there were the store rooms, which held stock. In one of these, the ham was cured and pressed, ready to be sold in the shop. There was a large garden, which ran at the back and also along the side. It was laid to grass, only broken, by some very large conifer trees and small fruit trees. There where four vast, dark green conifer trees in all. Two on either side of the lawn, as you looked through the kitchen window. At the end of the garden was the washing line, running from a fruit tree to a post. This is where I saw a greater spotted woodpecker, trying to get through the branch the line was tied on. I told Dad, who was more upset about the tree being mutilated than seeing the bird!!

To the left of the back lawn and behind one of the two store rooms, was a small piece of land with a shed. I was lucky enough to persuade my parents, mainly my Mother that I could keep some ducks there. Six were bought, but unfortunately one died in the first week. I had them for a few years and sold the eggs in the shop. There were two that really made their presence known. Tommy, who turned out to be female, laid quite a few eggs and was always the prominent one. Horace was bitten by a rat when young and doctored with brandy and soft mash, by Janet and Mum, as I was staying at Grandma's at the time. I was very pleased when he pulled through, but he was never the same. Whenever it was time for me to come home from school, all the ducks would waddle around to the side of the house and wait for me to appear. As soon as I was in sight, or they heard me, they would come running to the front hedge quacking away their greeting. Whenever there was a plane passing over, they would tilt their heads and peer at a dot in the sky, leaving a small vapour trail, and watching until it went out of sight, or they felt they were safe and did not have to worry about it.

Twice a week, my father would deliver orders that customers had placed in the shop. Sometimes on a Saturday I would go with him. I will always remember those rides, through the country lanes, talking to Dad, about everything and nothing. He was a lovely man. I have been told that I am a lot like him. I cannot think of a greater compliment to receive. He was always patient, would look at all points of view and was loving and caring. I feel honoured if I am half the man he was.

Most weekends, I would go to a nearby farm, with a friend and 'help' the farmer. We both had a fantastic time down there and did a lot of things others would only dream of doing. We managed to train a feral cat to be our friend, and whenever we went to the farm, he would turn up. According to the farmer, it was never around during the week. There was a pond at the farm and a pair of swans would take up residence each year and breed. Usually they had two signets. The first year, they would go for us every time we walked past to feed the chickens, if the signets where near to the bank of the pond. The second year they didn't bother and the third year we were able to reach down and talk to the young, whilst the parents stayed just a short distance away, letting us know not to harm them by giving an occasional hiss. We were always very wary, as we didn't want our arms broken, or worse.

On one occasion, 'Joe' who worked on the farm, and was an ex-jockey, was cleaning out the pig pen which held the boar. Suddenly, the boar shot out of the pen with Joe on his back, riding over the field as if on a horse, before being dumped into a large muddy puddle. Poor old Joe! We were laughing our heads off, as he tried to clean himself up. For some reason, he didn't see the funny side and came out with some very unusual words! The same words he used when trying to milk 'Helen', a good yielder, with high fat content and a very fiery temper. A quick kick was the usual way that milking started with her. When I wanted to try and hand milk a cow, I was given 'Helen' to try on. It was a good, or perhaps I should say bad experience.

One weekend, the local hunt, which set off quite near the farm, managed to flush out a fox. We saw it running down the field towards the farmyard. The next thing we knew, it was there with us. Quickly, we managed to get it into one of the loose pens and closed the door. Within seconds, the hunt hurtled into the yard with the dogs yelping at the door where we had the fox. Although the farmer allowed the hunt onto the land, he told them to get out of the yard, because if they had been in the open, the fox would have got away, as there was nothing wrong with him and he could have easily eluded them. Reluctantly, they left and the fox was released a couple of hours later. He dashed off across the fields and into the woodland, without stopping to say "Thanks"!

Across the road from the farm, there was a small stone bridge, which crossed a clear, fast flowing stream that ran from the pond. It was there that I saw my first Kingfisher. A beautiful coloured, but very small bird, its vivid blue back and crown of the head was more noticeable due to the equally vivid orange of its waistcoat, wrapped around the chest. It's long shiny black beak held a small fish. I watched for what must have been a full minute, before it flew away to feed its young.

The stream ran along the edge of a large field. Walking along the stream one day, I was kicking the mole hills that seemed to cover the area. All of a sudden, I was surrounded by wasps. I had kicked open a nest. In order to get out of the way, I tried running along the stream. Wasps don't give in that easily. They followed. The only way I could think off to get rid of them, was to get into the stream. I jumped in. Fortunately, the water was just deep enough to cover me. I turned onto my back, so I could see what was happening and also to surface and grab some air. I remember watching them swarm above me, for what seemed an age, until they gave up and went away. I waited for another minute or so, before surfacing and running back to the farm. When I entered the yard, everyone wanted to know what had happened to the lad who was dripping with water and out of breath. Fortunately I was only stung twice, but as I headed back home on my bike, those two stings felt as if they were covering my whole body.

One morning, we decided to get up early and be at the farm by 5.30am. This was so we could climb a tree above a fox den before it was light. We knew that if we approached from the wrong direction, the fox would stay inside and we would see nothing. After an hour of sitting in the tree, the vixen came out and had a look round. A few minutes later, she went back inside and came out with four cubs. We watched them play for a long time before they finally went back in. We then climbed down and walked back to the farm. The farmer was waiting for us. He had seen our bikes and didn't know where we were. We told him our story, but he wasn't impressed. He had been worried about us. If we wanted to do anything like that again, we had to tell him first. We accepted what he said and apologised for the worry we had caused him.

Along the road to the farm, were the pine trees that we had moved to be near to. In fact they were all around the area. Acres of them. My Uncle George in Yorkshire had always said that the problem with Surrey is that there where so many trees, you couldn't see the countryside. The countryside also consisted of large common areas. These are covered with a lot of bushes, various heathers, and bilberries. Pine trees, reaching high above the ground hugging vegetation, and lakes interspersed throughout. Some evenings, or on a weekend, I would get my bike out and cycle for miles along the country roads and over the local common. On one of these days, I noticed a family of adders, slithering their way across the track. There was a large one, which I assumed was the mother and two small ones. They went as quickly as they had come, disappearing into the heather and bushes along the paths made by other wildlife.

Further up the road from the shop and on the edge of the common, was a lake known locally as 'The Moat'. In the winter it would freeze over and the thick ice could bear the weight of people. At times they could be seen skating on it. My sister and I, would go up there and break off the ice at the edge We would then skim the broken piece across the surface, to see how far we could get it, and listen to the different noises as it travelled across, over different depths. I will always remember that one of the customers from the shop went to the moat for his holiday. At the most, it was two miles from the village. What a shame, that the gentleman never experienced going to another area. This was the furthest he had ever travelled. Travelling makes you appreciate your home, wherever that may be. You get to see different cultures and customs, experience different food, listen to other languages, see some magnificent scenery and wildlife. Whoever you are, if at all possible, travel. Life is short. Live it to the fullest.

2

MY new school in Surrey was Farnham Grammar, which was for boys only. It was a very large and imposing building, built in the l900s on 6 acres of land. In 1974, it became a college instead. The timing of the buses, which ran from Godalming to Farnham, meant that we always missed the morning assembly. I suppose that at times, if we had hurried, we could have got there on time, but we had a legitimate excuse for being late, so we used it to its fullest. It also meant that we could get away without having our caps on, or not wearing our blazers. One day however, the music teacher was sent to make sure that we couldn't get to the assembly. Fortunately, the bus was late, but he caught us all without our caps and blazers. Of course the headmaster was informed. We were duly reprimanded and warned that if it happened again, it would end in detention for us all. That involved staying behind after school, on a Friday for an hour, unless you had a double detention which was for two hours. Unfortunately, I got a double detention, but only the once. We were never caught without our caps or blazers again.... someone was always on the look out!

One morning we missed school altogether. A tree had fallen down across the road and it was blocked both ways. Needless to say, we stayed on the bus. When the headmaster found that the tree had fallen down only a couple of miles from our stop, he wasn't very happy, as we could have walked to school in an hour, but we got away with it.

Bonfire night, the 5th of November. The day that Guy Fawkes tried to blow up the British parliament, was celebrated in the usual way, with a bonfire and fireworks. As my parents sold fireworks in the shop, we normally had a good display. One year, there were quite a few left and Dad said that as a special treat, we could use them all up. I thought that was a great idea! As normal, Mum would make some parkin and treacle toffee and some friends came round. Dad had all the fireworks in a wooden box with a hinged lid. Remembering the fire at the garage, I thought that was a good idea! We had a number of rockets that Dad started the show off with, followed by a huge Catherine wheel. Next another rocket that seemed to go miles up in space. The colours and stars looked magnificent, against the very dark sky, lighting up all around as it drifted down to earth. The sparks went straight into the box containing the fireworks. The box was a great idea, especially if Dad had closed the lid. But he didn't! We were all ushered quickly into the kitchen to watch a fantastic display. Fireworks were shooting off all over the place. Illuminating the conifer trees, the ground, and occasionally the sky! The show was over in about 10 minutes. The red, yellows and blues, fading as quickly as the loud bangs that came from the box at various times. The evening, instead of lasting 2-3 hours, was over in about 30 minutes. Those minutes were packed with excitement and wonder, as well as glorious sights. Mum's parkin, tasted almost as good, when we ate it in the kitchen and the treacle toffee was as gooey as usual. The night had to belong to Dad though. What an impromptu performance!! A fantastic job Dad! Well done.

Janet, a friend of Janet's, whose mother worked in the shop, and myself, decided on a holiday abroad. We chose Opatija, which at the time, was part of Yugoslavia, but is now Croatia. It took two days by coach to reach our destination. It is a typical Mediterranean town on the Adriatic coast, close to the border with Italy. The beach was a stony bay, with huge rocks surrounding it. The large hotels along the coast were set above the sea, with steps leading down to the rocky swimming area below. As we had never been abroad before, it was very interesting to see the different architecture, hear the different language and eat the different types of food, which was nothing like we had back home in England. One afternoon I went for a walk around the town by myself. It was fascinating walking through the narrow streets. The dark golden brown of the stones, showed a lot of wear from erosion and occasionally there was a stone missing from a wall. The windows looked down onto the typical Mediterranean scene. It was strange to see the traffic on the wrong side of the road! It certainly made you think twice before crossing.

Janet and I were very fortunate, as we also went on a holiday to Switzerland with our parents, whilst living in Elstead. We toured Lucerne and stayed just outside the city, in the village of Kastanienbaum. The impressive hotel had views overlooking the lake, or the mountains on the opposite side of the road.

The dining room had a panoramic view of the lake. As you entered, it looked as if the lake was just outside the huge picture windows. There was in fact, a paved veranda area leading down to the large rocks, at the edge of the tranquil, blue, waters. There was a small type of jetty, where the ferry from Lucerne called, on its cruise around the lake, stopping at various villages and towns on the way. It was also possible to go swimming from a rocky beach. One day, it was so hot that the ground was almost burning my feet, as I dashed to dry myself off after a quick dip. I don't know what the rush was, as I dried pretty quickly in the intense heat. No wet footmarks were left, as they evaporated, as soon as my fleeting foot took the next blistering step, to the shade.

Switzerland is a country of green fields, the majority of them having back drops, of tall peaks, some showing the white of snow on them even in the summer, as the cold air at the top of the mountain, never warms enough for it to melt away, into the various streams and rivers, thousands of feet below. Moving down the mountain, from the ice and snow, the barren rocks start to show signs of life, as it becomes warmer for the alpine plants. The edelweiss is the national flower. The alpine plants start to merge, with the various greens and browns of assorted fauna and flora, before leading into one of the many green pastures. Waterfalls of varying height and flow can be seen as you travel along the winding road, leading from one set of high peaks, to another, through the various Cantons or regions. The wooded areas stood out as they brought further colour to the diverse shades of blue, green, and brown, that are broken by radiant shades of purple, red, yellow and white, from the flowers in the gardens, or the numerous window boxes, that adorn almost every chalet and picturesque wooden building scattered throughout the country side.

The ferry from Lucerne took us to Burgenstock, one sunny day. It was a peaceful sail on the steamer, looking down, at the clear water below. Occasionally, it would be possible to see the fish swimming around near the surface. Everything was still, apart from the ripples and small waves made by the ship as we relaxed on the deck. We looked at the mountains in the distance, as they drew closer, the nearer we got to our destination. Burgenstock is reached from the lake by a funicular railway. The steep track takes you to 1128 feet, with magnificent views over the lake and surrounding scenery. The area is actually a private estate, but has somewhere for a drink when you arrive. I believe there is a golf course up there now.

A visit to a glacier will always be remembered, with the gentleman in Swiss national costume blowing the long alpine horn, which has to rest on the ground because of its length and weight. The base of the long pipe turns into a large horn, giving notes of varying depths.

The coach journey took us along mountain passes, which seemed to narrow for it, as the front section and wheels seemed to disappear over the edge, as we travelled around one hairpin bend after another. It was a nice country to visit for a holiday, and I was fortunate to revisit there many years later.

The shop was sold, when dad was in his early sixties and we moved to Milford, another village nearer to Godalming. The large detached house was just round a corner on the main road. On turning left, you went through the open gates, up a short rise, to the top of the drive. The gates opened outwards, what a shame Janet didn't remember this, when she came home one night in Dad's car. She tried to push the gates open. She only realised they opened the other way, when the gate was taken off its hinges. Fortunately, there was not too much damage to the car, and I got the gate sorted out before Dad noticed. In the back garden we had an air raid shelter. Whenever you went inside though, it always smelt musty and it was only used for storing the odd items and garden tools. On a field that backed onto our garden, shire horses were still used occasionally, as they did not cause as much damage to the land.

For a short time, Dad worked for an engineering company in Elstead. It looked as if the time had come for the family to go its separate ways, so Janet suggested one last holiday together. We chose Tangier in Morocco. It was different from the normal resorts. Not only was there sand on the beach, it was everywhere else as well. At the back of the town, the sand spread into the distance. A huge yellow blanket covering the ground, with the hot sun bearing down, during the cloudless days, changing to various shades of brown, as the huge yellow ball in the sky, gradually turned into a dark yellow, then orange, as it sank below the distant horizon. It got so much cooler later in the day, that at night you would need a coat if you were foolish enough to set out into its vastness.

We had only been there one night, when sheep's eyes appeared on the evening menu. Dad had advised us to be careful with the food, until our stomachs had got used to the change in diet. I decided to try something else much to my regret. It was never on the menu again.

From the bedroom window, we could see where a beggar slept during the short night. His tin cans which he collected daily started clanging each morning. Walking down the hill towards the beach, on the corner of the main road there was a souvenir shop. Dad and I called in one day. The owner must have watched us walk past most mornings, as he immediately offered my father six camels for Janet. I jokingly said that was too many. I got a huge dig in the ribs from Dad, as he tried to explain that I didn't mean what I said and that Janet wasn't for sale. Shame! Just think how much money could have been made on the beach at Southport with camel rides!!

One excursion took us to Tetuan, this involved a drive through the desert before arriving at the town, which lies about 40 miles away heading south east.

Walking by the harbour one morning, we saw a day trip to Gibraltar advertised. We decided to go the next day. It was a lovely sail through the Straits of Gibraltar. The huge rock appeared in the distance, reaching over 1380 feet into the sky. It is six and a half square miles of British colony. Its income is derived from tourism, off shore finance and shipping. It doesn't take long to get around the colony. We walked along the main street and headed towards the top of the rock. Being energetic, we decided to walk. There was a cable car, which was first installed only a few years prior to our visit. Nearing the summit, we met some of the Rock's apes. Well to be accurate, they are monkeys. The Barbary macaques run wild in Morocco and Algeria, and the tale goes that they came along a passage under the straits. Dad told me the story, that if the apes disappear, the British will leave. At the summit you can view the runway below, which is also part of the road leading across the border to Spain, the large guns which once provided the British with the chance to control the straits, and the waterway, which separates the Mediterranean from the Atlantic.

One morning, Janet and I went for a walk along and round the huge bay. We crossed through a small river, on the right of the bay, and carried on with the walk. In the distance we saw some people with camels coming towards us. As the camel train, with the local Bedouins met us, they stopped. They asked Janet and I if we would like to ride back to the town with them. What a fantastic opportunity. Of course we said yes.

Two of the riders, got their camels to lie down and Janet and I got on behind them. We held on tightly to the man in front in the saddle, whilst we sat behind on the camels back. We were told by gestures to expect a sharp forward movement. That certainly was the case, as both of us almost shot over the camels head, then back over the tail. It was exciting, riding into Tangier on the back of a camel with the locals. It was also fortunate, as the small river had got much deeper as the tide was quickly coming in, and it would have been well above our waist. The camels just waded through. The water was nearly up to their knees. On arriving, we went through the backward and forward movement as the beasts lay down. There was a lot of grunting and some spitting, from the animals standing near us. A great experience! The Bedouin refused to take any payment, not only for the ride, but also for the flea circus that performed on the back of the men's dark brown woollen cloaks.

Our journey back home included Janet, but no camels. We also brought back something that was not wanted. Mum was taken ill soon after our return. She had got paratyphoid. This is a mild form of typhoid. We had to supply a list of all people we had seen since our return in order that they could be checked out for the disease. No one else became infected, but due to all the drugs given her at the time, she was subsequently unable to take any drugs except aspirin, without breaking out into a bad rash, or having problems with her throat. This unfortunately stayed with her for the rest of her life.

3

IT was from Milford that Janet and I started work. Janet went to work in Southport, which was close to where we lived in Lancashire. As for myself, I went into agriculture.

In 1962, I attended Merrist Wood Agricultural Institute in Worplesdon, three miles from Guildford, for a day release course in Animal Husbandry, whilst working at a local farm. After completing the course and getting the appropriate certificate, I enrolled for a full time course for the year 1964/1965. I carried on working on the farms and returned to the institute, for a further day release course, this time obtaining a certificate in crop husbandry. Merrist Wood is a mansion built in 1877. It is a huge house looking very impressive, sitting on a small hill overlooking the 400 acres on which it was built. On entering the large front doors, there was a dining room on the left and on the right, the common room. There was a lovely view from the bay windows, overlooking the well kept green lawn, with the yellow daffodils, bowing their trumpet type heads and blowing softly in the breeze. Trees around the house and garden made the view of the mansion look really picturesque, as it surveyed the fields and farm buildings that were further along the tarmac track, leading to the second entrance, which was near the main farm complex. The large, wide, wooden staircase facing the main doors, led up to the masters and students rooms. Turning to the left at the top, the long corridor with rooms on either side led into the new block. My room was the last one on the left hand side. The small room was large enough to accommodate a bed behind the door, a wardrobe and desk on the left hand side, and a wash basin at the foot of the bed. The window overlooked the asphalt drive, which looked grey, after all the traffic it had witnessed.

The woods which could be seen from the room were transformed in spring when all the bluebells changed the rugged brown and dark green floor covering, to a carpet of varying blues and greens, depending on how the sun forced its way through the canopy, of branches and leaves above.

One morning, I was dreaming about a waterfall, only to wake up to find that the student living in the room opposite mine, was pouring a glass of water over me to wake me up, as we had both had the same farming duties to perform. When the final exams got closer, we would wake up any time from 04.00am, to study. That wasn't too bad, it meant we got at least 2 hours sleep.

It was here that I met my life long friend, David Battershill. David got married to Jill a few months after finishing college. He worked on his father's farm in Copthorn, just outside Horley, near Gatwick airport, until they went to Canada. Unfortunately they couldn't settle and returned home after a year. I am pleased to say, we still keep in touch with each other and meet whenever we can.

I feel sure that all of us that attended the college really enjoyed ourselves. The majority managed to pass the course and receive the appropriate certificates. The National Certificate in Agriculture and a college certificate. The college was closed down in 1980. It is now home to a golf course, an equine centre, with stabling for 70 horses. But the horticultural side has remained.

I had numerous farming jobs after leaving 'Merrist Wood'. One involved an 18 mile bike ride and up a 1 in 10 gradient. By the time I got to work, I was ready to go home. The problem with going home was that the big hill I went up to work had a bad bend at the bottom of it when coming down. Therefore, I had to slow down from my 60 m.p.h. (according to my bike's speedometer) to 20 m.p.h. to get round the corner. Naturally I didn't work at that place long.

My second job was on the way to Elstead. I would head down the long, bumpy drive on my bike, being shaken to pieces, before I even started. The farmer was very good, but wanted the work carried out correctly from the start. I had no problem with that though. It was my duty to look after the calves and bull, as well as any other jobs given to me. One day I was cleaning out the bull pen when it came back in. I wasn't worried as his nose had a ring in it and the ring was on a strong threaded wire rope, leading from the back of the pen to the outside yard. On this one day however, the bull decided that he had seen enough of me, or perhaps not enough. As he walked into the pen, he blocked me from going out. No problem. There was a safe area in the pen that the bull could not get to. Phew. After about 10 to 15 minutes of his snorting and putting his head down at me, I was beginning to feel a bit anxious! Fortunately the farmer came to make sure I was alright and he got me out through a door, at the back of the pen. Next week, the bull was on his way to market. Evidently, once they have acted that way, they could turn on you again.

One morning the phone rang at home. It was 04.00am. The farmer was on holiday in Malta and his son, had broken his leg playing football. I was needed to do the milking. Although I had been in the milking parlour on a number of occasions, I had never done the milking all the way through. The farmer's son was there to greet me as I arrived, and gave moral support, whilst sitting on a stool at the top end of the parlour. Everything worked out well. When the farmer returned, he brought me back a wallet, with the Maltese crest on it which I used for years.

From there I moved on to a large farm which was close to home. I worked on the arable side, doing anything and everything. The potatoes we harvested were sent down to Portsmouth to fulfill a contract with the Royal Navy. One evening, we where working in a field close to the yard. It was harvest time and we were combining some wheat. As it was still dry and rain was forecast for the next day, two of us decided to stay on and get the straw baled. It was just gone midnight when we finished and I went home for supper. Mum had rung the farm to find out if I was alright. Yes, I had forgotten to get in touch with her, to say I would be a bit late. I was back at work the following morning on time, to try and get the bales in before it rained. We nearly succeeded.

On one of my early morning bike rides, which I had every weekend, I decided to go along part of the common land, about two miles from home. When I got there, I managed to see some badgers playing outside their set. Running after each other and tumbling about, but never straying far from their home. This was the first time I had seen badgers, and I was fortunate to watch them for ten minutes. How nice they looked, with their black and white coats. After they had gone back into their set, I carried on with my cycle ride. Not thinking properly of what I was doing, I put on my front brake, whilst going down a hill on one of the tracks. Whoops! Too quick! The next thing I knew, I was flying over the handlebars, ripping my trousers on the way. I headed back home. Trying to keep on the tracks as much as possible, as the tear was so big it stretched from near my waist to half way down my right leg. It was a bit of a breezy ride and I felt that anyone I saw was staring at this fellow on the bike with what looked like no right seat in his pants and half a trouser leg missing.

My next move was to a farm in Warninglid. This is a small East Sussex village, just off the main A23 London to Brighton road. It had a cricket green, a Post Office, a general store and a couple of public houses. The farm was owned by a hobby farmer. I was fortunate to have a farm worker's cottage. It was a 2 up, 2 down house. In the kitchen was a small Rayburn. A stove similar to the one my Gran had at the farm, but half the size. On the first morning, I was introduced to the dogs. Bob a Welsh sheep dog and an Irish wolf hound whose name I cannot remember. All I know is that it was the owner's pride and joy. It was as soft as a brush, but more useless. The only thing she could do was jump on our shoulders and try and knock us down!! The Foreman told me that if I could train Bob, then I could use him for the sheep. He was so easy to train and in a few weeks he was responding to whistles and calls. One time after the lamb-ing, we ended up with an orphan. I put it in the cool oven of my stove overnight and for the next few weeks bottle fed it, until it was able to feed by itself. At lunch time I would go down the hill to the pub, 'The "Trooper" for a meal. Bob always came along and when the lamb was strong enough, he didn't want to be left alone, so he came along with us as well. I had Bob on one side, the lamb on the other and we would go to the pub for a meal. Well, Bob had a beer, whilst the lamb drank some milk, courtesy of the landlord. One day, I asked why it was getting so busy at lunch time. Evidently, word had got around about the lad and the ani-mals going for a drink at lunch time, so people came to see us. That must have been my two minutes of fame!

4

I MOVED on from Sussex, after seeing an advertisement for a job with the Milk Marketing Board in Harrogate, Yorkshire. I was fortunate to get the post. It was the role of Fieldsman, which involved visiting dairy farmers to check the milk records they kept, and when required, to test their milking machines. My area was the old North Riding of Yorkshire, stretching from York in the South to Barnard Castle in the North and Ripon in the West to Malton and up to Bridlington in the East. It was a lovely area and I was paid to travel to the farms in this area to assist the farmers. If I finished early, I would drive to the nearest town and have a look round. I was often around the Whitby area. I travelled through the rolling dales, going over small streams that a lot of folk would never even get to, as they where off the beaten track, sometimes along roads that would be marked as impassable to vehicles or labelled as dead ends. It was then that I could appreciate what my Uncle George had said. You could see for miles, the heather clad hills, in purple and white, reaching to the next. Down in the valleys, small streams, bubbling over the clean, smooth and polished stones broke the silence.

Now and then, a grouse or a pheasant would call out. The shrill noise waking up the small mammals that occasionally ran in front of the car as I took in the lovely scenic views. The kestrel, appearing out of nowhere, to hover for a while, before swooping down on a field mouse running through the trails left by a fox or rabbit. Nearing the coast the seagulls would appear, squawking their greeting, or telling other gulls to get out of the way, as they all flocked to the same place, when someone threw food to them. You drop down into Whitby, with its picturesque harbour and fisherman repairing their nets or preparing to go to sea, willing to put their lives at risk, so we can enjoy eating the fish they would return with. The fish could be seen in the boxes ready to go to the market, the lobster pots still enclosing the crab, lobster and crayfish. Their claws were reaching out trying to gain their freedom, from the wicker basket that had claimed their lives.

Overlooking all these events stands the castle. Little more than a ruin now, but reminding us of the fortifications that surround the British Isles. Further down the coast you reach Scarborough, then Bridlington, both popular holiday resorts in England. The large beaches with promenades were waiting for the customers and fine weather, which will transform both towns into a hub of activity. Parents and children, flocking like the seagulls to certain areas which would either entertain them or look after all food requirements. Naturally the fish and chips restaurants around the area are really nice and come highly recommended.

Getting to Scarborough from Northallerton, which is where I was based, involved going through Thirsk and up a hill called 'Sutton Bank'. This hill, which is 1 in 7, also has a couple of steep bends as you ascended. Needless to say it was impossible to get up after a large snowfall, unless the snow ploughs had been out first. Winters could be a bit harsh at times. The snow made everything clean and pure, before man could get out and pollute it with salt and sand to clear the roads. One morning, I managed to get to the top of the bank, despite the snow which was gathering along the side and starting to lay its blanket across the road. I decided not to take a short cut at the top, as I would probably get stuck in the 8-10 inches of snow that lay on the ground. Turning the next corner I was brought to a halt by a snow plough. The wind at the top of the hill was blowing strongly and the road had been blocked by great big banks of snow. The driver asked where I was going. When I replied Scarborough, he told me to wait for about 2 minutes, then, follow him through. His was the third snow plough, keeping a stretch of 300-400 yards of the road open. They were going through at one minute intervals and he would advise the other drivers to wait for me, to get to the other end. After waiting for a short time I went on through. The walls of snow reached up at least 12 feet on either side. Towards the top of the snow wall, the sun shone through, giving a lovely sky blue colour. It was quite a sight to see! Fortunately no snow plough met me. Oh No Just a cattle transporter! The driver of the lorry shot straight into the snow bank and I gently crept by. How we got through I don't know. When I got to the other end, all the drivers from the snow ploughs were standing in a group, waiting to see if I was alright. The lorry driver had just shot past them and they had no time to tell him what was going on. I can assure you that seeing a large vehicle coming towards you, without apparently anywhere to go is a bit daunting.

On another occasion I had just gone through Guisborough on my way to Whitby when the snow turned into a blizzard. Suddenly I was in a white out. I could see absolutely nothing, just white all around. Everything went deathly quiet, and my mind started racing to find a solution. The year before, another driver was killed in a white out, within a few yards of where I was. If I stopped I might die of hypothermia. If I kept the engine running whilst parked, I might die from inhaling fumes from the exhaust. I decided to carry on. I couldn't see a thing. My car was starting to labour because of the snow gathering underneath. All of a sudden, it cleared a little and I saw where some tractor wheels had just gone through the snow. I followed them and after a short time nearly ran into the back of the tractor, which I followed for a number of minutes before reaching the farmyard. The farmer got out of his tractor and we smiled at each other; both knowing the end result could have been a lot worse.

As we looked back, through the clearing blizzard, we saw that we had come over hedges and ditches to get to the yard. I would never have made it without following the tractor. I had ended up in a completely different area to where I thought I was, at least half a mile north of the road I was travelling on. As they say, enough is enough and I headed back home before the snow came down again. Naturally, the farmer insisted on giving me a warm drink and some cake, before I set off, after thanking him for being where he was at the time.

Although I thought the top of 'Sutton Bank' was a beautiful area, I don't think it thought much of me. One day, whilst using a short cut at the top, the wind which was blowing very hard suddenly got worse. There was a huge crack and a tree came down in front of the car. They say that in this sort of situation, your past flashes in front of you. Well it did! Still applying my brakes, I just came to a stop before the main trunk of the tree. I looked round and saw I was trapped in by other branches. I quickly got out and started to frantically pull the pieces of tree away. Not very easy when it's a big branch, but it is surprising where your strength comes from, when faced with that kind of a situation. As soon as possible, I maneuvered the car through the branch I had torn away, and headed back to the top of Sutton Bank where there is a car park overlooking the plains below. I stayed there for what seemed like forever, unaware, of what was going on around me. After a while, I realised I had to start driving again. I cautiously set off back to Northallerton. When I returned to my lodgings, my landlady looked at me and asked what the matter was. Evidently my face was as white as a sheet. I told her what had happened and I was ordered to sit down, with a strong cup of tea, which had sugar in it. Aagh! I hate tea with sugar. But I drank it, thinking it would settle me down. I looked at my watch. It had taken me over 2 hours to get to Sutton Bank and back. It should have taken about 40 minutes. I decided just to run the car around the town, before calling off work for the rest of the day.

The majority of my time involved working between Thirsk and the Whitby/Scarborough coastline. The scenery was stunning. The old market town of Thirsk, with its cobbled market place, was mentioned in the doomsday book. Alfred James Wight moved here to open his first veterinary practice and lived here for the remainder of his life. He is better known for his James Herriet books, about a vet in Yorkshire. Another famous resident was Thomas Lord, who was born in the town in 1755 and was the founder of the Lords cricket ground, in London. On the edge of the town there is the race course, famous to those in the racing circles.

It was at a farm just outside Thirsk that I got trapped in the car. I had pulled up outside the door to the farm, after driving down a long straight drive way with trees on either side. As I was about to get out of the car, that is when they appeared from behind a tree at the edge of a small field and also from the side of the farmhouse, which was a two storey building built of traditional Yorkshire stone . They surrounded the car, as if that action had been performed many times before. The farmer confirmed this when he came out to rescue me. There must have been at least two dozen white, flapping, and hissing geese staring at me. Fancy putting up with that, just to see if the farmer was interested in any of the Milk Marketing Board's services! I don't know if you have ever been attacked by geese, well I have been chased by them, as well as trapped in the car by them. I don't recommend it. They make very good guards for a property. In addition to making a frightening noise, their wings can break your arms or legs, just like the swan.

Pickering is a small picturesque market town on the way to Scarborough. It is known as the gateway to the North Yorkshire National Park. The steam railway that runs from here is the longest in England and runs to Grosmont which is where the train is stationed. The next village along the A170 is Thornton Le Dale yet another beautiful place to visit. If time permitted, I would get out of the car and have a walk around, go along the street with the stream running by the side, call in at the local shops or have a cup of Yorkshire tea with a cake. Sumptuous. From this area you can turn left and head into the forest. This is a lovely drive, with pine trees on either side, reaching up to touch the sky. The fire watch towers looking down on the roadway, ensuring all is well.

My favourite area on this side of Yorkshire though, is around Castleton, Leaholm, Glaisdale, Grosmont and down to Goathland. The undulating brown, purple and white moorland only broken by the green of the pastures and in places the yellow buttercups taking over from the grass, to make a sunny looking ground, against a dull sky. One day, when near Goathland, I stopped to have my lunch before carrying on to my next call. I pulled onto the edge of the road and wound my window down. It was a bit of a dreary day. Although it was warm, the sky was covered with a thin grey blanket, only occasionally being broken by a patch of blue, forcing itself through, to smile on the sheep, grazing along the side and further into the heather clad ground. I was reading my paper, which I normally did during my lunch stop. The radio was giving me the news events of the day, and my cheese sandwich disappeared out of the open window into the mouth of a smug looking sheep. I don't know if she enjoyed it or not, but she didn't leave any for me. I made sure that when I ate my next one, it was mine alone.

The other side of my area was Bedale, Leyburn, Aysgarth and Wensleydale. Further North, I would visit Richmond, Grinton and Gunnerside, and on the odd occasion go to Barnard Castle. On one of the rare trips to Barnard Castle I joined the A 1 at Leeming Bar and headed North. I had only gone a few miles, when I passed part of a jack-knifed lorry. The large grey steel girders held fast on the trailer section by their shackles. A few yards further along, there was the torso of the driver with no legs. The head lay separately in yet another area. I have never witnessed such an awful and tragic accident. As I drove slowly along, the wailing sirens of the ambulance and police vehicles could be heard. The few cars around, were being driven very slowly, the drivers trying to come to terms with what they had just seen. I don't know what everyone else did, but I pulled off the road at Richmond to gather myself together, and have a warm black coffee. To this day, I can still envisage the scene of carnage caused by this horrific incident.

If you leave the A 1 at Catterick Bridge you would head towards Brompton On Swale. The quiet road runs over the River Swale, from where it gets its name. The river becomes very wide in this area after sweeping around a large bend. It is in this area that some boys unfortunately drowned, after a flash flood brought a huge wave of water gushing down from the hills above Richmond.

It was in Richmond where I took shelter from a terrible storm. As I was heading towards the town, the sky went an unusual dark yellow. I drove quickly into the centre and found one of the last parking places. By this time, it was as dark as night, everyone had to drive with their headlights on. Then, nothing moved. There was no noise, everyone was taking shelter and all cars parked. It was pitch black. Then, the roar of the thunder started, with the brilliant blue and white lightning announcing the coming rain. Time after time, the explosions of light and sound shook the parked car.

Then the rain came. To say it was torrential is an understatement. A river started to flow down from the hill, taking anything lying in the streets with it. It must have lasted at least twenty minutes, before gradually easing up and letting the sky show some light, through the ravages that had preceded it. The road started to gather bits of trees and soil brought down by the rain. After a further five minutes, I decided it was safe to get out of the car and go into the cobbled market place, which had shops and tea rooms reviving all those caught in the storm. The obelisk with its clock overlooked the area where the market is held. The town dates back to 1066, but was a settlement many years before.

A small road running from Richmond to Gunnerside, is well worth driving along. You will pass through Marske and Reeth before arriving in the quiet village, with its green, set on a small hill, looking down onto the traditional rows of houses, built with the local stone and offering peaceful views over the surrounding area.

The road from Bedale to Hawes leads you through Newton Le Willows, the village bearing the same name as the town I lived in, many years previously. Further along the road you arrive at Constable Burton. It was along this road, on a hot summer's day, that the tar in the road started to melt. As I drove along, I could hear the tyres pulling up the surface, with a sucking sound and the car being hit with stones and sticky tar, before coming to rest again on the boiling surface of the road. Heading through the lovely Leyburn leads to Aysgarth, with the famous triple flight falls on the left, rushing and leaping over the rocks before settling down again into the river Ure. One afternoon in the winter, I passed by on my way home to Formby, where my parents had moved to, and the falls were frozen solid. All along the road to Hawes, water was frozen to the sides of the rocks which ran along the side of the road. The green and brown of the fern, protruding from the clear ice, let me know that winter had arrived. Turning a corner before arriving in Hawes everything changed. Water could be seen running down the craggy rock faces and spreading along the side of the road, watering the plants and lodging in pools for all the small creatures to drink from.

The A 61 from Thirsk will take the driver to the old city of Ripon. The twin towers of the cathedral reaching into the sky beckon all those wishing to, to enter inside the large portals of the 1300 year old place of worship.

From Ripon the busy road leads on to Harrogate. This is the stretch where the accelerator of the car broke, whilst I was travelling at 60m.p.h.With the next roundabout looming fast, I slammed the car straight into second gear. The screeching of the engine was matched only by the noise of the tyres, as the braking started to slow me down in time to pull up and wait at the side of the road for the breakdown truck. Harrogate is a spa town. It is very pleasant and clean and at the time the road system was excellent. I haven't been back for a long time so I am unsure what it is like now.

When visiting the area office to see my manager, I was asked to take control of the testing of milking machines, for the whole of the old North and East ridings of Yorkshire, as well as the North of Lancashire, in addition to carrying on with checking the milk records within my old area. This involved more travelling and seeing different areas.

The first time I went to Beverley, I was impressed by the old archway you drive through to get into the centre of the town. It is really impressive, but nowhere as awe inspiring as the Minster. This monument of religion, built around the tomb of John, Bishop of York between the years 706-714. St. John of Beverly was canonized in 1037, following miracles attributed to him. The building was started in 1220 and finished in 1425.

I cannot say much about Kingston Upon Hull. It was then a typical city, with its rows of houses, streets that could be cleaner, and a dock area that needed tidying up a lot. I have not returned there since and I have no reason to do so. Malton, Norton and Driffield are typical Yorkshire market towns, which I did not visit very often, and I remember nothing in particular about them.

York is a different matter. Even though I did loose my car once and had to ask a policeman, after giving details of the area where I had parked, how to find it! The walls surrounding the city stand majestically, even though a type of construction was in place from the 9th century and the Romans had a similar type of defence even before then. You enter the city through the Barrs. When walking around them, you can envisage what it was like all those years ago when the fortification was needed to repel the attacking forces. Danes, Saxons, and Vikings. The arrow slits for firing through to the enemy. The enemy not only having a hail of arrows shot at them but also having rocks and fire or boiling oil, being hurled over the walls at them.

Just inside the city walls lies the impressive York Minster. It was built over a thousand years ago. The site being a place of worship even before the Cathedral was built. It was once the main seat of the church in England, and also the seat of government. As you approach the main doors over the paved area, you automatically gaze up at the South Tower, before going through the huge South doors. On entering the nave of the church, you appreciate how huge the building is. Seeing the crypt and chapter house you can't help but marvel at the architecture. Climbing the steps of the tower, you can look out at the city, 197 feet below.

Further into the city, you arrive at the Jorvik Viking centre. This very interesting museum gives a good insight into the Viking history. The castle museum is also a must. It is set out as the old city. Complete with streets, shops, bank, and a pub.

Near to the centre, is the old shopping area with its quaint black and white buildings, typifying old England. York is also famous for its locomotives and the National Rail Museum, with a dozen or more old trains, that you can look at or walk through. It is the largest rail museum in the world, and for a free exhibit it is marvellous.

On the A64 leading from the city centre the race course is on the left hand side before reaching the ring road. If you are within 100 miles of the area, stop to visit the city. There is something for everyone, and it is in such a beautiful part of the country. Have a week or two and visit some of the areas I have mentioned. The history, magnificent scenery and lovely coastline will ensure a pleasant stay.

On my next visit to the area office, I asked my manager for an increase in salary, because of the extra work I was carrying out. He refused and I handed in my resignation. With sadness I said goodbye to Yorkshire and moved back home with Dad and Mum. After I had started working for the Milk Marketing Board, they had moved back to northern England.

5

FRESHFIELD, is a small area of Formby, which is a town close to Southport, our old haunt. The large semi-detached house was next to St. Peters church, with a pathway between, that led to a road at the end. Formby is well known in the area, for its pinewood walks and red squirrel reserve. It is one of the few places in England that is home to the native red squirrel. In the marshes between the sand dunes, the natterjack toads can be found. The Formby family have been living in the town for about 600 years.

I started working at a farm in Halsall, owned by a friend of the family. The farmer's son had left to work in Trinidad and Tobago for the agricultural industry, where he lived until his untimely death, years later. One of his workers broke into the house and butchered him to death. It was terrible reading about it in the papers.

Although I enjoyed farming, I found that I missed using my brain to its fullest extent. Especially when carrying out all the manual work. So after a while, I took an exam and started to work for the Post Office.

During my time at home, I would go out with a friend most weekends. We had some great times together. Occasionally we would go to the Scarisbrick Hotel, along Lord Street in Southport, and just have a drink. My friend and I, along with his sister, and my cousin Jenny, would often go to a club in Preston on a Saturday night. It was usually late by the time we got back home. On one occasion it was a bit later than expected. My friend's sister had driven us all into Preston. My friend and I were late getting back to the meeting point after going for a coffee. The girls decided not to wait. It had just turned 01.00 am and the only bus we could have caught, stopped running at 10.00 p.m. We decided to hitch a lift back to Freshfield. It was only 20+ miles and we hoped to get a lift. It didn't happen! No, that's not true. We had a lift which took us about 5 miles into our trip. It was a good help. During the late sixties, there were not many cars around late at night. There weren't that night anyway. We only counted nine all the way back to Freshfield. It was almost 06.00am when I got home! Mum was just getting up for a drink of tea. She asked if I was just going out. I told her I had just arrived back and why. After managing a few hours sleep, Janet who was also living at home at the time, decided to mow the front lawn. She never mowed the lawn, but had decided to this time, to teach me a lesson for getting in late!!! Aren't sisters wonderful!

It was in Freshfield that I met my first wife.

Only a few months after we got married, Dad died. I felt as if I was starting to get close to him again, after being away from home for a few years. After suffering with lung cancer for a short while, it was a secondary tumour on the brain that killed him. Unfortunately, he had smoked a lot during his life and he passed away on 2nd December 1972.

We moved four times in 2 years, before settling down for a short time in Birkdale, a village which is part of Southport and has all you require and a very nice cheese shop. Red Rum, the horse that won the Grand National three times, was trained here by Ginger McCaine. Part of the training was carried out on the beach, and the horses could be seen being put through their paces. Southport is a lovely resort and popular with Scots travelling south for their holiday. There are many things to see and do in and around the town. It is known as England's golfing capital, because of the number of courses in the area. Apart from Royal Birkdale, which hosts many international tournaments, there are courses in Ainsdale and close to Hesketh Park, and various others within a few miles. Running along most of the promenade is the Marine Lake, a large boating and recreational lake which has the Lakeside Miniature Steam Railway running alongside it. At one end of the promenade is Hesketh Park, a large area which had a floral clock, as well as beautiful flowers, looking up and smiling at their visitors as they carry on along one of the many paths. The nearby Botanic Gardens have an aviary, boating lake and some nature trails. The ducks are always waiting to be fed. On a walk round, we would stop and have tea and cakes at the restaurant.

The far end of the promenade was the home to Pleasure Land, the ubiquitous fun fair found in all resorts. It was very good and kept up to date with all the new rides. The pier is the second longest in Britain, over a mile long. You could catch a train to the end, but it was a nice walk along the

wooden planks, that are just wide enough to see the sea below, as long as the tide is in. If not, get your binoculars out,
as it will be so far out you may not be able to see it. This is
due to the dredging of the River Ribble at Preston. The pier
has now been modernised and has entertainment buildings
and a restaurant at the end. The 34 acres of Victoria Park
at the southern end of the promenade, is where the annual
flower show is held. The displays are excellent, as are the
flowers within the tents.

Walking around may take you past a water garden, a
waterfall gently falling into a pond below, filled with purple, white and yellow water lilies. The Japanese or modern
day garden next door, shows the differences that can be
achieved with such striking effect with plants, bushes and
flowers, of such a wide description, that the average person
would not think of. It is amazing what can be achieved in
a garden of any size given the time and knowledge to do it.
Outside the park and running parallel is the road known as
Rotten Row. What a name for such a lovely drive. All along
one side, the flowers and bushes always appear colourful
no matter what time of the year you visit. Congratulations
to those involved. Lord Street is the main shopping area
with its imposing shops and Victorian balustrade fronts. It
is a lovely street to meander down. Pop into a café known
as 'Nostalgia' and enjoy an afternoon tea and scone. It is
highly recommended. The mushrooms on toast are really
good. Chapel Street and Eastbank Street also have a large
number of shops. The market leads off from Eastbank Street
and sells fresh fruit, vegetables and meat produce.

Our first child, John, was born in 1980.This was the start
of the sleepless nights, as most parents know only too well.

Just after we settled down to a good nights rest again, Sarah was born 2 years later.

Whilst we were living in Birkdale, there was a huge aerial fireworks display, put on by a large construction company, as a show of thanks to Southport for granting it a large contract to build a number of community buildings in the town. We were told the fireworks cost over £ l million pounds. Whether this was true or not, I don't know. I do know that the firm went bankrupt a few months later. I suppose that is what they mean by going out with a bang.

After a couple of years, the Post Office decided to split up its businesses. It was 1986, and I managed to get a transfer to Oxford. I really enjoyed my time working in the Liverpool Post Office, on the counter in the Head Office and managing offices around the area. Naturally, during this period, a number of events occurred which stay in my memory. Like the time I served someone, but I was unable to complete the transaction as the customer did not have sufficient identification. After a heated debate and a couple of return visits, I was physically threatened. I didn't think a lot about this, as it was an occupational hazard; however, when I was going home at night, there was the customer waiting. I was safely escorted from the building by the Manager and staff.

Fortunately I was early at work the next morning. When some other members of staff came in a few minutes later, the customer was again waiting. I was working at a different office the next day. After being in the Post Office for a few years, you were eligible for a duty in the Head Office, working in one of the various departments. Following 'writing duties' in the finance branch, counter branch and that for the mails, I was seconded to the security section. I thoroughly enjoyed my time there and it involved visiting every area of Liverpool and the Wirral.

We moved to a new house in Witney. This is an old Oxfordshire market town which was and still is, going through a huge expansion. It is a 20 minute drive West of Oxford, except in the rush hour when it can take over an hour. The town is on the edge of the Cotswold countryside and is famous for blankets that it has been making since the middle ages. In the centre of the town is the Butter Cross, a stone construction open at the base with pillars supporting it. It has a clock dating back to 1683 on top. This was the medieval meeting and market place, where ladies from the surrounding areas came to sell their wares, usually eggs and butter, and hence the name. Overlooking the green, stands St. Mary's church dating back to the 13th century. The west end is the old part of town with its antique shops and well preserved houses.

I had lived in a caravan at the edge of Oxford until the house was ready for the family to move in. Whilst in the caravan, it got pretty cold. One night, I had to sleep with the gas bottle in one of the two sleeping bags, so it would not go into a jelly type substance. I had put two layers of covering over the car engine, so it would not freeze. I got quite a bit of sleep despite the freezing condition. The following morning, my toothpaste was very hard to get out of the tube and the water had frozen enough, for the ice to have forced itself, to the top of the half full container; and the river Thames had frozen over at Folly Bridge. My car was fine, when I tried it in the evening when it was much warmer.

That weekend, as I drove back home, I called to see how things were progressing in Witney. Perhaps I shouldn't have done that. When I went to the back of the building and looked through the French windows, I could see the bath, wash basin, and toilet, suspended in mid air. The stairs were leading up to a vast space that should have accommodated the first floor. On phoning the builder the following Monday, I found out that the water tank had burst because of the cold weather. I was told there was no need to worry, as everything would be ready for us to move in two weeks later. To my surprise it was.

On my first day at Oxford district office, which was housed in a section of the old post office building in St. Aldates, I was introduced to my immediate boss. The two of us had to set up a cash management section for the region. Within a couple of weeks, with the help of two other members of staff the section was up and running. Our task was to monitor and set targets for the amount of money held in each post office within the region. It was thoroughly enjoyable and also involved visiting different offices, from Hemel Hempstead to Milton Keynes, Banbury and Burford and all points in between, giving advice and assistance where necessary. After a few months, everything was running smoothly and I became involved with certain security aspects of the district.

We had been in the house only a few months, when my ex-wife told me that her parents, who had moved with us, were finding it difficult to adjust to the place. We were on the move again. This time we moved to Cumnor. The village, lies just outside the city of Oxford up a long hill. It had a couple of shops, a Post Office and some decent pubs. The food in 'The Bear and Ragged Staff' was really good.

Unfortunately the family were unable to settle and although I enjoyed my work and was due for promotion I had to try and get a transfer back to the Liverpool area, because the family was unsettled. The Post Office was very good though and a transfer came through for Manchester after only a few weeks. Thanks to the Head of Human Resources, who knew me from when we both worked in Liverpool.

We bought a house in Ainsdale, another area of Southport closer to Formby. It was a modern, 4 bed- roomed, detached house, close to the boundary of the town. Although it was very spacious, it never felt homely to me. Perhaps that was because I was not there all that often.

Working in Manchester, involved me getting up at 05.30 every morning to catch the 6.15 train. On arrival, I ran to work in order to get in as early as possible as I worked flexi hours. I finished at 16.30 and ran for the train home. With any luck, the train would leave on time. I wasn't very lucky and most evenings it was delayed, or cancelled. Normally, I would get home between 18.30 and 19.30.lt was very tiring and most week ends I just wanted to relax.

Initially, I worked within the buildings branch, checking security procedures. Within a few weeks though, I was given staffing projects to carry out in various post office controlled establishments. These were very interesting and covered a broad section of working practices and environments.

My final area of work was assisting with the control of the 400 plus sub post offices within the region.

After a few months, I could no longer put up with all the travel and decided I had to do something different. Discussions followed and it was decided to move down to Eastbourne and I would work for my friend David, whom

I met at agricultural college. He was running a business in Hailsham, a small town 8 miles from the area we were looking to live.

I joined Dave and Jill in their company, Multi-Clean. It specialised in KEW pressure washers and vacuum cleaners, and he was the main agent for Sussex and Kent. We had difficulty in selling our house in Ainsdale. It was exactly 299 miles from home to home. I would leave Hailsham at lunch time on Fridays, arriving back home any time from 6.30pm. onwards. Sunday would see me taking to the road again, after an early evening meal, getting back to the caravan by 11.30pm. One journey saw me stuck on the M23 near Gatwick airport at 1.00am only snuggling into my sleeping bag at 2.15am.

6

NINE months passed and it was suggested that we look for a sub Post Office instead, so the family could get together again. I called into one near Oxford, on my way home. It seemed ideal and the owner wanted to move back up north, as soon as possible as his wife was not very well. He suggested an exchange of properties. This was agreed and everything was quickly sorted out.

On 7th September 1990, we moved into Yarnton Post Office. The office stayed closed on the Friday, but we opened at 9.00am on the Saturday morning, with all our personal belongings still in packing cases. It was a few months until everything was sorted out and unpacked.

Yarnton, is a lovely village with over 2,000 inhabitants. It lies to the north of Oxford, on the road to Woodstock and Blenheim Palace. It is an area that has been inhabited for a long time and an archaeological site, close to the railway line, had unearthed proof of a settlement from the Cromwell era.

The post office is situated in a slip road just off the main road. With the post office, there was a small store within the property. On taking it over we continued selling grocery items, cards and confectionery. As a large Sainsbury's supermarket had opened just a few miles away, sales were very poor. Consequently, we changed the items being sold on a few occasions, until we settled with cards, stationery, confectionery and gift items. At one time, we tried selling fresh fruit, vegetables and flowers. This involved a 4.30am start, in order to get to the wholesale market and return in time to open the Post Office at 09.00. The only problem was that during the summer, a lot of the villagers grew their own produce. After a few months of bad sales and wastage, it was decided to stop the fruit and vegetable sales. I continued my early morning trips in order to purchase the flowers, however this only continued for a few weeks before finally deciding that sleep was more important.

Janet had moved to nearby Northamptonshire with her two sons, Matthew and Neil after having problems with her marriage. It was nice to have them living closer.

I had increased the number of post office services offered to include datapost services, travel insurance, foreign transactions, with passport checking, and trusted I gave good customer service. The office grew, by the time I left, into one of the top 5,000 in the U.K. There were about 19,000 at the time and for a small village, I felt proud of my achievements.

After 9 years in Yarnton, I divorced my first wife. John went with his mother. He said that he would not have one of us living on our own, and I admired him for his decision.

Sarah stayed with me. I really appreciated her support and help. She pulled me up when I was down, and made sure we got out at weekends. Thank you Sarah!

We joined the National Trust and toured around the area, seeing new sights and going further afield to see what the countryside was like. We visited Dave and Jill. They were going to live in a penthouse in Eastbourne after selling their farm outside Hailsham. I really appreciate their friendship.

I received a lot of moral support from the villagers. A few couples invited me for some nice meals. Cyril and Gina Rumble were one of them. Cyril and I would often go for a glass or two of wine, and we still meet whenever possible to catch up with all the news whenever we are both in the country.

I decided it was time for a good holiday, so my children and I, along with my sister, Janet and sister-in-law, May, took ourselves off to Majorca. We rented a villa just on the edge of Puorto Pollensa. It was nice and relaxing, touring around the area or lazing about by the beach. On one occasion Sarah, John, and I hired bikes and set off up the mountain overlooking the bay. Half way up, we stopped to look at the view of the large bay, surrounded in the distance by mountains and the road running to old Pollenssa. The sea was full of holiday makers enjoying themselves in the clear, light blue water that had small fish swimming all around the edge of the beach. John turned back after enjoying the view, whilst Sarah and I carried on to the Cape of Formentor, with its rugged coastline and clean, white, lighthouse at the tip of the high hill, overlooking the bays below, that could only be accessed by boat. It was a great 'cycle' ride and we left our bikes on the sandy beach, to walk along the bay at Formentor which was surrounded by fir trees. On the return we stopped a number of times, not only to catch our breath, but also to look at varying scenery as we turned one corner after another.

One night, I woke up feeling itchy. After a few minutes I realised that it was something crawling over me. I jumped out of bed waking John up, to see hundreds of small black ants scurrying to and fro through the bed sheets. I sprayed the bed with an ant killing aerosol and went for a shower. No, that's not quite right! It took four showers and a lot of shampoo to get all the small, crawling insects out of my hair. I went back to the bedroom, John was fast asleep and so were the ants I had sprayed. A quick shake of the sheets and just like an ant, I crawled back into bed. The sheets had a good wash the next day. Janet saw to that! It was 1998 and the football world cup was being played. Needless to say, every evening we walked about a mile to the nearest bar and watched the action. England didn't win the world cup, but our holiday was fantastic.

Now I just wanted to get on with the remainder of my life. Following the divorce, the feeling gradually sinks in that the world is your oyster, only to be guided by the laws of the land.

Sarah and I went to see my mum a few times, before she died on a Friday night in June 1999 with Janet by her side. She was living in a Southport nursing home at the time. Unfortunately I was unable to be with her, as I was working in the post office and it was not possible to get away before the weekend.

In 2000 we returned to Majorca, but this time without my sister, as she was unable to get the appropriate weeks off work. We stayed in a villa in the centre of old Pollensa in a large Spanish type house, with a courtyard large enough to take a coach and horses. No ants to wake me up this time, but May had a bad fall and ended up at the outpatient's clinic of the hospital in Alcudia. It restricted us a little, as we had to go back a couple of times, to make sure the leg was healing alright. We were really impressed with the nursing care given.

After 2 years of being single I didn't know how I was going to meet anyone else to share my life with. All my time was spent working in the shop, or Post Office, so I decided to get monthly copies of the "Dateline" magazine. This introduced ladies to gentlemen and visa versa. I took the monthly copy with me on holiday. Whilst looking through it, I read the information about an Asian nurse who was interested in the same things as myself. I wrote a letter to her and posted it as soon as we returned back to England. Within a couple of weeks I received a reply. The lady lived in Kidlington. This was the nearest town to Yarnton, about 3 miles away. She could have been anywhere in the United Kingdom, but no, she was just a few fields away across the canal and railway line. That must be fate. She introduced herself as a 50 year old, who was born in the Philippines and lived with her two sons. I gave her a phone call and we decided to meet outside the 'Randolph Hotel' in the centre of Oxford.

The evening came for our meeting. I managed to park the car in St.Giles, which is only a short walk away from Oxford's famous hotel. It has been featured in television programmes, and looked after various Prime Ministers and Presidents, in addition to various celebrities. Boy was

I nervous as I approached the hotel. Believe it or not, but I had not been to many places by myself during the course of my life. Meeting ladies was a bit different! Zeni, turned the corner a few minutes after I arrived. I knew it must have been her, as she walked towards me in a light cream, suede coat. We passed introductions and went into the hotel for a drink and a good talk. She looked very attractive sitting across the table from me, and I found her very easy to talk to. She had the same problem as myself in meeting people. We talked about our likes and dislikes, our past problems, our children, our work and our aspirations for the future. Time passed very quickly, so it must have been a good first meeting. Zeni came into Oxford by bus as she couldn't drive I offered to take her home. Oh Oh!! Things could have gone a bit better. We got back to the car, and there on the windscreen was a parking ticket. I had been so nervous, that I placed the ticket the wrong way round! On our way back we made arrangements to get in touch again. This was the start of our life together. Zeni is a loving, compassionate, caring, and romantic, 5 foot Filipino beauty. I could think of no one better to share my life with. I can honestly say that since meeting Zeni, my life has changed for the better. It was obvious to both of us, that there was something magical between us. We just fitted into each other's life. Like a broken jigsaw, we had lots of pieces lying around, but gradually everything began to take shape and we could make out the big picture of our life together. I am pleased to say that when I sent a copy of my ticket for parking to those concerned, I did not have to pay the fine.

Three years before I sold the Post Office, I was approached by the owner of a garage down the road. He had decided to open a convenience store on the site, and wanted me to move my business into his. Terms were agreed upon and a few months later we moved the Post Office within his store. I took my two members of staff with me. One left but, Judy Welch stayed with me until it was sold. She was the best person I ever employed, and without her I would not have been able to have as much time off to start my new life.

I enjoyed my post office career, especially the years as the Postmaster of Yarnton. The contact with the customers, trying to help them and listening to their problems was really rewarding. I would like to thank each and every one of them, for the support and friendship they showed me, and for allowing me to serve them during my 13 years there. I will always remember this time in my life. My heartfelt and sincere thanks.

Book 3

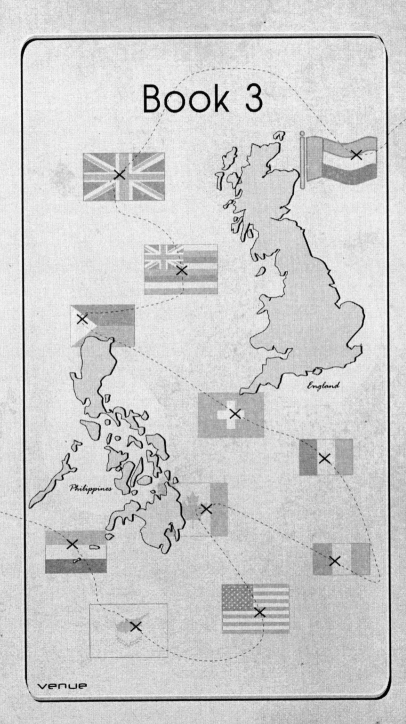

1

SOON after meeting Zeni, her friend Linda and husband Ed, came over from the U.S.A.. Zeni had known them for a long time and it was lovely listening to them reminisce and finding out more about Zeni's past life. At the weekend we took them to see my sister, Janet, who lives near the U.S.A.A.F. base, where Ed was working when he met Linda. We walked across and down the road, for a drink at the "Blackbird", the local for the Americans stationed nearby and where Ed used to visit when working there. It brought many memories back for them.

I really enjoy their company and we have met on a number of occasions since, in America.

A few weeks later we went to Heathrow airport, to meet more of Zeni's friends. Nimfa, Brian and Lesley, their daughter, along with Mariet were on a pilgrimage to Europe and stopped over in London for one night. It gave me the opportunity to make new friends and listen to some further events in Zeni's interesting life.

Sarah and I moved in with Zeni, and her two boys after selling the home in Yarnton. Zeni made sure Sarah had a nice room. It was in fact two rooms. An archway knocked through the bedrooms let Sarah have one as a bedroom, the other a living area, where she could study and entertain friends. She decorated the rooms, according to her taste and settled in very well.

Soon after Zeni went to Lourdes in France with her friends. She had booked the trip before we decided to move in together.

Whilst running the post office and before getting married we enjoyed many occasions which brought us closer together.

One weekend, we stayed at Express by Holiday Inn. Just off the M5 at junction 25 near Taunton. The following day we carried on to the Eden Project, near St. Austell in Cornwall. The huge 50 metre deep crater, left from a china clay pit, housed two biomes. These are huge honeycomb looking conservatories. The largest, houses trees, plants, shrubs and flowers from the humid, tropical areas of the world. It is 200 metres long, 100 metres wide and 47 metres high. On entering, as the heat hits you, the vastness of the place is appreciated. The rubber trees, bamboo and sugar cane, made Zeni immediately think of home. A hut was set out, as if in the Philippines, or other countries around the area. The colourful plants and flowers, often pointed at, with the comment " just like home". Fruit trees, not normally seen in England, were growing in the dome. It was very interesting.

After leaving this biome we entered another with different vegetation, from the world's warm and temperate zones, as in the Mediterranean, California, and South Africa. The difference was astounding, from the lush greenery, to the apparent barren areas. The stark contrast, suddenly made your eyes focus lower. The shorter olive trees, the bushes of tobacco and the vines producing succulent grapes for the table or wine for the carafe. The California poppy was adding a burst of colour to the arid land.

Outside, plants from the local area and cooler climate, on different stepped gardens brought the entire project together. There are over 4,500 species of plants growing in their natural surroundings. It was a fantastic week end. One day we will go back and see how the sight has flourished, since its conception. It was opened only a few months before we visited.

On other weekends we walked around Oxford and along the River Thames. Drive locally to the villages and towns of Eynsham, Witney, Burford, Chipping Norton, or Banbury. Stopping to walk through the town and have an afternoon tea and cakes, before exploring the surrounding countryside. Further afield Warwick with its castle and Stratford upon Avon, Shakespeare's birthplace as well as Leamington Spa and Tewksbury were a few of the other places visited.

Zeni and I discovered that we both wanted to emigrate to Canada, many years before. There was an exhibition, in Milton Keynes, regarding this. We really looked forward to the possibility of fulfilling what was almost a life long dream. A lot of research was carried out and we decided to use an immigration firm to help us. Everything was going well, until a couple of weeks before the papers were to be submitted to the Canadian Government. The rules were changed overnight and we had to find double the amount required under the proposed scheme. It had already cost us a few thousand pounds to get to this stage, but we had to stop the process. To say we were upset was an understatement. But these things happen in life and we continued to look to the future. We started looking at the possibility of buying a property in Canada and use it for our holidays. Many weekends we would look in magazines to give us more information regarding the idea.

On 25th January 2002, we caught Air Canada flight 861, at 11.30am, from terminal 3 at London's Heathrow airport, bound for Halifax, Nova Scotia. The flight stopped over at St. Johns in Newfoundland. About 10 minutes before touch down, we flew just a few hundred feet over the Atlantic Ocean, before landing on a snowy runway. The snow ploughs, with their blowers attached, scurried around to keep the areas clear. The blizzard, which had swept through earlier, had covered the trees with a white blanket, their younger and softer bows reaching to the ground with the weight. Lorries in the area were filled with snow and slowly edged their way from the buildings and runways to deposit their load in huge mounds on the airport's perimeter. Snow was blowing in small rivulets. The course changing as a vehicle, or the force of an engine, altered the wind direction.

After a short stay we continued our flight. The flight over Newfoundland and into Nova Scotia, appeared from above as if we were flying over a huge, starched, white sheet, torn by a frozen river below the rugged cliffs. This sheet was immediately repaired as we continued our flight. Then the sea, transformed by icebergs, slowly flowing and melting their way, to the warmer currents. On the opposite side of the plane, a small runway could be seen, stretching the full length of an island. There were a few houses in the distance, barely visible, as they blended in with the surrounding white of the land. For mile, after mile, the undulating sheet covered all below it. Only when we started to descend into Halifax, was it possible to make out the thousands of trees that had been hidden, by the pristine natural cover of the snow. A road appeared, seemingly from nowhere. The weather ensuring that few, if any, vehicles would use it that day. Frozen lakes and rivers emerged and intermingled with the forest areas. The winter weather tried to hide, then enhance the natural beauty below. As the taxi driver drove us to the capital, we were informed that 22 cm of snow had fallen overnight.

We had booked a room at the Holiday Inn, Harbourview for two nights with the intention of looking at a property in Digby. We were informed it was over an hour's drive away from the city. As we were having our evening meal, the decision was made, not to look at the property, due in part to the weather conditions. If it was an hour in good weather, how long would it take in the present road conditions, and would we be able to get back for the flight. We were not worried that we had flown for 5 hours and changed our mind on landing. The right decision is what mattered.

The evening meal was excellent and the corn chowder has never been matched. We have it whenever it is on a menu to see if any chef can achieve the same taste. We will keep trying! Afterwards the short walk in the deep snow, added beauty to the otherwise grey roads and pavements, and it was good to get back into the warmth of the hotel.

The next day we took a taxi into Halifax, from the hotel which was in Dartmouth. We went across the Angus L.

Macdonald Bridge, which stretches across the harbour estuary and into the city centre. We were dropped off along Barrington St., within walking distance of the ferry terminal. After having a drink to warm us up, we walked along by Purdy's Wharf looking at the water in the harbour below, and playing in the snow like children. Then back again, into Scotia Square and the streets nearby.

It was cold enough for me to buy a nice warm, insulated, head hugging hat. I felt a lot warmer as soon as I put it on. We meandered down to the wharf again and stopped at the casino at 6.00pm for a meal. The heat hit us as we entered, and the food was almost as good as the heat, inviting you to stay and see if you could beat the house. We declined and left after eating to return to the hotel. It wasn't what we expected to do during the day, but it was really enjoyable. The bedroom overlooked the harbour. It is the second largest natural harbour in the world. Sidney being the first. The cargo ships waiting to be loaded or unloaded as soon as possible, so they can be on their way to the next port of call. Ships from the naval base, could be seen further along in the harbour.

After a late start the following day, we took a taxi to the Mic Mac shopping mall. We enjoyed looking around the shops, before heading back again to the hotel for an evening meal. We would be leaving for home the following afternoon. Before that though, we took a nice walk down Aidemey Drive, to the ferry terminal on the Dartmouth side of the harbour. The airport bus picked us up from outside the hotel at 5.40pm, to arrive at the airport half an hour later, so we could check in for our 9.15pm flight back to London. The plane was a few minutes late taking off, as we had to wait for a passenger. The local Inuit was clad in her warm seal skin coat with her baby wrapped up in pouch. We both looked at one another and agreed it was the first Eskimo we had ever seen. It was easy to understand why they are so well prepared for the cold. Whilst looking at the television earlier, a temperature of -42 was forecast further north. The mother and child left the plane in St. John, Newfoundland, fully prepared for the icy blast that entered through the aircraft door. Zeni remarked that she hoped that they would both arrive home safely without getting frostbite!

We thoroughly enjoyed the long weekend, even though we didn't look at the house. It was our first holiday away together and one we will always remember. We came away more convinced than ever, that we would buy a property in Canada in the future. We were made welcome everywhere and greeted warmly.

It was on February the first that I proposed to Zeni. I made arrangements to get married as soon as possible. The date and time were to be memorable. The 22nd 02. 2002. The time, of course, was 2.00pm. We would have to leave our home, at number 222 half an hour earlier, or perhaps it would only take 22 minutes! On the 4th of February, we visited Biagio the jewellers, in Bicester and bought the wedding rings.

2

THE three weeks passed very quickly, and in what seemed like the blink of an eye, it was our wedding day. I went into work until 11.00 am and then left our trustworthy friend, Judy to look after everything for the rest of the day. We took Giles, Craig and Sarah with us and met Janet and John at the registry office in Bicester, a small town 8 miles from Oxford. It was a simple ceremony. I clearly remember how much happier I felt, than after my first wedding. Relatives and friends including Dave and Jill, Judy and her friend Ted, attended the evening reception at the Holiday Inn by the Pear Tree roundabout in Oxford. The food, cake, champagne and music were all good, and the guests made it a really enjoyable event.

I was awake at 3.30am, just thinking of the great day.

We got a taxi at 6.45am to take us on the first step of our journey to Paris. Arriving at the Waterloo railway station with an hour to spare, we checked in for the Eurostar train ride through the channel tunnel to the Gare Du Nord station, which is on the outskirts of the city centre near the Sacre-Coeur in Montmartre. The taxi driver, decided to take us for a trip around the city before we got to the hotel. He certainly went a long way round to get to the Holiday Inn at Garden Court, Paris-Elysees. What a good choice for a place to stay. Within two minutes, we were walking along the Champs Elysees after passing the Elysees Palace.

The stroll up to the Arc de Triumph took over an hour, as we viewed the different shops along the way. We looked at all the people drinking their coffee or wine, as they sat outside the café, under a veranda, some with fronts zipped on, in order to keep the customer warm and the cold air out. They in turn, were looking at the people strolling along the world famous thoroughfare, passing the time of day with the company around them. Upon reaching the Arc, we wandered back towards the hotel and went to visit a perfumery that Zeni had noticed earlier. Ladies have a remarkable knack for finding the most expensive shops! The store is situated on the corner of the Rue de Miromesnil, where the hotel is, and the Rue du Faubourg St. Honore, where all the designer stores are located. Also a few countries have their embassies located there. After half an hour in the perfumery, Zeni decide that she couldn't go to Paris and come away without some perfume. So she didn't!

For an evening meal we wandered up to the Champs Elysees and down one of the side streets, where we found a nice restaurant. Following breakfast the next morning, we decided to visit the Eiffel tower. Zeni is scared of heights, but even so she still managed to get to the top in the lift, by keeping her head pressed tightly into my jacket. It was definitely quicker than climbing the 1,700 steps. Designed by the same architect as the Statue of Liberty, the 320m high tower must be one of the most famous landmarks in the world. Stepping out of the lift, one is led into a covered section. Plaques describe and point to the area that reaches out to the horizon up to 75km away. After a few minutes, Zeni felt brave enough to venture to the outside walkway and go all around the top of the huge metal construction. She told me, that as long as we are together, she would go wherever I wanted as she felt secure with me. That made me feel as tall as the tower! We stopped off at the third floor before leaving the tower behind and wandering around looking for a restaurant. The food was delicious as you would expect in France. We went into a shop selling exquisite looking cakes, and bought some to eat there and then. Thinking of the family back home, we bought some more for when we got home later that night.

It started raining as we headed back to the hotel and by the time we arrived, we were wet through. As soon as we changed our heavy, rain soaked clothes, we took a taxi back to the station for our return trip home. It was only a brief honeymoon, but it was a very romantic, happy, and interesting excursion. Definitely worth a further visit.

Although the families had fitted in well, I wanted us all to go on holiday together, to bring everybody closer and feel more of the same unit. I asked John if he would come with us, but he declined. Cora's friend, Boots, was going to have a big celebration party for her 50th birthday. We were invited and naturally accepted. The party would be incorporated into our holiday. Of course I had to make sure the business was going to be alright whilst away. After Zeni and I had discussed the proposed itinerary, I talked to Judy about leaving her in charge, if I could get someone else to help her. She agreed and I felt relieved, knowing that everything would be in safe hands for my longest holiday ever, three weeks on the North American continent. Sarah decided that she would only join us for two of the weeks, so her tickets were bought accordingly.

On the 6th March, 2002, I booked the flights to Los Angeles. After further discussions with Zeni, we decided to incorporate a visit to Vancouver whilst on the continent. Flights were duly booked, from Los Angeles to Vancouver. Hotels were checked out and booked over the internet.

The Queen Mother died on 31st March 2002. She was 101 and the whole nation mourned. The Queen's sister, Margaret, had only died 7 weeks prior and sympathy for the Queen was profound.

On Sunday, 7th April, Zeni, Sarah and I went to London, to see Her Majesty's body lying in State. We joined a long queue of people, waiting to pay their respects to the Royal who was loved by all. It took four hours, before we entered the doors of the Palace of Westminster, and slowly wended our way to Westminster Hall. From there it took a further half an hour before we reached the large room, where the coffin stood on its plinth. On arrival, we looked towards the coffin. At each corner, stood either a Gentleman at Arms or Yeoman of the Guard, looking resplendent, yet solemn in their official dress uniform. Their heads were bowed, with hands gripping the ceremonial sword resting the tip in front of the feet. The Vigil of the Watch. The long line of mourners stretched down the stairs and around the coffin. White flowers adorned the lid of the coffin, along with Her Majesty's crown. Its Ko-I Noor diamond set within, making the ceremonial head wear priceless. We paid our respects and went home. Just three of the estimated 200,000 people that managed to do so. The funeral took place at Westminster Abbey on the 9th April, with the precision, timing, dignity and ceremony required of such an occasion. The bell tolled once every minute, for each year of her life. The Massed Pipes and Drums, the gun carriage carrying the coffin, the Royals in their respective military uniforms, followed the carriage. It was such a sad, memorable, yet resplendent procession, in all its glory and sorrow. It is estimated that a million people were either at the Abbey, or along the route to Windsor Castle to pay their respects, and millions around the United Kingdom observed 2 minutes of silence when the coffin reached the castle at 11.30am. The last Queen of Ireland and Empress of India was finally laid to rest, next to her husband in St Georges Chapel. Monarchs, Royalty, and Heads of State who attended from around the world returned to their respective countries, their respects paid, as ours was, a few days earlier.

A much happier event took place during the first week of June with Her Majesty the Queen, celebrating 50 years of accession to the throne. Jubilee celebrations stretched over 4 days with official pageantry, and religious services, culminating in the people's show of love and affection. As the celebrations also included a public holiday, it was on that day, Monday 3rd June, when Zeni, Sarah and I headed off to the capital. We caught the bus from Oxford in the morning to give us a few hours around London, before the main event later. The road to the palace from the Royal Mews was closed off for the day. Instead of vehicles there were people. It was strange to be able to wander around the road without noise and fumes. I kept checking to ensure nothing would come along with the horn blaring away. We walked down The

Mall, the thoroughfare leading from Trafalgar Square and Whitehall to Buckingham Palace. The monarch's London residence, acquired for the crown in 1761. Since then it has been redesigned and enlarged. Even though it was bombed in the Second World War, the then King and Queen, (the Queen Mother who had just died) decided to stay there and be amongst their people. We went in and around St. James park, stopping for a drink at the café there. It was starting to get busy with people. Happy souls, talking, laughing, running, strolling, sitting, and playing. The St. John's Ambulance members were there to assist with any sudden health problems, along with the ambulance crews. There were police everywhere, helping, talking, and listening, as the public poured out their problems, or asked for advice. Never obtrusive. Always vigilant. Enough people around now, to say that, the crowd was starting to sit wherever they could, to get a view of the evening's event. Around the Queen Victoria Memorial into Constitution Hill and Green Park, along both sides of the Mall, into St. James Park and Birdcage Walk people were gathering. Yes, it must be time to settle somewhere with a television monitor within sight. We managed to find a spare piece of the kerb, about a quarter of the way up the Mall from the Palace with a monitor opposite and a view right up to the Royal Residence. Radio's talking or playing music and impromptu singing from various groups of people. The monitors were frequently being tested. Everything and everybody was in place for the concert of the year.

Up on the roof of the building, a 'lone' guitarist starts the proceedings. High above the crowds outside and the audience in the garden behind, Brian May, from the group

Queen, played the National Anthem. It was so spectacular, so moving, and a brilliant start to a concert, which included such famous names as, Sir Cliff Richard, Eric Clapton, Ozzy Osborne, Rod Stewart, Joe Cocker, Ray Davies, (from the Kinks) Brian Wilson (the Beach Boys)and Sir Paul McCartney. A great show! Everyone seemed to enjoy it. Then the fireworks. 2.75 tonnes of explosives leaping into space, from the roof of the palace. The colours burning their way, high into the night sky. During the concert, the front of Her Majesty's palace was changed in appearance, with the assistance of laser beams depicting the Union Jack the nation's flag, changing the colour of the brickwork and then spelling out the message endorsed by all. GOD SAVE THE QUEEN. We managed to make our way together with the other million or so spectators to our transport home. We remembered as we went, the other events that had taken place during the celebrations. The parade of people dressed in costumes and the decorated vehicles. The world's largest gospel choir (5,000). The Concorde and Red Arrows fly past. Also the religious ceremony with all the dignitaries. I can't remember what time we got home, but needless to say it wasn't early.

3

O N the 19th July, Craig, Giles, Zeni and I, arrived at Heathrow airport, bright and early, after getting a taxi at 3.00am, to catch the 6.20am flight from terminal 2. An unusual terminal for a long haul flight, but we flew via Zurich, before heading off to LAX, Los Angeles airport. We arrived in L.A. on time, to be met by Ed and Linda, and Nori and Mariet. It took about 1 hour 15 minutes, to drive to Ed and Linda's house in Duarte, a town between San Bernardino and Pasadena, along the famous Route 66. The new house has a lovely garden, with lemon and lime bushes, as well as the largest magnolia tree I have ever seen. The San Gabriel mountain range rose high in the sky on the near horizon. It was HOT. I had never experienced such heat and was very grateful for the air conditioning inside the immaculate, warm and friendly home. Giles and I went for a walk along Oak Drive. It was strange to see the large palm trees, oranges and lemons, growing in gardens. So unlike England.

We got up late the next morning, to find Ed and Linda waiting for us to start breakfast. Most of the morning, was spent catching up with the news and events from both sides of the Atlantic The afternoon saw us wandering around the town, down Route 66 and getting ice-cream to try and cool us down. It didn't work.

For the evening, Ed and Linda had organised a Hawaiian party for us. It was a lovely evening with a pig roasting on the spit, and tables covered with all sorts of different food, both Filipino and American. All the drinks being kept in big bins, to ensure they kept cool. Hannah and Mitchi came over from their new home in Long Beach. Belen arranged for family and friends to perform an Hawaiian dance for us. It was a night to remember.

I had never dreamed of going to Las Vegas. It was one of those places that you hear of but never expect to visit. That changed. Mariet, Nori and Belen decided to treat us all for three days. WOW! We set off at 3.30pm the next day. Later than anticipated, as the hire car we were going to use, had been run into at the back, and was out of service. We waited at Nori and Mariet's, until Jing, their brother, turned up with the vehicle over an hour late. Then another eye opener. We drove over the San Gabriel Mountains through the San Bernardino National Forest, on Highway 15 into the Mojave desert. I had heard of the desert, but never thought I would see it, let alone drive through it! It was going through the desert that made me realise just how large America is. The barren land with the mountains seemed to go on forever. Mile after hot mile. It was incredible. As we went through Baker, the largest thermometer in the world, reaching high into the never ending blue sky signalled that the temperature was an incredible 127 degrees Fahrenheit. We drove past a sign post showing Death Valley. I had heard of it, but

DAVID & ZENI TARLING

had no idea where it was. There we were. Going so close. Now I know why it got its name. We stopped off at a rest area. A train appeared from behind one of the mountains, it seemed to go on forever. Its last wagon, eventually, came into view. It looked about a mile away from the engine. A long metal snake, moving across the desert floor with its tail following. Winding along and through the parched land, to its next place of rest, goodness knows how many miles away. We passed a large casino on the Nevada border, giving a brief insight into what lay ahead. Then it came into view. An ensemble of huge buildings in the middle of nowhere. We drove along The Strip. The roads with more lanes of traffic than the British motorways, hemmed in on either side, by buildings of various shapes and sizes, but none small. We entered the "Stardust", where we were staying through the car park entrance, passing through a seating area, then down a couple of steps towards the reservation desk. Zeni and I stayed in room 11502 in the West Tower. It was on the 15th floor. How tall are these buildings? There was certainly nothing this tall in Oxford. It would have dwarfed all around it. The bedroom was bigger then most living rooms back home. The shower could have held ten people!

Ed, Giles, Craig and myself had a walk around, after leaving Zeni playing the slot machines with her friends. It was hard to believe what we saw. The casinos, with varying themes, stretching high in the sky as wide as three, four, or even five English hotels put together, and much, much longer. Around midnight we gave up and went to bed. It was still 88 degrees outside, warmer than many an English summer day. Zeni had WON!! The following day, most were playing in the casino, however Giles and Craig went off by themselves, and Zeni and I decided to wander along The Strip. Stardust is near the far end and we decided to walk the full length to the Mandalay Bay , which was then one of the first casinos on entering the city centre. It was still hot! We managed to get past the Frontier, before entering the new fashion area that was under construction. It was in the shade. Oh! The luxury of shade! On walking past Treasure Island, it was decided to call in at every casino to try and keep cool. We just walked through the entrance of Mirage, which is set back off the street. After this, we carried on to Caesars Palace and went in to have a look around. It is so difficult to describe the vastness of these structures. There are villages within each building! As we walked into the place, there are shops on the left and right hand side, as you reach a square. There is a replica of the Trevi fountain in Rome with café 's around it. We carried on to the next large building 'Bellagio'. Wow! Outside, the huge lake area has musical fountains that entertain the visitors of this unusual city in the desert. A spectacular sight! We called in a shop as we passed near Monte Carlo for a bottle of water. I had wondered why a lot of people were carrying a bottle. Although seldom seen in England, it is an essential part of life in a desert environment. The temperature had reached 117 F. New York has an area like Times Square within it, with small streets leading off. We only had time for a quick visit to Excalibur, before calling in at Luxor, the pyramid along the strip for a nice meal. On entering, there are huge Egyptian statues as if in the front of the tombs. Into Mandalay Bay then quickly back. We had to get the mono rail to Excalibur, then crossed over to MGM with the white lions behind the well cleaned glass, at the edge of the vast area of slot machines. Time was passing far too quickly and we had to get a bus to Paris, the casino with a copy of the Eiffel Tower. It was half the original size, but still large as it looks over the street below. There was hardly any time left to call into the Venetian, with its gondolas taking you for a ride through the water, if you so wished, to the Italian interior. That was it. No more time. Belen treated us to a show for the evening as a wedding present. The Wayne Newton theatre at the Stardust had the person it was named after performing. First though, we were all treated to a Chinese meal in the restaurant. What a lovely gift and such a kind thought. We thoroughly enjoyed the show and were so grateful. The next day, the four of us went with Ed and Linda and started at the Mandalay Bay. They showed us the Shark Reef aquarium, with the pool outside with sandy beaches, and the magnificent restaurants. A quick Hello to Luxor, but time to take a ride 'In Search Of The Obelisk', then we visited New York before catching the mono rail to Bally, and a walk to Paris for a lovely drink in one of the French cafes on the stone cobbled street. Then time was up. It was back to Duarte, through the desert again with the tumble weed blowing in the wind. We drove by cattle, about 5 cows, despite everyone thinking I was seeing things or I was utterly mad, up to the top of the pass, 4,726 feet above sea level, before finally dropping down to the plains below. What a fantastic few days in a larger than life city. The streets were busy 24 hours of the day. The journey was incredible. The vastness! The heat! The memories! The following day we took a quick trip to Ontario. No, not Canada, but another town half an hour's drive away, where we had lunch. A family meal finished off the day.

What next! A day out to San Diego. Ed and Linda, the four of us, together with Linda's family, set out on the 2 ½ hour drive along the Pacific coast. We were off to Sea World. There are so many things to see and do. Shamu the killer whales show. It was absolutely fantastic. Be prepared to get wet if you sit in one of the front rows. There are turtles and flamingos and a manatee rescue centre. Of course, Ed and I, together with Zeni and Linda, had to go into the Budweiser beer school. We still have the certificates to prove we are now certified beer masters. As we started to enter the polar bear enclosure we noticed the time. Sarah would be setting out to join us. The polar bears looked so content in their large enclosure with a deep swimming area. They looked better and cleaner than any I had previously seen in various zoos. On the way home we all stopped at Applebee's for a meal, courtesy of Brian.

Flight SR 106 carrying Sarah, touched down late. Even so, an hour and a half after her due landing time, her smiling face appeared through the arrival area, to be met by, Zeni, Linda, Ed and myself. We drove back to Duarte, to await Giles and Craig, who had gone out with their cousins around the Hollywood district. At 8.00pm we were bound for our next destination. Ed and Linda, Mariet and Nori, took us all to 1520 South Harbour Boulevard, Anaheim. We said our goodbyes. We thanked them for a really fantastic holiday. Thanks didn't seem adequate. What more could we say, except that we were looking forward to seeing them again, at the end of the holiday before flying home. After they had left, we settled into our rooms at the Park Inn. Our room, 315, was just as big as the one in Las Vegas. Everything is done in a big way in America! The hotel was directly across from Disneyland, and as we went out onto the corridor, we could see the fireworks exploding in the sky. Cliff and Belinda, with their children, Katy and Tyler along with Katy's boyfriend, Mike, met us downstairs. We had made arrangements to meet them soon after booking the holiday. It was nice to meet more of Zeni's family. After deciding where to have breakfast in the morning, (one of the important things in life), we all left for our various rooms, and a good night's sleep. The following day was spent naturally at Disneyland. Following an evening meal, close to the hotel, we returned. Craig, Giles, Sarah and I watched, as the others re-entered Disneyland, whilst we went to the entrance on the other side. This took us into California Adventure. We wanted to experience the bigger rides. On the roller coaster ride 'California Screamin'', we were expecting a slow start, but the small train shot up the first steep incline taking us all by surprise. We did a complete circle. I am pleased to say we survived all the rides even after going at break neck speed, vertically up a square metal structure to such a height, that we had a good view of the whole district. It didn't last more than a second or two, before we sped down to the ground. Maliboomer, as it was called, was so quick. 180 feet in 4 seconds! It stopped me talking in mid sentence. It takes something to do that. Then, the 'Parade'.

The evening show was full of razzmatazz, music and Disney creatures, showing themselves off. This was followed by the fireworks. We managed to get a late drink of coffee, listening to jazz, as the darkness of the evening surrounded us.

Another day and another place to visit. This time we caught a coach to 'Universal Studios'. We walked past the huge stainless steel globe, bought our tickets and carried on through the archway, advising us that we were in the right place. Once inside, we met up with Belinda and her family. Hannah and Michi also joined us. Where to go? What to see? The area is vast, as are the events. We took a coach tour around the sets. We were told how the facade of the building could soon change, according to requirements. We were shown where 'Jaws' lived and thought we would be washed away in a flood. We entered an earthquake zone. Most of all, we found it all very interesting and enjoyable. A show, reflecting the film 'Waterworld', entertained us with the high power jet ski stunts, water soaking everyone in the front rows, explosions, and believe it or not a plane landing in the small lake in front of us. Incredible! We saw E.T. as he cycled off home. An Egyptian mummy made Zeni jump out of her skin. She was walking past the statue, when it suddenly bent down to say hello. I have never seen anyone move back so quickly. We had a meal next to Jurassic Park, before going on the ride that ends with a vertical drop of 84 feet, to the water below. A ride on the escalator is an experience in itself. It must be one of the longest in the world, leading from the top section of the studios to the lower level. Another excellent day.

On Monday 29th July, the Airbus A320, left LAX at 12.05pm and landed in Vancouver, Canada at 2.40pm, the next stage of our incredible holiday. It was cheaper to get a stretched limousine to the Holiday Inn, Vancouver centre in Broadway, and Randy dropped us off there 15-20 minutes later. The 16 floor hotel was very welcoming, as we entered and found out which rooms we would be in, for the next stay of our travels. We soon got out and walked to Granville Island which is situated just below the Granville Street Bridge. It is a mix of an area. The market offered a huge variety of fresh fruit and vegetables, meat and fresh fish, bread and cakes. Cafe's and restaurants abounded. Studios and Galleries, intermingle with retail outlets, maritime services, and a brewing company. In the early evening, we set out for an exploratory walk around part of the city of Vancouver. Along Broadway and over Granville Bridge, turn right then up Cambie street, turn right along East Pender St. turn left, soon after and you will find China Town. We followed the instructions and found a good restaurant in the second largest Chinese community in North America. After the meal, Giles and Craig went back to the hotel by taxi. Zeni, Sarah and I decided to carry on looking around the city. We set off for Gastown, the old Victorian part of the city, where 'Gassy Jack' Leighton, the Irish publican, set about establishing the city of Vancouver. Somewhere, I took the wrong turn and ended up where we were advised not to go!

As soon as I realised we had turned right instead of left, it was a quick about turn. The stroll turned into a fast walk, as we passed through the more unsavoury side of the city. Even so, we never felt as if we had anything to worry about. However, it was a bit of a relief, as we turned a street that led us down into the Gastown region. As night encroached upon day we returned to the hotel. It was the Broadway area the next morning, and a snack in the Wendy's restaurant. Giles and Craig decided to stay around the city in the afternoon, whilst Zeni, Sarah and I took a trip. The first call was the Capilano Salmon Hatchery. The man made salmon ladder, assisting the salmon to return up the river to spawn. It was just the beginning of the migration for the fish, and only a few were actually trying to ascend the concrete steps to reach their place of birth. We found the talk about the salmon's life very interesting. The building is set amid a cedar forest. A short walk leads to some fantastic views, with the fast running water, falling, splashing finding its way between the trees and rocks as it heads down the mountainside.

Next, we were off to the Capilano suspension bridge. A 10 minute drive from the city centre and you can walk over a 450 foot bridge, swaying from side to side, as you look over into the river, 230 feet below. It was in 1889 that the first footbridge spanned the gorge, enabling the owner to cross over from one side of his property to the other. I am pleased to say it has been rebuilt since then. The new one has steel cables in concrete blocks holding the secured planks. Zeni was going across with me. I could tell she was really frightened, but as I wanted to go, nothing was going to stop her, even when I said I would wait with her whilst Sarah went over. She stuck to me like glue, mainly because some people started to sway the bridge from side to side. A voice boomed out from a microphone telling them to stop, which they did. On the way back over, after walking around the forest path, Zeni felt much better. It seemed as if she may be overcoming her fear. We received certificates to say that 'We Made It' across the hair raising, moving, passage way, with the breath taking view many feet below. The totem poles have been in the park for 60 years, after being carved with their insignia of events, and given by the indigenous population. They look new, so must be well maintained. It was only a further 5 minutes to our next destination. We got out of the coach and caught the Sky Ride to the Peak of Vancouver, Grouse Mountain. The 8 minute ride in the cable car, took us over huge Douglas Firs, reaching up to touch us, from their roots many feet below. The view 3,700 feet above Vancouver is sensational. You can see over to Vancouver Island, the Fraser Valley, Richmond, with its International airport that serves Vancouver. The mountains to the back and sides of us are breathtaking! We walked straight along the wooden walkway, into the Peak Chalet complex. The Theatre in the Sky was showing the film 'Born To Fly', an eagle's eye view of Vancouver and its surrounding countryside. I enjoyed the film so much that I bought the video and the sound track tape. That tape has been played so many times since! We strolled on to the area where bears are given refuge after being orphaned or badly injured. It is a huge enclosure. The bears are allowed to wander freely around, and are fed daily with salmon and other food thrown into the compound. As they will be returned to the wild, as little human contact as possible is essential. We were fortunate to see them run out for the food, before taking it back into their forest home. Back and down the hill a few yards to watch the lumberjack show. The speed with which the chain saws were handled making wooden figures or seats was breathtaking. Sarah carried on to the chair lift, taking her another 400 feet to the peak. Zeni and I went back to the main chalet for a drink and a snack.

We met Sarah outside. Whoops! Zeni and I were a bit late. Fortunately, Sarah was there to usher us along to catch the last cable car down, in order to be in time for the coach journey back. We stopped off at the Capilano reservoir and

Cleveland Dam, before going to Lonsdale Quay Market to catch the sea bus across the Burrard Inlet and docking in Vancouver. The coach driver was waiting for us as we got off to take us back to our hotel, after a really marvellous day. It still wasn't finished.

We had asked around for a good place to eat with a good view. At 8.45pm we took a lift to the 42nd floor of the Landmark Hotel, in Robson Street. It was a good recommendation. As we waited for a table, the Jazz band was playing nearby. We ordered our drinks and decided on what to eat. We were shown to our table and started to enjoy the well prepared and delicious food. We sat by the window of the revolving restaurant, giving a 360 degree outlook, that takes 1 hour 10 minutes to complete one revolution. Our view began by looking across at two peaks high in the sky. The lions, as the 5,400 and 5,200 foot mountains are called, can be seen from many locations around the city. The Lions Gate bridge built by the Guinness brewing family and opened in 1938 enabling the North Shore to be linked permanently with Downtown Vancouver. Moving slowly round and Grouse Mountain came into the centre of the panoramic view. It is just possible to make out the cable car and supporting pylons. The ski slope cut out between the Douglas firs showing a green belt stretching towards North Vancouver. A small mountain of yellow sulphur was waiting for export. We saw Lonsdale Quay where we had caught the ferry previously, Mount Seymour and the port area stretching along the Burrard Inlet. The towering cranes in one of the busiest ports in Pacific America. The Gastown area, and way below us Robson Street. The mountain peaks in the background. The district of Burnaby and

Vancouver. Vanier Park leading to the wooded area around the University of British Columbia. English Bay flowing to False Creek. Finally Stanley Park. The largest urban park in North America with one thousand acres of absolute heaven. Inside there is a temperate rain forest, marsh land, ordinary woodland, Lost Lagoon and Beaver Lake. The largest aquarium in Canada, Totem Poles, beaches, restaurants all linked together with intertwining trails. The 5.5 miles seawall walk, takes you past Brockton Point, Prospect Point, and Ferguson Point, all with varying views. It was 3 hours later, after completing a succulent meal that we returned to the hotel. We were exhausted, but what a day.

Time for a lie in! NO. There was too much to see and do. The itinerary for Wednesday 31st July 2002 was Whistler. The ski resort, reached after 76 miles along the Sea to Sky highway, is one of the most famous in North America, with evidently some of the best snow. Our coach ride took us along the waterway known as Howe Sound, with huge rugged rocks on the other side of the highway. We stopped at Shannon Falls, around 1,100 feet of falling water. What an impressive sight. Carrying on to our destination we passed the Stawamus Chief, evidently the 2nd biggest free standing, granite rock. We then passed Squamish, the sporting area of British Columbia, if not of Canada for rock climbers, wind surfers, mountain biking, water sports, winter sports, walking. There must be a golf course nearby! A short time later we pulled into Whistler. The large village, which comprises of chalet type hotels, restaurants, retail outlets and homes, sits at the base of the 6,000 foot mountain. The gondola ride to the top was really enjoyable, especially as we were never too far from the ground for Zeni. The view on arrival is spectacular. No matter which way you turn, the landscape is awe inspiring. From Blackcomb Mountain, to all the varying heights of different peaks, making up the horizon. After a quick walk round, we headed back down to meet Sarah. Instead of going to the peak, she hired a mountain bike and caught a lift half way up. The trip down for her was pretty demanding. At least she only fell off once. We just had time for a quick meal before heading back. We stopped off on the return trip at an ecology centre, and for a forest walk. We saw two trees that were 2,000 years old. Unfortunately, they had blown down a few weeks previously in the bad winds. Pretty old for a living thing. The walk was very informative and we enjoyed it.

Going through Stanley Park on the way back to the hotel, we asked to be dropped off there, ready for the fireworks later in the evening. The Symphony of Fire is an annual festival of fireworks, where 3 countries from around the world compete to give the best display. It is carried out over a few nights, with each country giving an evening display, culminating in the final day. All the events take place aboard ships in English Bay. What a display! Even better than the impromptu one Dad gave years earlier. Yes; it was that good. Zeni and I had a meal in the Fish Restaurant whilst waiting. If you love fish food, which we do, you will love it here. Magnificent, succulent, fresh fish, cooked to perfection and accompanied by British Columbian wine. After the display it was a matter of getting a taxi. Somehow or other we managed and got back to the hotel for a rest, as the next day it was off to Vancouver Island.

We caught the B.C. Ferry from Tsawwassen, after catching a Pacific Coach Line bus from near the hotel. The one and a half hour sail was like a mini cruise. Outside, we watched as we passed a number of small islands with the cool breeze in our faces and the blue sky showing through the patchy cloud. On landing we caught a bus to Victoria, the capital of British Columbia. Sarah and I wanted to go whale watching. The rest didn't fancy the small dinghy on the wide open sea, and elected to have a look round the city instead. We got kitted out ready to go. A large, floatable wet suit was donned, along with boots and waterproof hats. We certainly couldn't run far in them! We waved the others off as we set out into the ocean. We passed by a small rock full of sea lions, then carried on to find the whales. The person in charge of the large dinghy, kept in contact with others to find out if any of the huge mammals had been sited. They had. Off we went towards their last sighted position. We saw them, blowing water high up into the air. They were all around. Suddenly, one headed into our direction. The cameras were ready. It was heading straight for us. Where was it? A shout! It had gone right underneath the boat, and we just witnessed the huge tail as it disappeared again below the waves. WOW! We sailed around for a few more minutes before returning a bit early. We had heard over the radio that bad winds were on the way. We turned and headed quickly back. We didn't make it in time. The waves got bigger, and we kept manoeuvring in order to avoid the big crests heading our way. We were constantly asked if we were all O.K.. It was great, like a roller coaster. Suddenly a huge wave appeared from nowhere. It looked colossal as it bore down on us. Whoops! The boat was manoeuvred along, through and over the great wall of water. That was a ride. When we returned to the jetty, poor Zeni was worried sick. We had turned around early, and arrived back almost half an hour late. Sarah and I had a quick bite before we all headed back for the boat. We managed to catch the 8.05pm boat back to Tsawwassen after the bus ride.

That was it. Our last day in Vancouver. Where did the time go! Somewhere along the line, we had also fitted in a game of pitch and putt, shopping in Vancouver, as well as another trip to Gastown. Phew! Next. The birthday party.

Air Alaska, flight 574, left at 10.38am for San Francisco. The Boeing 737 flew for 2 hours 22 minutes before landing at 1.00pm. Cora and her friend Boots where waiting, and drove us to the Hampton Inn, Daly City, on the outskirts of San Francisco. In the afternoon we had a walk around the vicinity to find the BART station ready for the next day. BART is a rapid transport system, (electric train) which runs through to the bay area. Like the good tourists that we are, it was first a visit to Pier 39, a large complex with the usual souvenir shops and restaurants. It was also a mooring place for dozens of boats. One set of moorings was taken over by sea lions. There were so many constantly moving in and out of the water, it was difficult to count them. They had taken refuge from the sea, when the last earthquake had sent them scurrying to seek shelter. Then on to Fisherman's Wharf. This area dates back to the gold rush days. There are attractions for the family, shopping and sightseeing possibilities. We decided to book a boat trip during our stay. After passing a square on the right selling fresh fruit and vegetables, we crossed over and walked up Hyde St. to Russian Hill. On the left we came across Lombard Street, reputed to be the most crooked street in the world. We walked down it (with care) into Leavenworth Street. Went back to Russian Hill and caught a taxi to the Pan Pacific Hotel in Post St., along from Union Square, the venue for the party.

As we drew up, a doorman quickly shot forward and opened the door. On entering the hotel, which is reputed to be one of the best in the world, we were advised to take the glass lift to the 2nd floor. We changed in one of the suites Boots had booked for a couple of nights. It was a formal dress affair and I think we looked quite smart, especially the ladies. Following the Hors d'oeuvres we entered the main reception room. Zeni looked stunning in her new pink evening dress. Tables were laid out around the dance floor, awaiting the hungry guests. The four course meal was excellent and so was the Italian wine. The meal was followed by a display of the 'Argentinean Tango', which was enthralling to watch. Then the ladies candle wishing ceremony, when a candle was presented to Boots and a brief talk, on where and how, the lady met Boots, was given. The microphone didn't work when Zeni attempted her talk! Following some dancing, it was the gentleman's "50 Roses Dance". This is where a gentleman presented a rose to Boots, and had a short dance with her. I was 5th in line. A good evening was had by all. I can't remember what time we got to bed, except to say it was late again.

Yes, we had a lie in the next morning! It was Sunday, a relaxing day. We went into San Francisco and Union Square. Zeni bought a bag at Macy's. That was it. A quiet day and an early night.

Cora and Boots picked us up at 8.45am on the Monday and took us to the pier ready for our trip. We first stopped at Angel Island and a bus took us around. A lot of the historic sights dated back to the Second World War. If that is old, then so am I. O.K. perhaps you are right, but what about the sites in Rome, Greece, and Egypt? It makes you realise how young America is. Just over 200 years old. When we had a drink before leaving, some raccoons came around the tables asking for food. We were advised not to feed them, or try and touch them in case they bit us. Fine. I just looked at them. I hadn't seen them in the wild before. Going across the bay we got a good view of the Golden Gate Bridge. Then ALCATRAZ. Most people must have heard of this infamous prison. The penitentiary, set on the island in San Francisco Bay, was within sight of the hustle and bustle of the city. However, the swift moving currents ensured that to try swimming across was a foolhardy scheme. If you thought it possible, the water temperature of 45-50 degrees should make you think twice. It did. Well almost. On 11th June 1962, three prisoners attempted an escape. Were they successful? Who knows? What is known is that they were never seen again! Al Capone, 'Machine Gun' Kelly, and the 'Birdman' of Alcatraz, Robert Stroud, were all taken to 'The Rock'. Various films have been made depicting the times, events, and unsuccessful (and perhaps successful) escape attempts. As we set foot on land, everywhere looked bleak and uninviting. On walking up to the main compound, the guard posts stared down, making sure we were safe to carry on. I'm glad there wasn't an armed guard up there at the time! Inside the cell area you can only imagine what it was like. Sarah stood outside a cell for a photo. It showed how little room there was for the prisoner. We saw the cell where Al. Capone was kept. Fourteen cells closed at the same time, with a metallic sound, letting all know they were going nowhere until that sound was heard again. The dining room overlooked the city, tempting those inside to go and visit!

The recreational yard still looked foreboding. As for the isolation cells used for solitary confinement, I dread to think what it would have been like to be locked inside a cell with no natural light or anything else, come to think of it! The prison opened in 1934 and closed 29 years later, after gaining a notorious reputation. It housed only 1,576 during that time mostly murderers, counterfeiters, and bank robbers. The visit was very good, and came highly recommended, but I'm glad it wasn't an enforced visit. After getting back to the mainland, we caught one of the famous cable cars to Union Square. Zeni and I stood on the back, so we could look down the hill at the islands we had just visited. We met Cora and Boots, who had bought some items for her home, and also a gift for Zeni and I. We were taken back and treated by Boots to a good Chinese meal in Daly City.

It was 7.00am when we left the hotel. The bus on scheduled route 6845, was to leave the Greyhound Coach station in San Francisco at 9.15am. Before that, we had to get our bags sorted out and loaded for the 8 hour 5 minute journey back to Los Angeles. After a long wait, we were on our way. The large lady driver, set out the rules for the journey before we got started.

If we didn't get back at the stated time, we wouldn't be on the bus. It's a simple as that. We made sure we were never late. She meant what she said! The route took us along Highway 5. It was interesting to see the different areas of California. The arid, brown, tall hills were too dry for the cattle to be on them, the fields with varying crops, looking sad in the heat and the rugged rocks. We eventually reached the urban areas around Glendale, before arriving at the Greyhound coach station in L.A.. After all those miles we arrived early. Good going for a journey of over 400 miles. Within a few minutes, Linda and Ed's niece, another Sarah, arrived to take us back to Duarte.

In the evening we went to Nori and Mariet's for our last party. This is where I saw my first humming bird. It was next to Brian, and the small bird was flapping its wings so hard, in order to get the long beak and tongue close enough to extract the pollen from one of the flowering bushes. We ate in the back garden, sitting around the swimming pool. We told them all about our Canadian holiday and our time in San Francisco. After the meal, we had to bid farewell to all of Linda's family, in the hope that we would see them again before too long.

The following day, Ed's niece, Sarah, took Zeni, Sarah and I around the Hollywood area. As Giles and Craig had already been, they went to Santa Barbara with Nimfa's daughters. We went to Beverly Hills, which was very smart, the Walk of the Stars, and the shopping place for the stars, Rodeo Drive. Evidently the shops have the highest rent in North America. We finished by travelling along Highway 2 to Santa Monica, a really clean and smart town, just outside the Hollywood district of Los Angeles. We had a drink and a snack along Third Street Promenade, before wending our way back, to see where Sarah was studying to be a film director at The University of Southern California. The site, where the Oscar ceremony is carried out, was shown to us as we headed back to Ed and Linda's, just in time for a lovely barbeque that had been arranged for our last night in America.

On our last day, we had some more photographs developed, before having a quick lunch prior to boarding our flight home. The journey to the airport wasn't terrific. We were caught in an accident along Highway 10. It delayed us by more than half an hour. I was so pleased when we got under way again, as I was worrying about catching the plane home. OH DEAR!! Another accident! This time on the 405. Another delay. We eventually arrived at the airport just as the desk for the flight was closing. The staff had heard of the accidents and we were quickly dealt with. After saying our fond farewells and hopes that we would all meet again soon, we went through customs and security to board our 3.00pm Air Canada flight back to Heathrow, England, and home. We landed the following day the 9th August. What a shame all our bags were not on the flight with us! There were two cases missing. They were eventually traced and forwarded to us at home two days later. I certainly will never forget the marvellous holiday. The friendliness of Zeni's friends and family will always remain as a huge contributing factor, to a time that others would only dream of. To you all. Thanks. Back to work even though it took a few days to get over the jet lag.

4

CORA had asked Zeni on a number of occasions, to visit her, and after the Christmas period we were able to make the trip. We were off on our travels again! The British Airways flight 718 took us from London to Zurich, on 6th January 2003. I left work at 9.45am, in time to get changed and arrive at Heathrow for the 3.00pm flight. Unfortunately, the flight left an hour and a half late due to frost on the runway, an activated fire alarm which fortunately wasn't justified, and the plane in front that had just gone down the runway experienced a burst tyre. This required a full sweep of the runway as a precautionary measure. On arrival in Zurich, we transferred to the railway station, which is just below our flight arrival point. Zeni phoned to tell Cora we had eventually arrived and we were on the way to Bern. The capital of Switzerland is surrounded by mountains. That is why there are no large commercial aircraft flying into the small airport. A legend has it that the city is named after the German word for bear (Bern), after its founder killed one on the peninsula. It was 9.30pm when we eventually arrived at the station where Cora was waiting to pick us up for the drive to her flat. It was nice to meet another of Zeni's sisters. Naturally a lot of talking was done before we went to bed. The next day, Tuesday, we went to visit a friend of Cora's who lived in Herbligen. The house was a typical Swiss chalet. I never realised they were so large inside. We set off for Lucerne, the city I had visited many years before. We enjoyed a walk around the area, before having a coffee and a snack, prior to our visit to a glass factory just below Mount Pilatus. Glasi Hergiswil, is the oldest glassworks in Switzerland. It dates back to 1817. Outside, it was a bit cooler than Las Vegas! So different, so beautiful, so serene, so natural, so cold.

I had heard of Gstaad, as the winter playground of the rich and famous. It has been visited by such people as, King Constantine of Greece, Margaret Thatcher, Elizabeth Taylor and Sir Elton John. After parking the car, we wandered around the picturesque village, which consists of one main street, the majority of shops being jewellers and fashion stores. The soft, pure, snow covered the area like a white tablecloth with the small serviettes atop the seats. Waste bins, and other small objects in the centre of the picture book, traffic free, street were also transformed. We stopped to look at the statue of a calf, carried on to the end of the street, then passed over a small stream. The banks showed the clear crystals of frost and icicles. The white covered trees behind, helped to make the water look very dark, against all the white of its surroundings. It was minus 10° c when we arrived at the railway station village of Chateau D'oux for a fondue meal. We got through a lot of bread and cheese during the warm and inviting meal, as well as some good Swiss wine. Yes, they have some nice local wines in Switzerland. We carried on to Buile for a cup of fresh brewed coffee.

Our next day's outing was to Interlaken, via the old town of Thun. The river runs alongside the road and through the centre of the town, over the weir and below the wooden bridge. Icicles were hanging along the side of the road from rocks. Solid masses of ice, stuck to the rocks like mirrors, glued onto the black rocks and any fauna that gets in the way, as temperatures drop low enough to stop the ice cold water in its tracks. We entered the Hotel Metropole and ascended to the top restaurant for a cold beer and cake. Well, it was warm in the Hotel. Afterwards, we walked to the casino with its frozen fountain. With the light disappearing we set off on our return journey. The meal that Cora's friend had prepared at home was wonderful.

The following morning, after a good breakfast, it was time to take a trip into the Capital city, which had only 130,000 inhabitants. It is one of only a few cities in the world to be designated a World Heritage Site by UNESCO. The tram had a terminal just across the road. Nice and handy! We walked to and around the Cathedral. We could see how Bern was surrounded by the River Aare, as it wound around the old town. We looked over the city roofs, to the Alps beyond. Our walk down to see the bears, led us under the impressive clock tower, Bern's first western city gate, between 1191 and 1256 and down the main street. The bear is the symbol of Bern and a number are kept in a large enclosure. It was a bit cold even for them, and they thought it better to stay in their rock homes which afforded relief from the cold wind. It was too cold to head up to the rose garden, even though it could be seen on top of the hill. We walked back up the main street, stopping at a restaurant for a warm coffee and cake. It was even cold in there, so we kept our coats on, as did everyone else. Time to go home to Cora's nice warm and comfortable flat. Lovely!

Saturday morning we were taken to Interlaken again. This time Zeni and I were off to the top of The Schilthorn. The frozen waterfalls, on our way to and at the base of the cable car ride, were spectacular. It is the longest aerial ride in the Alps and was completed in 1967. It took four separate journeys to get to the peak of the 9,842 foot mountain. The first transfer was at Stechelberg. The second was in the beautiful and picturesque, mountain village of Grimmelwald, before our final transfer on top of Muerren. The restaurant at the summit was used for the James Bond film, 'On Her Majesty's Secret Service'. Going outside to the viewing area enabled us to see the Jungfrau, which is 13,642 feet, the Monch, 13,448 feet, and the Eiger, 13,025 feet above sea level. We looked across the mountain range, known world wide as the Alps, with views of over 200 peaks, all eventually leading to the valleys way down below. None of these could be seen though, because of the cloud at about 7,000 feet, blocking out all possibilities of seeing anything beneath.

We were up and out of the house, by 6.45am the next morning, for our journey, via Zurich to London, then home to Kidlington. Thank you Cora for a great time. I hadn't had many holidays before I met Zeni. I am certainly making up for it now.

The first year of our marriage had gone by so quickly! It was February already. Over a brilliant St. Valentines day meal at the Holiday Inn at Oxford, we decided as we had our Aphrodite's Syrup (coffee and mints), that an anniversary visit to Paris would be ideal. That was it then. Off to Paris for a return visit. We used the Eurostar again, as it was a lovely ride through the countryside. By the time we took into account, waiting at the airport and transfer to the city centre, it was almost as quick as a flight to the capital of France. We trundle through the London suburbs, before picking up a bit of speed, down to Ashford the channel tunnel station, not far from the underground passageway, 31 miles long, with an average depth of 150 feet below the stretch of water, dividing England from France. We decided to return to the Holiday Inn near to the Champs Elysees. As we left England in the late afternoon, it was 9.50pm by the time we booked in. This time a better taxi driver knew where he was going, and it didn't take long to get from the station. There was an African summit on at the time and the hotel was full of journalists and other representatives. After taking our bags up to room 209 on the second floor, we went out for a quick walk up the famous avenue as a reminder of our previous visit. It was nice to be back in the city of lovers.

In the morning we walked down the twisting staircase to the breakfast room. Helped ourselves to a buffet breakfast then headed into the centre of the city. We turned the opposite way out of the hotel then walked along Boulevard Haussmann. On arrival at the Galeries La Fayette, it was too much of a temptation for Zeni, so in we went. The shopping area, houses some of the most famous names in beauty products, fashion and accessories. The middle of the impressive building houses a fantastic glass dome. The supporting metal strips, spread out from the flowered centre leading down to the four floors. The open galleries look out onto the central floor below. Such an impressive building! Zeni and I decided to go to the roof area and look across the city skyline. There was a Chinese week being held within, so we decided to have a Chinese meal. It was very nice, but expensive. We left La Fayette and walked through some of the smaller streets in the area. Zeni was so pleased we did. Looking in one of the shops, she noticed some lovely trousers. We came out of the shop with four pairs, as well as four tops. All greatly reduced as it was the start of the new fashion week, and everything was being cleared out. She bought all of them, for the price of one pair of trousers back home.

Our walk back to the hotel, took us past the St. Madeleine church. The outside looked like a hall or Greek temple, but it was magnificent within, with its gilt and marble. Three domes let in the daylight. We looked down and walked to the Place De La Concorde. The obelisk, having been brought from the Temple of Ramses, in Luxor, Egypt. The square was renamed after the revolution. It was here that Marie Antioinette and others were executed by guillotine. We turned and walked through the Jardins Des Tuleries leading to the Louvre. Then back along the banks of the Seine, into and along the top end of the Champs Elysees, turning right past the Elysees Palace, and into the hotel. We had a nice meal off the Champs Elysees, went for an evening stroll, and then to bed. Saturday the 22nd February was our anniversary. What a fantastic year. I am so pleased we met each other and we get on so well together. The next day we went along the Seine, before crossing over the bridge to Notre Dame. It took 150 years to build the Gothic structure which was completed in 1345 and lies at the end of an island, surrounded by the River Seine. The impressive interior has some magnificent stained glass windows. There is a huge crucifix in bronze, which was presented by Napoleon. Zeni had confession with an English speaking priest and bought some rosaries from the store inside Notre Dame. Many tourists were already at the site and the queue to climb the tower was quite long. We decided to walk down the street at the side and have a drink and some crepes, instead of climbing the 387 spiral steps to the top of the tower. Crossing the river then turned left into Rue De Rivoli, it took only a few minutes to arrive at another famous landmark, the Louvre. Where had the time gone? It was 3.30pm already. We quickly presented €10, for our two tickets and entered the vast building, through the entrance, into the huge glass pyramid, with its 793 panes of glass and into its huge reception area below. This is where the problems begin. There were 30,000 exhibits of art! It was off to see the most famous of all, the Mona Lisa. There she was smiling at us with her eyes seeing all from behind her bullet proof glass encasement. Needless to say, we were not the only ones there, but we managed to get in front of the painting then view it from either side. Just to make sure those eyes did follow us. The second floor has exhibits of paintings from France and other European countries. The works of art are indeed masterpieces. It was soon six o'clock, the closing time. Perhaps, if we come back for a few months, we could see most of the exhibits! It was time to get back to the hotel ready for the evening meal. A special night; so a special meal. We got a taxi to the Port de la Bourdonnais, where at the foot of the Eiffel tour, we boarded a boat for a dinner cruise along the river. We set sail heading towards Notre Dame. A leaflet was given out showing what sites we would pass, before and after we turned back at the Charles De Gaulle Bridge. The Notre Dame looked very impressive, as we slid past the structure, lit up by floodlights. The Eiffel tower had lights along its 18,000 metal sections. Turning to dock we went around the Statue of Liberty, a small bronze version, (of that given to New York), erected for the world fair of 1889, the year the tower was opened. We had a four course meal with an excellent choice on the menu. Zeni started with a slightly cooked, smoke salmon steak with spices and herbs, as well as Brioche bread with a sorrel fondue. I opted for marinated scallops with bacon and green lentil cream. The cod gratin and caramelised carrots with an orange flavour, looked good as Zeni started her main course. My Chateaubriand steak with a liquorice wine sauce, on a bed of artichokes, tomatoes, onions, garlic, shallots, and rosemary was so good. The steak was done to perfection. Numerous cheeses from France followed, before we both finished with the cold lychee soufflé, with lychee liqueur and red fruit sauce. Somehow, we managed to eat all this whilst looking at the sights, and listening to either, the violinist or female singer serenading us all. It was an excellent night, to round of, what must be, one of the best years in my life.

Before catching the 11.45am train back home on the 23rd, we had a meal at the station, whilst looking down at fellow travelers as they came and went, along the platforms, and concourse; with trains leaving and arriving, from other countries, across the continent of Europe. It was the first time we had travelled through the French countryside in daylight. It was another interesting journey, as we sped towards the hole in the ground leading home.

During the previous year, we had visited Dave and Jill, in their lovely penthouse in Eastbourne. They told us about their holiday to China. A cruise along the Yangtze and the Three Gorges, before flooding took place for a new huge reservoir, the water then covering areas forever. It sounded an ideal holiday. We booked up through Saga travel and waited until 10th April for the experience. April 9th arrived. Unfortunately so had SARS! The holiday was cancelled 24 hours before departure. Now what? I had made arrangements for Judy to look after the Post Office. In addition, someone was coming to help her out. We decided to have a look on the internet and see what was available. Not a lot. It was Easter and hotels around the world appeared to be booked up. From Hawaii to Florida, Borneo to Bermuda. From the Maldives to the Seychelles. If we found a room, it was difficult getting a flight. Where do we like? Vancouver. We got a room in the Crowne Plaza. (Hotel Georgia). Yes. British Airways had seats. That's it. We were off the next day.

Flight BA 85 only left Heathrow at 5.00pm, so we left home for the airport at midday. It was a good flight, which ended will the best landing we had ever experienced. We couldn't tell when the wheels touched the tarmac. Applause for the Captain resounded around the cabin.

Whilst flying across the Atlantic and over the vastness of Canada, we decided to have a look if there were any properties for sale. The hotel, which is situated in downtown Vancouver, faces the art gallery. We had been given a large room, at the side of the building, overlooking the Pacific Centre Mall. Zeni wondered if Elvis or Edward The Prince of Wales had stayed in the same room. We decided we were

Vancouver

not as well known as them, so it was very unlikely! A meal in one of the hotel's restaurants was followed by a walk around the area. It was great to be back. As we had decided to buy a holiday home, the next day we strolled around the downtown district, looking at available property. We walked miles to what seemed like every new apartment block being built. Next, was a taxi across Burrard Bridge, up the hill, then right into 10th Avenue. There where some duplex houses being built there. We had a walk around to make sure we liked the district, then set off to see the houses. It wasn't quite what we wanted, so we went back to the hotel. We bought a paper on the way back, to see what other sales there were. There was no doubt in our minds. We love Vancouver, and were now utterly convinced about our decision to buy property here. Despite all the walking the previous day, there was a site we had missed. We went along to the showroom in Seymour Street to find out more about the new apartments being built. We liked what we saw and put a 48 hour hold on one of the few remaining units. That's it. We will have a good look around and make our minds up finally in two days.

Time for a coffee and snack in Urban Fayre, the food store is unlike any I had seen before, with fresh fruit and vegetables from around the world. They had an excellent cheese counter with innumerable types of nuts, a ready to eat section, with hot and cold food to take away, or have at one of the tables. Zeni kept showing me items she had eaten, when at home in the Philippines. There were even pieces of sugar cane. It must have been an hour later, when we went back out into the rain. If SARS couldn't stop our holiday, rain was certainly not going to stop our enjoyment. Just a few yards from Urban Fayre and we were at False Creek, the mass of water stretching from English Bay to the dome of Science World. The huge glass structure was a reminder of the world trade fair, Expo '86. Turning right we walked along the pathway at the side of the creek. Despite the rain, we could just see Granville Island, which we visited on our holiday with the family. Past the David Lam Park, then back up Homer Street. By now we were thoroughly wet. We went to the hotel for a nice shower and meal. We enjoyed ourselves, as we got to know areas of the city better. Robson Street, Georgia Street where the hotel is situated, B.C. Place stadium, the Pacific Centre shopping mall, the Hudson Bay Company, Sears, Chapter's book store. Granville Street and Robson Square, set below street level. Robson Street is the shopping street to be seen on, and the opportunity to see the rich and famous when they are in town. It is the Rodeo Drive of Vancouver.

Decision day! First though, let's try out the light rail system, the Sky Train. The fully automated train drew up, and off we went to New Westminster. A mistake! We should have been going to Coquitlam. We caught the next train back and then the right one to Coquitlam. We went into Sears at Lougheed Mall where Zeni bought some shoes. We had a quick walk up the hill, before going back to the city centre. The decision was made. We went to the show area and confirmed that we would purchase a suite in the Brava residence. It was also going to be the site for the International Film Festival. The area houses a 185 seat cinema, production and other facilities. This is set between the two towers which accommodate the apartments. On top of the film area is a swimming pool for the residents of the buildings. South Core Park is sited just across the road. We were so happy with the decision that it called for a celebratory meal. To us the only place for this meal was Cloud Nine, the revolving restaurant. During the next few days, we stayed in and around Downtown Vancouver. On one of them, we walked along Georgia Street into Coal Harbour Road and around Coal Harbour towards the rowing club, then under the main road to Lost Lagoon in Stanley Park. We walked around the water, stopping on the way to take a photo of a black squirrel with a nut in its mouth, as we headed towards second beach. The white blossom of the trees stood out against the various shrubs, bushes and trees. We then took a leisurely stroll along the seawall promenade. As we neared third beach, we met someone making stone sculptures. There was anything between three and ten rocks standing on top of each other. One had a large old branch across a small stone, then another larger stone on top. It looked strange seeing large stones balanced atop smaller ones. Returning along the other side of Lost lagoon, we sat on a bench to look at the picturesque view. The water reflected varying colours of green. The trees had light green leaves, which had recently burst from the buds to look at the water below. The darker coloured firs and spruce reached up to the mountains behind. The mountains, with their peaks covered in snow, blended into the pale blue/grey sky. Suddenly there were seagulls in the sky just like the ones in Yorkshire and the world over, flocking to the edge of the water where someone had thrown some food on the ground. They were much quicker than the ducks that came waddling up, after most of the food had disappeared.

One morning, when looking out of the bedroom window, we saw thousands of people. It was the fun run around the city. Hundreds of contestants set off with their particular group. The next group was already in place before those in front had gone a hundred yards down the road, with a person with a gold costume bringing up the rear. A few of the runners were highlighting the fact that Vancouver was trying to get the Winter Olympics in 2010.

Directly across from the hotel is the Vancouver Art Gallery. At the time the building was being used for making the film Scooby Doo 2. The city is frequently used by film makers. We visited Gastown, close to the area where we got lost on our first visit. A statue of Vancouver's founder, Gassy Jack stands at the junction of Water Street and Carrall Street, the site of his first wooden shack. Walking up Water Street, the main area of Gastown, we stopped off one day and had a meal in the Old Spaghetti Factory. An old wagon, set out as a dining area lures the children and adults alike. The food is good and a reasonably priced. We carried on after eating, and came to the steam clock, the centre piece of the district. The two ton clock is powered by excess steam, from a company that provides it as a heating source to some buildings in the vicinity. It gives a rendition of the Westminster chimes, and can be heard every quarter of an hour. It is always a main attraction for visitors. Canada Place is close to Gastown and the main terminal, for all the cruise ships that visit the city that are going to or coming from Alaska. The view from the top encompasses part of Stanley Park, the Lions Gate Bridge, Grouse Mountain and the surrounding area, North Vancouver, Lonsdale Quay, and Mount Seymour. There is a café next to the IMAX cinema, where we had a coffee and took in the scenery, spread out in front of us. Vancouver Exhibition and Convention Centre as well as the World Trade Centre are also within the complex. The Pan Pacific Hotel sits above all. Its entrance leads from the doors to the escalators, which stretch high up to the reception desk. There is also a nice restaurant on the same floor looking out over the harbour. We returned to the Crowne Plaza. I don't think we could afford a night in this five star hotel.

Grouse Mountain deserved another visit and when at the summit, Zeni bought me a new hat. I had lost the one from Nova Scotia. We had hunted high and low for a similar one with thermal lining with no luck. What a good excuse to go back to Halifax! Not for a while though. The snow around the chalet was 2-3 feet thick. Even so we had a walk around. Skiers and snowboarders, set off for their particular slope, enjoying the fast ride down, and then the journey back up. A snow mobile! Now that looks fine for me. What a shame you can't rent them. It was an employee going about his work. The wooden sculptures stood out against the snowy background. How realistic they look. The men with the chain saws had been busy again. Unfortunately, there was no view as the cloud was too low making the air quite cool. It didn't stop us from visiting one of the restaurants though. From what we have heard the Observatory is very good, but we decided on Altitudes. There were no complaints. The meal was very good indeed. We had seats by the window, even if there was very little to see. As we went down in the cable car, Burrard inlet came into view, then the remaining scenery, as the low cloud dispersed and the hazy sun spread its tentacles on the city below.

It was raining when we went to the aquarium in Stanley Park. This is a place to be visited. The Beluga whales looked strange in their all white guise, performing tricks. How do they manage to get their weight out of the water? They look so friendly. I think a lot has to do with the way they can turn their heads, unlike most other whales whose neck vertebrae are fused together, making the movement impossible. From the viewing gallery below, their blubber can be seen moving around, as they return into the water. Two sea otters lay flat on their backs and lovingly holding hands, without a care in the world. There were pacific dolphins, sea lions and seals, and vast numbers of fish, showing off their colours as they swim around their tanks. Long ones, short ones, fat ones, thin ones, striped or plain ones.

The rain forest section had anacondas, boas, alligators and piranhas. It was a really enjoyable visit. When finished, it was off to the Fish House restaurant for a very late lunch or early evening meal; but the heavens opened again. We felt like fish out of water. Drenched to the skin, we squelched our way back to the hotel instead.

It was a good 15 minute walk along Georgia Street, then into and along Howe Street, to catch the 8.30am bus service to Seattle, which left from the Holiday Inn Downtown. The scheduled bus service took 4 hours to cover the 150 miles. We arrived with 20 minutes to spare. The schedule calls for a stop at Vancouver airport, Campbell River Store, which is just before the U.S.A. border, Bellingham airport and Everett before arriving in Seattle. It was a good journey until we got to the border. It was the weekend before Easter and there was a flower and garden show only a few miles away. Instead of the normal two coaches waiting to pass through, we were sixth in line! In addition, there were more cars than normal clogging up the lanes leading into America. The usual 20 minute crossing, took over two hours before clearance, and the coach resumed its journey to Seattle. We left the coach, and a ten minute walk took us to the Space Needle. The 605 foot tall tower was built for the 1962 World Trade Fair. Our ascent took around 45 seconds to the observation deck, 500 feet above the ground. The panorama includes the bay and harbour areas, mountains in the distance overlooking the city and the State of Washington. Mount Rainier stood proud above them all. Looking down towards the city centre, we saw the Monorail taking its passengers to the Westlake Centre in Fifth Avenue, ten blocks away. We descended and visited the shop before leaving the tower. It is a tall concrete structure, held to the ground by 72 bolts. Each bolt is 30 feet in length. The tower is well and truly anchored. We went into the Centre House. Children were letting off steam in their play area, which also had a funfair inside. The International fountain was nearby. We had no time to go into the city centre because of the delay at the crossing. We wandered slowly back to the bus stop to make our return.

We made it to the Fish House Restaurant before going home. The evening flight home gave us the opportunity to see both the sunset and the sunrise. The yellow morning sun crept round the curvature of the earth, before flooding the land we were flying over with its life giving properties. Another day bringing forth the vast number of experiences it yields to all that inhabit this planet earth.

We had only been home a couple of weeks, when a telephone call from California, announced that Lourdes's daughter, Michi, was getting married, and we were invited. Could we go? Arrangements were made and we were off. Nothing could stop us now, we had caught the travel bug. It's great.

Michi was getting married in Las Vegas. We took a flight to Los Angeles again, this time with American Airlines. Nori and Mariet picked us up at the airport, as Linda was working until 5.30pm. We were greeted with the usual warmth and affection we receive from all Zeni's relatives and friends.

On arrival at Stardust, Las Vegas, we went straight to the island Paradise Café for a meal. A prime rib dinner. The prime rib was cooked slowly and served with a baked potato, whipped butter, sour cream and chives, and the vegetable of the day. We had soup as a starter and the meal cost only $8.99 each. The steak was huge and about 2 inches thick. In England it would cost at least twice as much. Zeni and I set off for the Stratosphere afterwards. All the family members that had managed to make the trip were meeting there. The view from the bedroom was of the flat plains of Las Vegas surrounded by the mountains. The plains looked almost cream, as the warm sun spread its light across them. Although we went to the top of the tower, 833 feet above street level, I did not have a ride on the roller coaster sited on the top as time ran out. Rosemarie and Fabri from Italy had arrived, and I met more members of the family. In the afternoon and evening, Zeni and I took them around. We have been here so often now, we are like locals! On arrival at Bellagio, Fabri had a good look at the expanse of water, where the fountains give their spectacular display. He told me that it looked just like Bellagio on Lake Como, close to where they live. I didn't know there was such a place as Bellagio. It was evidently reproduced down to the last outcrop of rock. The children enjoyed seeing the rain fall inside Aladdin, but Fabri didn't think the coffee in the Venetian matched up to what they had back home. Saturday 14th June was the wedding day. Before then, Zeni and I went to Aladdin to see Michi. We took a few photographs, then had a look around before we were picked up by Nori. She had kindly offered to take us to the chapel where the wedding was to take place.

Michi married Gene. The best man was there giving support to Gene. His happy and friendly manner put a smile on everyone's face. The young boys, Mark and Ian were page boys, with their black suits and waistcoats. T.J. was not outdone with his long black trousers, white shirt and bow tie. Gene was in a black suit and waistcoat with a rose bud in his button hole. He was talking excitedly to his best man, whilst waiting patiently for his bride. Michi looked lovely, in her long white strapless dress, the white veil covering her shoulders. Walking down the aisle, her long white gloved hands, held a beautiful bouquet of white roses. Cliff was by her side, ready to give her away. Hannah looking radiant and attractive in her pale blue satin bridesmaid dress. Close at hand to make sure her sister's day went well, Vanessa having flown from Brescia to be the youngest bridesmaid, was in a dress of the same style and colour. Lara, Gene's sister and a friend of Michi's made up the bridesmaids. All looking resplendent and beautiful in their matching dresses. It was a nice ceremony, followed by a lovely meal. It was a large family reunion bringing together, most of the sisters and their husbands. Cora from Switzerland, Fabri and Rosemarie from

Italy, Mary Jane and Mother who were then, living near Long Beach, Lourdes, who was staying with Mary Jane, Cliff, and Belinda from Kansas, as well as Zeni and I from England. It is fair to say that we all had a good time.

On the Sunday it was a 5.15am.start. We met Ed and Linda, who had made arrangements for a day out. The coach took us along the road to Boulder City, the town built for the construction workers at the Hoover Dam. As we drove through the town, I was surprised to see a waterfall. The water moved over the stones to the small pool below. A man made stream flowed along through the golf course that was made in the middle of a desert. Not what I expected! A few minutes, later we arrived at a small airport.

The twelve seater plane took off, with Ed offered a view from the co-pilots seat. We flew over the Hoover Dam and along a small section of Lake Mead, a 115 mile long expanse, of crystal clear blue water in the desert. Water sports are catered for at various sites along the 550 miles of shoreline. Then it came into view. One of the seven natural wonders of the world, the Grand Canyon. Reaching out as far as we could see were the rugged mountains and a deep gorge. The granite rock strata at the base, 1.8 billion years old, was reaching up to the Kaibab limestone, a mere 260 million years. The small plane landed at the airport serving Tusayan, the arrival point for our tour. Following a short visit to the town, we carried on to the South Rim and the Grand Canyon Village. Walking to the rim trail and Mather Point, no one, on their first visit can be prepared for what lies ahead. The 277 mile long canyon that in places allows you to see a small blue winding water course, one mile below. The Colorado River looks like a piece of rope, placed on the ground at the base of the huge rigid forms of rocks. At the widest point, the gorge between the two land areas is 18 miles. To say it is awe inspiring is an injustice to the huge monoliths created by nature over the millennia. It makes you understand how strong nature is, how small man is. How in comparison, we are on the earth for a mere blink of the eye. It is impossible to describe the beauty, the ruggedness, the vastness, the humbling form of nature that spreads out in front. We walked along the rim trail to the other side of the village. The steepness of the drops was astounding. There were guard rails to ensure that visitors didn't get too close to the edge. As usual though, some completely disregard rails and warning signs, thinking a picture is more important than life! The previous two or three days, condors had been flying around the rim. Unfortunately, none where sighted on our visit. A packed lunch marked the end of our stay and a return to the small plane. The plane that accompanied us, with other sightseers could not take of because of engine trouble. As we settled into our seats, the pilot warned us, that heavy turbulence was forecast. How right he was! Zeni and Linda were petrified, and Zeni held my hand so tightly as she normally does when nervous. The lady in front was violently sick. The downward currents changed into upward blasts of air so suddenly. We were all pleased when almost 45 minutes later, we taxied along the airstrip to the reception area. In 1919, Grand Canyon National Park was created. Since then tourists have been visiting the park. The Grand Canyon Lodge opened in 1928. There are now six lodges in the park, and one at the bottom of the canyon for an overnight stay. It would be wonderful to stay and watch the sunrise and sunset on the rocks. Not this time though. We neither had the chance to go rafting in the waters of the Colorado River. Another fine steak finished off the day nicely.

Ed and I popped into Excalibur for a good freshly brewed pint of beer, whilst Zeni and Linda went to buy some shoes. Then we were off home. Whilst on the continent, we wanted to see other parts of California. This is why Nori and Mariet drove us, the next day to the Holiday Inn in Long Beach for a three night stay. On arrival we left our comfortable room and got the complimentary shuttle car to Pine Avenue, the heart of the city for a meal. There is a good selection of restaurants along the street, and in the end we decided on where to eat, before walking back. Sitting on the sofa in the hotel, were Mary Jane, Lourdes, and Cora. They had arrived in two cars, so we could all go to Mary Jane's rented apartment. Within a few minutes Fabri, Rosemarie and their children arrived. We were off to Huntingdon Beach. We took a brisk walk along the pier, looking at the coast line made famous in the Bay Watch television series, before our return to the hotel.

Redondo Beach is another famous beach within a short drive of the hotel, and we all went to explore the area. Parking near Basin 111, the pathway leads along the side of the harbour with various types of shops and restaurants overlooking the water, sprinkled with boats available for cruises. We came across the fish section which had live crab, lobster, shrimps, mussels and oysters. When walking towards the pier, I spotted a number of pelicans on a rock nearby. Wouldn't you guess! I had run out of film in the camera, and my spare ones were back at the hotel. Finally, we walked along the pier, before deciding to have a meal in Tony's. The fish restaurant supplied both a good tasting meal, and a view looking over the water and across the beach, where children could be seen jumping, playing and swimming in the sea. The water so clear the sea bed could be seen 3-4 ft below. On the way back to the car we stopped and bought two large lobsters from the Quality Seafood fresh fish market. Rosemarie, Fabri and the children joined us at Mary Jane's apartment. Fabri took charge of cooking the lobster and had also brought a nice Italian wine.

The complimentary shuttle car from the hotel is a great service. We were dropped off at the harbour and told to ring when we were ready to go back to the hotel. The Queen Mary is the old Cunard passenger liner that used to ply between European ports and America. It arrived in Long Beach in December 1967, thirty one years after her maiden voyage. During her lifetime, she had also acted as a troop ship, during the Second World War. In May 1971, it was opened as a tourist attraction and has since welcomed more visitors than when she ploughed the seas. It is rumoured that ghosts walk along the passageways! After lunch we were picked up by Mary Jane and Marilou, Lourdes best friend from the Philippines, and driven around Los Angeles. We were shown the fashion and jewellery districts, the place Bobby Kennedy was assassinated, and other recognisable sights around the city. We finished the tour in the Hollywood district. The cars were parked up and we went to Hollywood boulevard and piled into Tommy's, the original hamburger bar. The burgers were full of meat, and were delicious!! After watching all the expensive cars go by, it was time to head for the airport. As our flight was 3 hours before that of Fabri's we said our goodbyes first and Mary Jane and Lourdes took us to the airport. Like the last time, we got stuck in a traffic jam, so Lourdes phoned Marilou to tell her to start her journey with Fabri. I don't know why I was starting to worry, the flight eventually left almost 3 hours late, just before Fabri took off. The main thing is we arrived home safe and sound, ready for our next adventure.

5

WITH Zeni having relatives and friends around the world, we are more fortunate than most. A holiday in a lot of instances involves only the cost of an airfare. We book tickets at the earliest possible opportunity, and are prepared to change flights in order to cut costs. Evening and night flights are cheaper. We get very little sleep on these flights, but we think it is worth it. The earlier the payment is made, the better. Without doing this, we would certainly not have been able to travel as much as we have. We were also very fortunate to have Judy, as someone we could completely trust with running my business.

Dubai, in the United Arab Emirates was our next port of call. Another place and another airline. This time we fly with Qatar Airways from terminal 3 at Heathrow. It was Thursday 9th October. The night flight, left half an hour late at 10.00pm, instead of 9.30pm. A menu was given to every passenger for the evening meal. I decided on the Chicken Chasseur with roast potatoes, green beans with garlic, and glazed carrots with sesame seeds. It was followed by a slice of raspberry brulee, then a roll and butter with cheese and

biscuits. I finished it off with a black coffee. Zeni decided on
the fish syadich with sauce, rice, grilled eggplant and zuc-
chini , instead off the chicken. We changed planes at Doha,
and were quickly ushered through to the departure lounge.
We bought a lottery ticket for a BMW X5, and had a drink
before flying on and landing in Dubai at 9.45am. As we
walked out of the airport, the heat hit us. It seemed warmer
than when we were in Las Vegas. We noticed a small bus
with "Holiday Inn" written on the side. It was a courtesy
bus picking up other clients. I had missed the availability
of the service! Following a word with the driver, 5 minutes
later he confirmed we were customers and included us on
the journey to the hotel. Different country, different airline,
same hotel group! We were satisfied with our previous accommodation with the group, and knew we could rely upon
their cleanliness, professionalism, and friendliness. Dubai
has grown quickly since it joined the other six Sheikdoms
to form the United Arab Emirates in 1971. Abu Dhabi is the
capital. Dubai's late ruler, His Highness Sheik Rashid bin
Saeed Al Maktoum laid the foundation for the marvellous
development of the Emirates. Dubai creek has expanded on
both sides.

This is the central business district, although develop-
ments along the Sheikh Zayed road include the Internet
City, and the Finance City. The Sheikh Zayed road is the
main route through Dubai and onto Abu Dhabi. Everything
changes quickly in the Emirate. Ideas are thought out and if
agreed upon will be enacted almost immediately, whether it
is the construction of the world's tallest building, the largest shopping mall, largest indoor ski area or the best hotel
in the world. When you visit Dubai you will be astounded

by the new buildings completed or under construction, the beauty of the architecture, and the innovative projects. Most people will have heard of The Palm. Three massive projects. Islands in the shape of palm trees, reaching out into the Arabian Gulf .The World is another project of islands in the shape of the countries of the world. If you want to own a country, go ahead you can! Shopping centres abound. Most major sports are catered for, such as golf, horse racing and show jumping, motor racing, tennis, water sports, and camel racing. Whatever you want Dubai has it. It is the most incredible place we have ever visited. It was only a ten minute drive from the award winning airport. The air conditioned small coach, brought relief from the dry hot air outside. In no time at all, we were checked in and our bags had arrived in our room, number 417. We took a quick nap to catch up with our sleep then went downstairs to have a snack in the lobby restaurant. It was then time to explore. Down the road, the heat was not giving up. It meant walking in the shade wherever possible. The beautiful coloured trees stood out against the buildings. Plants, grass, flowers and trees, all looked very healthy, thanks to tender care and automatic watering systems installed at the time of planting. The evening meal in the Bistro was excellent. It was still early, about 9.00pm, so we went to one of the many shopping malls. By the time we got to bed, it was past midnight. It must have been the night flight that made us sleep until 9.50am.

The restaurant finishes serving breakfast at 10 o'clock. We made it by 10.05. No problem though, I had got the time wrong, they served food until 10.30am. It certainly made us get a move on though!! A taxi took us to the Jumeirah

Beach district. It is around 25 kilometres along the Sheikh Zayed road. A lot of construction was going on in the area. Huge blocks of apartments, most with sea or water views. The Jumeirah beach area has fantastic hotels. We called in at the Jumeirah Beach Hotel for a drink. The 26 storey hotel is in the shape of a breaking wave. The interior based on the four elements of, air, earth, fire and water. After passing the Wild Wadi water park, the Burj Al Arab hotel came into view. We had heard of the hotel, and wanted to have a look at it and see the inside of it. No luck though as I was wearing sandals. You need to be in correct attire to enter the hotel, unless you are staying there, so we will go back on another day.

Following a meal at the hotel we set out for the gold souk. It was a fantastic experience. The shops displayed bangles, earrings, cuff links, bracelets, necklaces, and rings. Then the items you don't expect to see, wide gold belts, waist coats and head gear. There were huge lengths of gold dangling everywhere. When the sun catches the metal, the whole area shines! Of course Zeni bought something from one of the largest gold markets in the world.

For the evening I had booked a diner cruise along the creek in a dhow. It was still light as we set sail from Jaddaf. The Dubai Creek Golf Course appeared on the right of the boat. There appear to be a number of golf courses in the deserts throughout the world. It reminded me of Las Vegas. The marvellous grass is a special selection, that when temperatures are very high, the greens need cutting twice a day in the summer! Of course the building is special. It is in the shape of a dhow with full sails. For the evening there is a 9 hole floodlit course. The food was great and there was so much of it. The creek is a bustling water course, with water taxis, shooting back and forth from bank to bank. It seems overcrowded, as they dart in and out between any other boat in the way. Evidently there is a code for the creek. I could never work out what it was though. The buildings along this prime location are to be marvelled at, like the National Bank of Dubai. The two large towers appear to be holding huge mirrors. As the setting sun caught the glass, it was reflected across the water. The water and buildings are reflected on the windows, of the towers reaching high into the sky. It is truly a sight to see. It was an evening I would never forget.

After Zeni had a sketch of herself drawn at the nearby Dana Centre, we were off on a desert safari. First stop, a camel farm. Camels were wandering around, and in pens. Baby camels, were being reared in outdoor wire enclosures. The drivers of the vehicles took the opportunity to reduce the air in the tyres ready for the trip over the desert. The four by four vehicles sped up and over the sand dunes. On reaching the top of the dune, the sand would start moving to the side or fall back behind the vehicle. This gave the driver the opportunity to change direction depending on which way the sand was flowing. A great experience! As evening beckoned, it was lovely to see the sun set over the undulating sand spreading miles before us. Then, quite quickly, it became dark as the golden ball of fire said its farewell before disappearing below the horizon, so far away. In a lot of places around the world, it is nice to see the stars in the sky. When you are in a place with very little, or no light pollution, the sky is lit up by so many stars. Hundreds more than you ever see when in a village, town and certainly a city. This was the time to visit the Bedouins. The local Arab tribes had set up a camp, to entertain us in their traditional way. After a welcoming cup of coffee and very sweet cake, there was an opportunity to try on the Arab dress, smoke from the Hubbly- bubbly, experience henna painting or watch the falcon training. Whilst enjoying our meal and afterwards, we were entertained by a belly dancer. As we set off back for the hotel, Zeni made a remark to the driver, that it was a good job he had his headlights on going over the sand dunes. Not the right comment!! He turned them off. We were shooting over the dunes not knowing which way the vehicle would turn. The expertise or foolhardiness of the driver came across once again, as he showed he had complete control. Perhaps! After a few minutes, the headlights shone again, as we joined the main track and the rest of the party. We joined the main E77 road, then onto the E66 back to Dubai. Another great time!

It was our last day in Dubai. At least we were catching a late flight back. We took a taxi back again to Jumeirah beach. I was correctly dressed this time. We saw the security guard who allowed us to enter after paying the admission fee. That is not quite correct. The amount we paid can be used for a meal or drinks in the hotel. The Burj Al Arab, (Arabian Tower) is on a man made island, 280 metres out to sea. The worlds tallest, most luxurious hotel, (7 star), built in the shape of a sail. At 321 metres, it is taller than the Eiffel Tower. On entering, the opulence hits you straight away. 22 Carat gold leaf finishes abound. The escalator moves up to the main lobby of the hotel. On the right hand side is the AL Iwan restaurant. Behind that and overlooking the beach, the Sahn Eddar serves refreshments during the day. The centre piece is the fountain. Jets of water, dance from one side to the other, in perfectly round flows as if in a tube. Every twenty minutes, water shoots 32 meters into the air. It comes down within a few inches of where it started its skyward journey. Within seconds of the water completing its display, if any splashes had ventured out of the pool, they were quickly mopped up. Cleaners are always around, looking very smart and unobtrusive. Dusting and cleaning wherever it looked necessary. This is a credit to the management. We caught the elevator, giving us a view of the Arabian Gulf, to the Al Muntaha Skyview restaurant, where we had a drink whilst looking across at the city of Dubai in the distance and 200 metres below on the bar side. The building of the Palm Island is on the restaurant side. We sat in the luxurious chairs enjoying a fruit cocktail. I have still not come across, anywhere in the parts of the world we have visited, a place that can match the delicious, thirst quenching, great tasting drinks made from a combination of so many fruits as we had here. When we entered the building, I tried to book a table at the Al Mahara Seafood Restaurant. This is when you take a short submarine ride, to the undersea fantasy restaurant, to enjoy a meal with fish swimming outside the windows. As there where no free tables, we decided on the Al Iwan. Before entering, we just sat and looked at the fountain, then upwards to the top of the hotel. There were suites on either side, meeting towards the gulf, with stars appearing in the last column giving it a marvellous effect. Meal time. Within seconds, we were shown to table 14. We had decided on a buffet. The food was from every continent. There was so much food. It was so colourful, so well presented, and delicious. The service could not be bettered. We had three waitresses. Sadly, after finishing we had to leave! We had decided, we could put up with the luxury. What a shame our pockets couldn't!

What a place to visit. We could not complain about anything. The locals were very friendly, and pleased to welcome you to their country. It was a pleasure to go there. Our flight back was due to take off at 11.45pm. This gave us time to have a look around the airport. Within a few years, it has been established as a major hub, and won many awards, including the best airport in the world. We can't argue with that. The flight was 2 hours late leaving. What about our connection in Doha? We switched flights, from 115 to 119. The London flight was waiting and left as soon as those transferring were on board. We arrived at Heathrow only 15 minutes late, at 7.15am. Just after 11.00am British time I was back at work. What a great long weekend. By the way we didn't win the BMW X5!

Cora's friend Nyle, who lived just outside Los Angeles was visiting her at Christmas, and she wanted us to join them if possible. If we went on Boxing Day and came back on New Years Eve it would be possible. So this is what we did. It meant an early start as the flight left at 09.05am.We were up at 3.30am, and out earlier than necessary, as Sarah was going to Rome to have a look round. We left Sarah at Terminal 1 for her flight at 7.20am then we carried on to Terminal 2 for ours at 09.05am. As before we caught the train from Zurich Flughafen to Bern, and Cora and Nyle picked us up. Our first day was spent relaxing at Cora's, and catching up with all the news. We didn't stay up late as the next morning it was a 5.30am start. The train left Bern at 7.34am and arrived 3 1/4 hours later in Milan, Italy. The journey took us through the Alps. The scenery was magnificent, as the snow gave a picture postcard effect. The mountains overlooked the chalets below, with the long wooden buildings housing the cattle and stock at one end. This enables the farmers to milk, feed and look after the stock, without travelling in the deep snow that is experienced around the country. The villages and towns with snow on the roofs, had smoke from the wood burning fireplaces spiralling upwards into the grey sky, then blending in, as the two colours merge into one. We went through the tunnel in the Alps, and out into Italy.

Customs officers are on the train to check the relevant documents as we speed towards our destination. Passing Stresa, we view Lake Maggiore on our left, then carry on and arrive at Milan Centrale on time. This gave us 15 minutes to get to the right platform and catch the 11.05 to Brescia, our final destination. It was the town where Zeni and Cora's sister, Rosemarie, her husband, Fabri and their children live. There are a number of medieval and Roman monuments in the city, which has shown signs of habitation since at least 197 B.C. There have been battles in and around the town, between 197 B.C. and 1945, including a visit by Napoleon. Fabri was at the station to meet us all and take us to their home. Rosemarie had a pasta meal ready. Bread and cheese followed. There must have been at least five different types of bread, and even more varieties of cheese. Fabri opened different wines to compliment the food being eaten. Fabri had booked us into the local hotel for the night, and we went there for an hour for a quick rest. During the afternoon, we visited the town centre and toured around the Cathedrals.

The old cathedral of the 12th century was very interesting. It went below the square outside, and also has some old Roman baths. The streets and main square are worth a visit. In fact, it would be a really nice place to live. In the evening, we were treated to one of the best meals I have ever had. The surroundings, the family get together, and the excellent food all contributed to make this a memorable time. The food was served in small portions, at least twelve of them, enabling the food to digest and the talk to continue. We were served marvellous wines, at least five different ones, to compliment the meal, as before. All the food and drinks were chosen by Fabri. A grappa rounded off the 3 hour evening event. Brilliant, absolutely brilliant!

Following breakfast, we were picked up and shown Fabri's business. The family own a building supplies company. The inside of the warehouse was so clean and tidy it would have put many houses to shame. The office building was most impressive with a marble staircase.

It was the 13.37 train we caught back to Milan, allowing us a few hours for a quick sight seeing tour. We caught the subway as far as the Duomo, Milan's cathedral. I was looking forward to seeing the lace type architecture of the building, with its 135 spires. We walked up the steps and into the square. Oh No! Looking through the pouring rain, the whole of the front was covered with scaffolding and huge sheets. Restoration was being carried out. What timing. This didn't stop us from looking around inside though. Then just across the square into the Galleria, a building full of majesty and elegance, having shops around the edge of the glass roofed arcade. There were a large number of bars and restaurants and a huge Christmas tree overlooking the centre piece. We had a meal before heading back to the railway station. The 18.10 train was late leaving, and we had to change at Brig, on the way back with only a 10 minutes change over. No need to worry. The connection was waiting. When we left Italy and entered the tunnel, it was pouring down. On leaving the tunnel in Switzerland there was snow, lots of it.

Nyle was not feeling well the next day, so it was just Zeni and I that set off to have another look around Bern. As it hasn't changed over the last 500 years, I knew it would be the same as when we had visited almost a year previously. This time we walked around the parliament building, before going into the city centre and the old square. Across the river, it was still cold, but not as severe as the last time. We had a lovely meal, before catching the tram back.

At 8.11am the following day, we bought the tram ticket, for our first stage of the journey back home. The plane landed 10 minutes early at 1.50pm, and by 4 o'clock, local time, I was back working in the Post Office.

6

AT our Valentine Day dinner (the Holiday Inn again) Zeni and I, had a good talk about the future. First of all, our anniversary trip was decided. That was easy. What about the rest of our lives? The house had been put on the market a few months ago, but was proving difficult to sell. It would reduce our huge bills, as Zeni's large ten bedroom place was costing too much to run. The sense of adventure had gripped us. Why continue doing the same old things day in and day out? What else can we do? Where shall we live? We could live in Rugby, an hour and a half drive from Oxford, and still keep the Post Office. What about the children? We would have to make sure they were alright, then did it matter where we lived? The "children"! Giles was now 24, Craig 20 and Sarah 22. Zeni and I had both left home by the time we were their age. We both agreed that it made better people of us. It gave us more confidence and ability to manage through life. We talked it through with them and they were all in favour. The biggest headache was over. We would see what unfolds and make any alterations as necessary. Should I carry on as the Postmaster of Yarnton, or do something else? That would depend on where we decide to live. What about living abroad? We had wanted to emigrate to Canada, but had no success. What about another country? France, Spain, Italy, or elsewhere? After researching different countries, we ended up with Southern Italy and Dubai. As we had both got used to the nice weather in the States and Dubai. Sunshine won. Dubai it was. As soon as someone showed a positive interest in the property, we would take more decisive steps. Until then we would carry on and continue enjoying ourselves.

For our anniversary we had decided upon a sail. Only a little one! A weekend, well nearly! After finishing work on the Saturday, we drove down to Portsmouth. The overnight ferry left at 8.30pm for St. Malo, France. Well it would have done, if strong winds in the channel hadn't delayed the service by an hour. These things happen; it's no use getting upset about it. A number of people get really angry over delays. They start shouting and abusing. It gets them nowhere and they do themselves no good. We finally boarded and found our cabin, number 6309. An inside 2 berth with a shower and toilet. Nothing else was needed except some food. Off we went to the restaurant. Afterwards we walked around the ship. The bar area had entertainment going most of the night. Fantastic! We just sat down and enjoyed the events. It was well past midnight when we got to bed. Arrival in St. Malo was still as scheduled at 08.15am. We disembarked as soon as possible, to have a look around, as we were catching the same ferry home. It was leaving at a new time, at 10.30am and we had to be ready for boarding no less than 45 minutes before departure. Along to the roundabout, turn left and head towards the old walls and the town within the

20 foot thick walls. It was a good view from the parapets, as we looked across to the port, the hill rising behind. Another of natures natural harbours. There was a sandy beach between the port and the castle. Turning around we saw the very old streets of the town. It was founded in the 6th century by Welsh monks. After a quick walk through the old narrow streets, still quiet as it was only 9.30am on a Sunday morning, we wandered back to the ship, reported in at the departure desk, and then bought a drink at a shop close to the customs/departure gate. The wait in the large hall like reception and booking area, was cold as the automatic doors kept opening and closing as people came from and went out into the cold winter air outside. We passed through customs and waited for a bus to take us to the ferry.

As soon as we got on board, we left our overnight bag in the cabin. This time it was room 6061. The ferry, M.V. Bretagne, run by Brittany Ferries took about 10 hours, to complete the channel crossing. We spent a lot of time outside, just enjoying the cool air, and looking out to sea. When it got too cold, we would go in and explore the ship. We would look around the shops, have a cup of coffee and spend some time in the lounge bar listening to music. We docked at 6.30pm, went through customs, then along the inner road, to the passengers car park, onto the motorway and home. It was a lovely weekend and cost just under £150 for both of us. That included the petrol.

At the end of November, we had discussed what to do for Craig's 21st birthday. We had taken Sarah to the Bear in Woodstock for her meal. Zeni wanted to do something special which they would all enjoy and remember, as if it was their individual twenty first birthday treat. The boys fancied a trip to New York, Zeni wanted to return to Las Vegas, and Sarah did not go with us all the first time. How about if they paid for their own air fare, and Zeni would contribute to Craig's as part of his present. This was certainly something that would have to be looked into. How much would it cost, if the children paid for their air fare and we paid for everything else? Time to check everything on the internet.

7

IT is said, the most stressful situations in life are divorce and moving. Well, I can't disagree with these sentiments.

Selling the home that once housed the Post Office also proved hard. The builder who bought the property, was very awkward and difficult, and had no thought for anything else, except for what he wanted. We were now in the position where our Kidlington house had been on the market for a while. Although a developer was interested in demolishing the property and building a number of flats on the land, we had been waiting months for completion of the sale. There were always delays. Planning permission and access to the property were agreed upon. Still all sorts of other excuses were made, when we enquired about progress. There seemed to be no end in sight. Each week, we were advised that the signing would be soon! At least he seemed more humane than the previous builder.

However, more important issues had to be discussed. Life is too short to let it pass by.

The question of Craig's 21st birthday was resolved. We would go to New York for a week, then to Las Vegas for 2 days.

Thursday the 18th of March 2004, just before 5.00am, Giles, Craig, Sarah, Zeni and I got into our loaded Land Rover Discovery and headed for the airport. This time, our departure was from Gatwick South terminal, London's second main airport. I had already paid the £58 fee, which allowed us to park our car there for the duration of our holiday.

Continental Airways flight CO 19 left at 10.30am, and arrived in Newark (for New York) at 1.25pm. The yellow New York taxi, with its friendly owner set off for the Crowne Plaza hotel at the United Nations, on the corner of 304 east and 42nd street. Conveniently situated, it was within walking distance of many famous land marks. It was another of those days with the traffic. As we went through the tunnel from the New Jersey side of the river to the New York side, we joined a conglomeration of cars, vans, and buses going nowhere. I was informed that it was characteristic of the city. Most days there was a head of state, or a high ranking dignitary arriving to address the United Nations or leaving. Whichever way we turned, the taxi driver met a wall of traffic. Finally he decided to go past Madison Square Gardens along 7th avenue, turned into 14th street and through numerous back streets before arriving on the famous 42nd Street. From there, it was a quick stop and start to the hotel.

After the transatlantic flight and an hour and a half journey to the hotel, we were happy to get to our rooms. Within half an hour though, we were hitting the streets of New York, the land discovered by Henry Hudson in 1609.

The twelve mile long island of Manhattan was then occupied by the native Indian population. The Dutch invaders christened it New Amsterdam, and when the British left in 1783, it was already named New York. A year later it was recognised as the Capital of the United States.

It was getting dark after we had finished our meal at the restaurant, across the road from the hotel. We headed for the Empire State Building. The building reaches 1,250ft above its base on 34th street. Upon entering, the enormity and grandeur is so noticeable. The marble slabs on the back of the lobby wall, depict the building against a map of New York State. It is hard to believe that it took only 1 year and 45 days to build from the first blast into solid rock on 7th February 1930. The rock blasted to a depth of 55 ft. 4,000 man hours per day, (a total of 7million) were used for the construction. There are 73 elevators ready to swiftly take their occupants to the required floor, much better than using the 1,860 steps. I can't imagine that any of the 4 million visitors a year, use them either. After paying our $11, it only took a minute to be whisked up to the observation deck, 1,050 ft above the city. The lights of the cars below looked like pieces of gold travelling along a cream, straight lane. Frequently stopping, as the red garnet clusters come and go, when brakes are applied to the small moving boxes. During a clear day, it is possible to see for 50 miles. At night, we get to view the lights on the numerous sizes of buildings, twinkling and shining their different colours, highlighting the innumerable and varied structures leading to the horizon. We could see Chrysler Building with its magnificent stainless steel spire, the darkness of Central Park, more noticeable due to the surrounding street lights. There was constant traffic, moving back and forth over the three bridges leading to Brooklyn, across East river. The blackness over the Hudson River was broken by the flashing light of a ship, heading into, or out of the harbour.

Over the following days, we visited many of the well known tourist attractions. We spent hours walking around the city. Macy's on the corner of 34th and 6th avenue. We walked along 5th avenue taking in all the shops, stopping at Tiffany's to buy a huge diamond, from one of the three floors selling exquisite and expensive merchandise. Well, actually it was a piece of crystal, cut into the shape of a diamond. The nearest we could afford to the real thing. Craig had wanted to look in the shop, that is known worldwide, and most people will have heard of the film "Breakfast at Tiffany's".

We went down to the Rockefeller Centre building, through the Channel Gardens. In front, there was a skating rink being fully used by the locals. Their gliding forms expressing their happiness and freedom. Then whoops, showing how to get up from the cold, slippery, frozen water. The golden statue of Prometheus oversees the events below.

In 1856, the city paid $5.5 million for the 340 hectares known as Central Park, reaching between 5th Avenue and central Park West and from 59 street to 110 street. I wonder how much it would fetch today at current real estate prices! There are horse drawn carriages on hand, to provide a leisurely ride through the green open space. Four lakes, the Bethedsa fountain, with the angel of waters statue, one of many fountains in the park covered by 32 miles of footpaths. The great lawn is near the centre, with Sheep's meadow across the lake. Trees abound as do roller bladers, walkers, cyclists, and the occasional horse rider. It was very cold during our visit, as our wrapped up bodies took in the sights and sound, of one of the most famous parks in the world. The waterless fountains looked forward to performing for their audiences, as soon as the warmer weather makes the buds burst forth on the trees and spring leads into summer.

Grand Central Station must be one of the finest stations in the world. The ¾ ton clock, 15ft in diameter, above the main entrance guides you onto the 48 acre site, set between Lexington and Madison Avenue. Opened on 2nd February 1913, the 380 ft wide and 340ft deep building, 8 stories high, has 500,000 people passing through each day. The huge arch windows, 60ft by 33ft in the main concourse, allow in the light from outside, so you can view the vaulted ceiling showing a sky mural. The 10,000 panes of glass in the structure come from as far as Italy, France, Belgium and Germany. We had a cup of coffee and surveyed the comings and goings of people, rushing for trains, or meeting relatives and loved ones, from across the tracks, or other parts of America. Some were from other countries on the continent, or beyond.

Wearing our warm, waterproof clothes, we set off for Battery Park, at the tip of Manhattan Island. At 12.35, we bought our tickets for the Circle Line Ferry and boarded the ship which first stopped at Ellis Island, the initial point of entry for migrants into the New world. Then on to the Statue of Liberty! Zeni and I had seen the smaller scale model when we were in Paris. This lady though, stands 150 feet high and has a 35inch thick waist. A gift from France in 1886, it was originally intended for the entrance of the

Suez Canal in Egypt. The Lady with the torch stands majestically on Liberty Island, less than 2 miles from our departure point.

Of course we had to visit Times Square and Broadway. Why it is called Times Square though eludes me. It is a triangle of roads! The lights, sound, sights and people, make the atmosphere like that in all large cities from London to Vancouver, Paris to Manila.

As we were staying on 42nd Street, we decided to see the show with the same name. Tickets costing $41.25 each, gave us balcony seats, for the 7 pm musical, which was showing at the Ford Center for Performing Arts. It was a spectacular, colourful, extravaganza which we really enjoyed.

Afterwards, we had to go into Coldstones. Evidently, it is famous for all its different varieties of ice cream. There was certainly a good selection, with a rousing song from the staff every time they were given a tip. A nice rounding off to another good day.

The United Nations building is just down the road from the hotel, between 42nd and 44th street and First Avenue. The 18 acre site, which backs onto the river is the world's home. The meeting place for all nations, where friend and foe alike, meet to discuss their concerns, ideas and ideals, for their respective country and the world as a whole. All the countries flags fly outside the building, with visitors searching to find the one that represents their homeland and place of abode.

Halls, portray gifts given by different nations. There are rooms everywhere. Sizes vary dramatically, from the small, for one or two people, to huge conference rooms. The General Assembly hall has seats for all countries represented. Rooms for interpreters overlook the vast hall. The occupants relating all to the representatives in a language they use at home, or are easily conversant with. We sat in the now empty seats, and as many people as normal listened to my dialogue! NONE! Perhaps nobody had told them we were visiting. The family got fed up with me talking, yet again, so we left the world to be looked after by those in office.

The Security Council chamber is not as large as the general assembly hall. Only those countries elected sit there. At the moment, eight nations with the advice from the general assembly, decide on the issues involved. It is the most powerful organisation within the United Nations and can impose sanctions and military action against any nation not adhering to the policies of the General Assembly. As we leave, portraits of all the Secretary Generals look down at us, with the dates they served showing below.

During our time in the city, we went our separate ways on a number of occasions, enabling us all to make the most of the stay. On one occasion, Zeni and I met up with Sarah, opposite 81st street on Central Park West, and went to the American Museum for Natural History. Our purpose was to visit the Rose centre for Earth and Space. We entered the Hayden Planetarium after paying a $12 fee. It was an excellent 2- 3 hours. We saw how the Big Bang occurred and how the earth evolved. Fascinating stuff! It is surprising how you visit these exhibits, whilst on holiday, yet rarely see the same whilst at home.

After leaving, we passed by the Dakota Apartments, where John Lennon was killed. Opposite, in Central Park, there is a memorial to him. Strawberry Fields.

Naturally, our wanderings took us along Wall Street, one of the finance capitals of the world. The pin stripe suited gentlemen were going to and fro, from the building. Why though, do some have to wear trainers? It spoils their appearance of professionalism.

A visit to the site of the 9 - 11 disaster, the old world trade centre, was slightly disturbing. Knowing that all those people had died there made me feel uneasy. The list of names and numerous bouquets of flowers, remember those that lost their lives. Then, when you see how people are cashing in on the disaster, it becomes distasteful.

The children decided to treat us to a meal on different days. Giles choice was the restaurant we visited first, across the road from the hotel. The dimly lit interior, made way for the tables and comfortable, black leather, dining chairs, set within the large room. There were televisions on the wall showing sport for those interested. We had a good meal, and it was not far to walk either.

Craig decided on Chinatown. So one late afternoon or early evening, we set off to walk around the Chinese district, looking for a suitable restaurant. Tucked away on a small back street, was the answer to our stomach's feelings. The small basic restaurant provided us with the fayre we expected and enjoyed. On leaving there was just one question to be asked. How do we get back to the hotel? It took a couple of wrong turns, before we realised where we were and started heading for the comfort of our rooms.

Sarah opted for Mars. You must admit, it was a bit ambitious, but being intrepid travellers, we are not going to be put off by a few million miles. Before I could look up the best way to get to this far off planet, Sarah led us to

1633 Broadway at 51st Street. There, we found Mars 2112. Our space ship, train ride, took us down to the floor below, where we were greeted by a friendly New York Martian. He directed us along the large room of the restaurant that was set out to look like Mars. At least I assume it was meant to look like the planet. I will let you know of the resemblance, if and when we ever get to fly around the universe. The Martian named meals resembled our own earthly food! It tasted good and after saying goodbye to the nearby Martians, we returned to reality with a walk back to the Crowne Plaza hotel.

At 19.15 on Wednesday the 23rd of March, flight CO 468 took off for Las Vegas.

New York was a great experience. We all enjoyed our stay, but now we were off to celebrate Craig's 21st birthday in style. At 21.53 our flight landed and we were ready to meet our friends and relatives.

Zeni and I stayed in Harrahs casino, along with Ed and Linda. Sarah stayed with Marriet and Nori in their room at Stardust. Giles and Craig also had a room there. The rest of Zeni's family stayed along the strip, except for Cora and Nyle, who were in the old town at the California Hotel.

The next day, 25th March was Craig's birthday. Ed and Linda had been excellent at choosing a place for a meal, and had sent us a copy of the menu when back home in Kidlington. We were all meeting under the headless statue of Lenin in Mandalay Bay, for the mid-day meal. It was a great get together. All Zeni's relatives from California were there, also Cliff and Belinda from Kansas. The buffet meal in the Bayside restaurant was excellent. It was a good family reunion, and sometimes, only sometimes, there was more talking than eating. Don't worry though, the talking never stopped until we got on the plane to head back home.

We showed Sarah around and along the strip. The main road running through the city with Casinos and varying sights, you would expect to see in other countries and continents. Every time we have visited, the musical fountains outside the Bellagio drew me to them. The synchronised movement of erupting water, to varying immense heights, with the addition of music, leaves me wanting more every time. It is a spectacular feature that draws crowds to the outside of the vast building each time it performs. Every one of the free shows, from Circus Circus to the white lions at M.G.M. draws crowds. The erupting volcano in front of the Mirage, and the pirate show in the waters of Treasure Island, are always popular. Fantastic, free entertainment for the whole family! In the evening, top name stars perform throughout the city in song, comedy, dance, music or magic. Somewhere, there is just the show for you and the family.

Late nights, early mornings, what is the difference when you are enjoying yourself? Oh yes! It matters when you need to get up early the following morning, Friday 26th March to go and meet Marilou and her husband, Jim, at a house they are staying in belonging to her cousin. We go north, along the strip, turn left at Stratosphere, along and up the road to the outskirts of the city. As we head along the last street, we run parallel with the strip, almost 2 miles away. Yet still the sights, sounds and atmosphere, somehow seem to reach out to us. Marilou and Jim had put on a fantastic feast, and there in the centre of the table, was a huge chocolate birthday cake! Craig's second 21st celebration! The time and effort put into the occasion was appreciated by all, as we talked, laughed, ate and drank our way through the last full day of our holiday. We fully enjoyed the company, surroundings and air conditioning, as the temperature outside reached heights unheard of back home in England.

Ten o'clock in the morning on 27th March, with the goodbyes, thanks, good wishes, and hopes to meet again in the not too distant future said, our plane heads for George Bush International airport in Houston, Texas. Following a long taxing run along vast open spaces, we arrived with an hour to get our connection to Gatwick Airport. Our foreign trip ended when we touched down at 7.55am.

El Gouna

8

ABOUT a year earlier, Zeni and I had taken the decision to sell the Post Office in the near future. It was a very hard decision, as this was my main source of income and Zeni was now working part time, whilst spending the rest of the day looking after her enlarged family. As soon as I got home from work, a meal would be on the table. If Sarah was late, due to her college course, or any other reason, Zeni would be there, making sure she didn't have to wait for her food. The families fitted in very well together. Naturally, we all had our ups and downs, but everything taken into account life was treating us very well. It was the end of February, the beginning of March, that the business was finally put up for sale.

Within a week or two, we had an interested party and following the necessary procedures, a date of Friday 14th May was agreed as my final day as a Postmaster. It was the end of an era. My work had been my life for so many years. It had been enormously pleasurable, made so by the many great customers and the enjoyable aspects of the work, such as selling stamps, paying pensions, issuing car tax discs, banking, bureau de change, passport applications and insurance requirements. The camaraderie would surely be missed, especially the interaction with the customers. I would also miss my talk each day with those working in the petrol station, where the Post Office was now sited and Judy listening to my moans and endless natter. There is no doubt, without her, Zeni and I would have found it a lot more difficult to establish our relationship. No long weekends or holidays in which we got to know each other, inside out.

I often look back and always think how lucky I have been to have met Zeni. She has made my life complete, with love and understanding, caring and thoughtfulness, and happiness and sincerity. It is the complete bonding of two individuals. It is so different from my first marriage. Deep in my heart, I know that as long as we are together, the future holds nothing but a good and successful life. I count success in health and happiness, not economic terms. How could I feel insecure with so much going for us!

Before finishing at the Post Office, Zeni and I had been to an exhibition for buying homes abroad. We decided to view some houses in Egypt. There was a relatively new resort, selling all types of properties, from one bedroom apartments to luxury villas. Our visit was booked on the 11th of March and we were flying out on 21st May, a week after finishing work at Yarnton.

Our charter flight left Gatwick 2 ¾ hours late, after being delayed whilst flying in from Florida. The international airport at Hurghada, on the shores of the Red Sea, finally welcomed us. Transportation was waiting and at 11.30pm we finally arrived in El Gouna. There was a street party along the road, in front of the hotel where we were staying. What a reception!

After travelling for nearly 16 hours, all we could do though was collapse into bed.

A lovely view greeted us the next morning, as we stepped out onto the veranda. Abu Tig marina formed in the shape of a bay. A restaurant, jutted out into the turquoise water. Its umbrellas giving notice of the heat we could already feel, as the sun baked balcony reminded us it was time to get a drink and some breakfast.

Carol, the sales representative, had left a message to advise us she would call in later in the morning. On her arrival, we were given information of the area, the transport within El Gouna, and certain privileges given to property owners in the town. The rest of the day was now ours. We started by getting a weekly bus and boat ticket. This cost 10 Egyptian pounds (£1 sterling) for unlimited travel around El Gouna. A bus into the centre of the town took just over 10 minutes. By the time we returned to the hotel for an evening meal, Zeni had decided the place was so nice we had to buy a property there. I was still reserving my opinion until later in the week, after we had seen some apartments and got to know the area better.

I could understand Zeni's decision though, influenced by the imposing front entrance with its huge rocks on either side, with water flowing down them to give a tranquil feeling. The turquoise, warm, calm, clean, sea and the 18 hole golf course, looking resplendent in the desert setting. (We were getting used to these now.) The lagoons, in front of every property, the clear water inviting you in for a cooling swim. The cloudless sky, enticing you to linger at one of the restaurants or cafés, for a drink or meal. The boutique type shops offering their wares, everything required to live in the town or souvenirs for the tourists. The area is excellent for Scuba diving and snorkelling. The night could be spent in the casino, bar, or restaurant, overlooking the town centre, marina, or the sea. Every Friday night, the road around the Abu Tig marina is closed off for a street party. Also top hotels offer entertainment. The town has all the necessary amenities, including its own desalination plant, and has one of the best hospitals in the Red Sea area.

We spent the following morning looking at apartments, with Carol showing us different sights and explaining customs of the region. There was certainly no pressure to buy. Perhaps because the town sells itself and the relaxed atmosphere encouraged us to stay longer.

Yes, we saw a small apartment we liked and to cut a long story short, we decided to buy. I was convinced that the town was a good investment, and perhaps we could rent the property out to holiday makers, when we are not there. We booked a couple of trips, one to Luxor, the other, a sail to one of the remote islands which sounded really nice. We were up at 4.00am and on our way to Luxor an hour later. The first part of the 290 mile trip, took us by coach to the town of Safaga, which was over an hour and a half drive away from El Gouna. At 8.00am we were heading across the barren and in places, rocky desert. We were in a small coach, in a convoy of 200, with Police guarding the front, middle and back.

It was every coach for itself as we set out at breakneck speed. We only passed through one large town. All the traffic had been stopped to let the convoy through. Militia, police, or the army in full control of the road they were in charge of. I think we slowed down then, but I cannot be sure! On every road, through every village, we were afforded the same protection. The same measures were taken on our return. The Egyptian authorities certainly take the safety of their tourists very seriously indeed.

The heat hit us again as we got off the coach in Luxor, and we were introduced to our English speaking guide. First, a visit to Karnak, just a few hundred yards from where the coach was parked. The largest temple complex in the world, greets you with its enormity. You cannot help but marvel at the colossal pillars, and statues, reaching into the cloudless sky. In the Hypostyle Hall the hieroglyphics depict plant life from when time began, still etched deep into the circles of stone, reaching all the way to the 30 feet top stone. 134 columns needed to support the sandstone blocks that once formed the roof. How on earth could these vast stone monuments, be moved and carved with such precision, all those thousands of years ago? From 2,000 years before Christ! This place is truly awe inspiring. The only comparable feature was that of the Grand Canyon. One created by God, the other created for Gods.

Our wanderings took us to a temple. The priest opened the doors to its followers, as the sun reflected on the gold altar. It gave the effect that everything was covered with the precious metal. We saw Cleopatra's Needle, one of three such obelisks, the other two having been transported to London and Paris years earlier by historians of the times. The enormous statues of Ramesses II, with Queen Nefertari looking an insignificant height as she stands in front of his legs. After all her statue was a mere 6-7 feet tall! The chambers, the rooms, the enormity of such vast pillars, quite close to each other, in order to support the huge weight of the roof. The passage way to the temple of Luxor lined with Sphinx.

We stayed for hours, but it didn't seem long at all. Another day and we may have been able to take more in of this vast memory to the Gods and kings of ancient times. Now for lunch at the Old Winter Palace Hotel! Not as old as the temples of Karnak. It was only built in 1886. The lobby is resplendent with its pillars and central chandelier. We were shown into the vast restaurant divided into different rooms. The cleanliness and magnificence matched that of the buffet lunch.

All aboard for our next journey, to The Valley of the Kings. On our way, we stopped to see the Colossi of Memnon. Two huge statues, 59 feet high, standing in what seemed the middle of nowhere, depicting King Amenhotep III. It is thought their original height was nearer 65 feet!! The statues faces worn away with time, towering above the mere mortals below. The mountain behind, with trees at the foot, breaking the dry sand coloured scene, as the intense heat bore down. It was a relief to get back into the coach!

Our next stop was Medinet Habu, or the mortuary temple of Ramesses III. The temple is in marvellous condition, considering it dates from c. 1184 -c.1153 BC. The carvings, hieroglyphics and painted columns, stand out, against the stonework. Even on the entrance wall, there are carvings showing the king killing his enemies and them being offered to the Gods of the day. Another truly remarkable sight.

Our arrival at the Valley of the Kings hailed another hot spot. It was over 42c, as we followed our guide into the area.

Six in our party started to walk around and look into various tombs, leaving out that of Tutankhamun, as evidently little was left in there to see. There was a slight smell of mustiness, inside the great burial chambers. As you would expect, the paintings and hieroglyphics looked remarkable after all the years.

The vastness of the tombs, carved out of the rocks for royalty of the day. We walked through the wide entrances, down the long corridors, leading to the chambers and anti-chambers, of this vast hole in the rock. The workmanship was masterful. The Valley of the Kings is surely that. Mountains on each side and the rear, make this single entry site stifling with the heat. There is no cool breeze, or relief from the searing sun here. Three of us made it to the end of the tour. The others having to seek shade, as the erupting, yellow powerhouse in the sky, reached down, with all its mid-day strength, reminding us that rain was something that fell in other places, certainly not in most parts of Egypt.

I must admit, that with great happiness, we entered the air conditioned coach. The coolness, started immediately to revive our hot, weary and very parched bodies, back to life. What a relief. Pass the water please.

The way back to Luxor involved going past the Tombs of the Noblemen. These were reputedly even better, than those of the Kings, as all the noblemen at that time were the sculptors, painters and architects, as well as scribes. The Valley of the Queens was also nearby. The guide started summing up, with his profound knowledge of Egypt, both ancient and modern.

Before leaving, we just had time for a quick sail down the Nile. The expanse of the river was appreciated more as we approached the centre, of the longest river in the world. It stretches from Lake Victoria in Uganda, 4,184 miles, to the shores of the Mediterranean Sea.

The drive back took us along the same roads. The Lower Nile area is very well cultivated. Tomatoes for export around the world, along with the sugar cane and other vegetables are grown on this very fertile stretch of land. It is irrigated by one of the great rivers of the world. There were mud brick houses waiting to be completed. Others appeared to have no roofs, but there again who needs one when it doesn't rain. I expect that if woken at night by huge spots of water falling on their heads, there would have been great pleasure among the locals. We passed donkeys being ridden. The rider try-ing to usher them along with a small stick, or what looked like sugar cane.

On our return to the hotel, at 10.30pm, all we could think of was our bed and the astounding sites we had seen and visited. A relaxing sail to a remote island is about as far away you can get to the historical temples of Luxor. The sail to Gobal Island should have been so relaxing. We were ad-vised that as Zeni has a fear of water, the owner of the yacht would let us stay on board for the meal. Unfortunately this couldn't happen, so Zeni spent the whole time worrying about transferring to a dinghy, in order to reach the island for the barbeque meal. Naturally, I reassured her as best I could, and offered to do anything which would make her trip less daunting. As I have mentioned previously, if Zeni thought I wanted to do something, then she would do it also irrespective of fear. Nothing would persuade her not to take the trip. This shows what an exceptional person Zeni is, and also how fortunate I am to have such a wife. We arrived at the island and the crew was really kind and caring. We went over with the last group in the dinghy. Zeni was obviously pleased to be on dry land, but was now worrying about the trip back.

The island itself was very barren, as we walked across the top, looking over to Mount Sinai, another ancient place. We did see one small plant hugging itself close to the ground. From there we could see the view down to the bay below, with the yacht sitting just out at sea, in the pale blue water, which turned darker depending upon the depth and the sand, or rocks below. The small, brown cocker spaniel dog, which accompanied the crew on each sail, wagged its short stumpy tail vigorously, whilst running along the white sand, close to the waters edge, looking at the small waves as they very gently lapped in from the warm, calm sea. The most important thing though was the barbeque. The crew had everything up and running, ready for the meal. There was no way we could do any running though, certainly not in that heat. Our slow walk back to the beach, ensured that on arrival, all we had to do was walk up to the barbeque, get some food and drink, then sit under the canopy put up for shade. After everybody had eaten their fill, and drunk their drinks, it was time to start our way back. Zeni and the crew, made sure that we were in the first boat ride back to the yacht. Once on board, I could feel the sense of relief that overtook Zeni. The sail back, was so much more relaxing than going out. We actually moved around the boat, and at one time, gallantly walking by the rail at the side, we watched six dolphins swimming along by the side of the yacht. They looked as if they were playing. Different ones took up the lead, as we headed towards our home port of El Gouna.

The remainder of our time in the town was spent walking, swimming, well actually paddling, as Zeni was too nervous to go further, once it had reached the top of her ankles. A massage on the beach got rid of all Zeni's tension from the sail, whilst I had to suffer a long, ice cold beer, whilst waiting for her. The time and beer seemed to vanish into thin air.

A walk round the marina ended with us talking to the occupants of two small boats, both crews sailing around the world. One man was by himself in such a small boat, it couldn't have been more than 17 feet long. I certainly didn't envy him, as he had wrestled with storms and strong winds so far. In two and a half years he had sailed from Vancouver to Australia, stopped over in Malaysia, parts of Africa, including now, Egypt. Next port of call was Europe. The other crew had sold up and left Australia to sail around the world. Both crews were deciding where to meet next.

All good things come to an end. So it was with our trip to El Gouna. At least we had the knowledge that with buying an apartment, we will be back sometime in the near future, giving us chance to explore not only Egypt, but also the surrounding countries of Africa and who knows where besides.

9

OUR future very much depended on where we were going to live and work. We had decided on Dubai, so it was a matter of getting a job over there. A customer and friend from the Yarnton days, told me that her friends son, was working out in Dubai and perhaps he could help us. We were kindly introduced to her friend and arrangements were made for us to meet Richard, when we got out there. The Lufthansa flight to Frankfurt left Heathrow an hour and a half late. Consequently, our connecting flight to Dubai was missed and we were to be transferred to an Emirates Airline flight instead. We were told to run to another gate, over 5 minutes away, and they would inform the airline that we were on our way. What a pity they didn't do that. As the few of us who arrived at the desk were told it had just closed. They got in touch with the pilot, but as everything was being secured, he did not want late comers on board. With security as it is, we understood, and were given seats on the next plane out.

A shame it was 5 hours later, but, these are the joys of travel. Our arrival in Dubai was 10 hours later than scheduled. To make it more frustrating, one of the cases didn't arrive. We called at the Emirates Airline lost luggage section, and they were excellent at sorting it out. The bag arrived the following day. Full marks go to the Emirates airline for stepping in and looking after us. The service on the flight was excellent, as well as the food.

Richard, is a really nice guy, and was very good at helping us look for work, as well as advising us of the different customs and laws.

I got in touch with a number of work agencies, as well as contacting firms direct. A lot of time was spent writing and sending letters with an accompanying C.V., all to no avail. What I did fancy was a job at the airport. Having gone through so many in recent years, I enjoyed the buzz and thrill of the travellers coming and going around the world in search of business or pleasure. The atmosphere is really exciting. However it was deemed not to be. Whilst there, Richard took us to the camel racing track which had the camels, cantering, if you can use that word for camels. The young jockeys hung on hard so they wouldn't slip off the back! One didn't hold on tight enough though, and he was trying to catch his mount. He looked so small next to the big beasts. I believe they now have mechanical jockeys!

Of course, we found time to look around a couple of the malls, Deira City Centre and the Wafi Shopping Mall. Another day out, was a visit to Al Mamzar Park, which borders onto the Emirate of Sharjah. It was very hot, and the beckoning water, soon saw both of us, taking advantage of a small, insignificant, cooling down process. We ran out of the water to the shade of a palm tree. It may have provided shade, but the relentless heat drove us to the restaurant area, after only half an hour! The flower garden bloomed from the daily feed of water! We needed more than that, so we returned to the Holiday Inn, air conditioning, cool drinks, and fine food looking at the view of colourful red trees and tall sleek buildings. One building had a huge golf ball perched on top. Yes, this can only be Dubai.

A week had flown by. No success on the job front, but Richard found an apartment we could live in on our return in September. The U.P. Tower stood majestically along the Sheikh Zayed Road. So we said goodbye to the land that we were ready to call home, when we returned in September. Why September? Well Zeni's sister, Cora, was getting married. Of course it had to be somewhere different! We were invited. Could we go? You try and stop us! Zeni will explain all later.

Before then though, it was a matter of keeping on top of everything. We had finally sold the house. Not to the builder, but to someone else who crept in at the last minute and signed the necessary papers. To say the builder was not amused, is an under statement. He had months in which to sign, but opted to wait until all the I's were dotted and all the t's crossed. You have to take a risk in life. At last it was all over and we decided to take the family, Giles, Craig and Sarah, for a day out to Calais.

We drove down to Dover, leaving the car in a multi-storey car park. We caught the P and O Ferry, Pride of Calais at 10.45am. The whole sail only cost us £15.75. I thought that was a pretty good deal for 5 folks, having a 2 hour sail there, and the same back.

We walked around the town and finally decided to have a meal at "Le Calice". It was a lovely day, as we sat in the garden eating our meals, talking about all our futures, both Zeni and I worrying if everything would be alright for them after we left.

Zeni and I took a trip into London on one of the frequent bus services that run from Oxford. We spent time around the Westminster area and finished with a trip on the London Eye. The giant observation wheel is the world's highest at 135 metres. The 32 pods which can carry 25 people in each, take half an hour to complete the circuit. It overlooks Westminster and the Houses of Parliament, St James Park and Buckingham Palace, Scotland Yard and the Ministry of Defence, Charing Cross and the Embankment, Waterloo Stations and Waterloo Bridge, the Aquarium, St. Thomas Hospital and Lambeth Palace. In the distance, on a fine day, it is possible to see Windsor Castle, 25 miles away. It has become one of London's main attractions.

It is fair to say, that there was quite a bit going on at this time. The house was sold and completion of the sale was 26 August. Just under 2 months away. Of course, that involved packing up the furniture. We had some earmarked for our apartment in Vancouver, but it would have to go in storage for a few months. Boxes were being packed for Dubai, and we had decided not to take anything to Egypt. It was a small apartment, and we would furnish it over there. Then we hit a bit of a problem! The furniture could only be sent to Dubai, if we had a job there. There had been no success on that front at all. I had been making phone calls and sending faxes since arriving back home, all to no avail. I was again advised to go there and keep trying until I was successful. As they say, this was crunch time. The decision had to be made soon, in order to plan our future lives. If we moved to anywhere in the European Union, we could automatically work and live. That sounded like a good idea! But should we, or is it worth trying further for a job in Dubai? Zeni, had received a phone call from her sister a few weeks earlier and we would be out of the country until just before the completion of the house sale. At least it gave us something to think about!

10

ONE evening in May, after a hard day at work, I was relaxing on the sofa, watching television with David. The phone rang and I went to answer it. It was Cora, my sister from Bern. Of course we had a long chat and she invited us to a spiritual wedding in Hawaii! She told me that her American boyfriend had offered to marry her.

As this was a bit of a surprise, she decided to go for a spiritual wedding. This is a marriage performed by a lay preacher, without an actual marriage contract. It is the bringing together of bride and groom bound together by marriage, but with no legal standing. Cora was a bit apprehensive at first, but was reassured when Nyle told her they would go for a legal ceremony as soon as the correct papers were completed.

As you can imagine, I was so excited. It was a marvellous excuse to visit Hawaii, the place I had been dreaming about, since my childhood. My dream holiday to the Paradise Isle.

The island that has the hula dance and grass skirt costume.

I had seen the Elvis Presley film, "Blue Hawaii", on a number of occasions. The thought of the stunning, tropical scenery made me feel excited about going there. I told David the good news. He was speechless for once. I was so thrilled after talking to Cora, that I spent most of the night tossing and turning. My mind was thousands of miles away, thinking of the beautiful Hawaiian island. A paradise for lovers, just suitable for David and I. It would be another honeymoon. It is just a few months, weeks, days, until the day in July when we will be off to Hawaii.

We fly to Hawaii via Los Angeles and the same on the return flight, so we will visit my other sisters, whilst there. The exciting moment came. Oh dear, what is the matter. We are called over to the flight desk. We confirm our names, show our passports and get up graded to business class!

Thank you United Airways. They must have known how much I was looking forward to this holiday! Wine was served soon after getting aboard, as well as the daily papers. Now this is service. If only we could afford it every time. This was truly a luxurious, trans-Atlantic flight. Although I don't like flying now, the service and huge seats, made me forget my worries as I relaxed for the next few hours. After transferring at Los Angeles, we were given a seat in the main body of the plane, but with extra legroom. We had travelled United before, and we would certainly check their prices every time we fly now.

On arrival in Oahu, the main island of the Hawaiian group, we took a taxi to Garden Grove Hotel, located two blocks away from Waikiki beach. Nyle had told us about the hotel, as he stayed there every year, when attending a surfing contest. On our arrival, Cora and Nyle met us. We talked for a long time over drinks, before going to bed absolutely worn out. That's what happens when you travel for over 24 hours.

The next day, as we walked down near the beach, the view was so tropical, so real, so much like home in the Philippines, with tropical fruits, the coconuts, the flowers, and the scenery. No wonder there are a lot of Filipinos living on the island.

Whilst talking to Cora, she gave me a surprise! I was to meet Annie a neighbour from back in the Philippines so many years ago. I had not seen her for nearly 32 years! I remembered her vividly, as Cora continued talking about her. She was living here in Hawaii with her husband, now retired from the military. They had got married in the Philippines, when living in Quezon City where we used to live. I remember her as a teenage girl. She was a friend of Cora and Lourdes. They often went to parties together during holidays and after school. What a shame, we were only here for 2 weeks. During our stay they were so kind to us. Even after Cora and Nyle had gone back to Los Angeles, they took us around the island. We really enjoyed their company, and were so upset when we got back home and couldn't find their address or telephone number. They were moving back to Washington State, and we were hoping to see them when we visited Vancouver. Unfortunately this never happened. One day we sincerely hope to meet them again.

We had been talking, on our way to the International Market Place, along Kalakaua Avenue. The avenue starts at the foot of Diamond Head Beach Country Park, winds its way along Waikiki beach, inland to the Royal Hawaiian shopping centre, across the Ala Wai canal, passing the convention centre, before stopping at South Beretania Street, which in turn runs into downtown Honolulu.

The International Market Place has huge banyan trees inside the area. One of these large trees has dozens of tendrils trailing down from its branches. These in turn, have taken root, giving an umbrella affect around the now shaded area. The pond below had golden orfe and koi carp swimming in the cool water. There was a Hawaiian lady with her stall under the tree, full of fresh flowers to make the traditional garland, the lei. Shops and stalls wind through the area until they reach the food court. This turned out to be a favourite place for Cora and I, as two or three of the outlets only sold Filipino food. Needless to say, we had something to eat, before Nyle took us to one of Honolulu's most famous tourist stores.

The free shopping shuttle bus took us to Hilo Hattie's. As we entered, we were all given a shell lei. As elsewhere in Hawaii, we were always met with the customary greeting, which is heard throughout the Islands, "ALOHA". The fresh ice cold drinks, welcomed us into the big store, selling everything associated with Hawaii; tropical shirts and dresses, hats and sandals, wooden kitchen requisites and coffee, not forgetting the macadamia nut, the round, hard nut, synonymous with the Hawaiian Islands. It sold Hawaiian music on c.d. or tape as well. What a truly Hawaiian experience!

Cora and Nyle had decided to get leis made for their wedding, by the lady in the blue Hawaiian dress whose stall was in the International Market Place. They were made with plumeria flowers, which have a lovely scent and grow all over the island.

The wedding took place on the beach beneath palm trees. The vastness of the Pacific Ocean spread out behind them, before reaching the shores of other Polynesian Islands, Japan, and onto the Philippines. Cora was in a white ankle length dress, wearing her leis. A ring of fragrant yellow and white flowers adorned her head, with a longer one around her neck. An additional one in purple and white flowers matched that of Nyle's. Nyle wore traditional Hawaiian attire, made up of shorts and a white shirt, with an embroidered flower motif around the chest. I was wearing a sky blue dress with a flower and leaf pattern.

The bespectacled lay preacher, one of Nyle's friends, performed the ceremony in the shade of the palm trees, with David and I, and their friends looking on. It was exciting seeing Annie again and we had a good talk, catching up on old times, recollecting on our lives since leaving the Philippines and looking at where our lives had taken us. How I enjoyed those talks with Annie whilst in Hawaii. David and Annie's husband seemed to get on well together also. I will let David relate the good times we had on the Island, as well as the trips we took. Without Annie and her husband taking us around, the holiday would have not been as enjoyable.

Following the beach wedding, we all set off for a celebration meal at a restaurant of Nyle's choice. The talking and celebrations continued until late in the afternoon, when everyone went their own way. Cora and Nyle, Zeni and I were taken on a drive around the island the next day. Hanauma Bay is a Sate Underwater Park. One of the main beach parks on Hawaii and is part of a sea crater from an old volcano. People go there in their thousands every day, to picnic, swim and snorkel. The bay is full of tropical fish, with coral covering the area. The one road going round the island has sea views almost all the way. The rugged rocks reach into, or come out of the sea. Waves splash high into the air, before plummeting back onto the rocks or returning to the turbulent ocean. By contrast, tranquil bays, perfect for swimming or sun bathing. There are surfing beaches all around the Island.

Most evenings, Cora and Nyle, Zeni and I would walk down to the Sheraton Princess Ka'iulani Hotel located along Ka'iulana Avenue. We would sit in the central court near the swimming pool, with a Hawaiian cocktail, listening to the Hawaiian music, or watching the Hawaiian dancers performing to an appreciative audience. A singer/pianist would then play requests, or sing well known songs.

At times, Nyle would go surfing, to get ready for a contest later in the week, whilst Cora, Zeni and I would either be on the beach or looking around the local shops. How ladies love the shops! Especially Zeni. One group, ABC, was everywhere. They had a shop on every block. All Blocks Covered.

One afternoon, Zeni and I visited Diamond Head. This old volcanic crater has been dormant for 150,000 - 200,000 years and lies at the end of Waikiki beach. It can be reached with the local bus service, (no.58), or by walking past Honolulu Zoo, which is what Zeni and I did. The signs, soon lead you off the roadway, up the steep hill, round the corner to the entrance. The 761 foot peak is reached by a walk through, up and around the pathway, in the crater to where the first steps meet you. 99 of them, but don't think that is it. Another 76 await you before entering a 225 foot long tunnel. After negotiating the old gun emplacement, we walked out into a view of Waikiki beach and the tower blocks of Honolulu, with the green grassland of Kapiolani park on the right, and views of the island with Kuli'ou'ou beach park and in the distance Koko head crater on the left. A magnificent view all surrounded with the pale blue serenity of the calm sea. White waves, breaking on the clean cream sand. In places, the sea was so shallow that few or no waves appeared to exist. Immediately below, were the rock formations covered by water, before reaching the sand, in front of the million dollar homes. The single yacht, with its white sails standing out against the pale blue background. It was already a long way out and still heading into the horizon, where the blue sea and sky became one.

By the time we returned to the bottom of the crater, I can assure you, we were ready for a drink. The heat and exertion when climbing made us feel utterly exhausted. We caught a bus back to the hotel, where we recovered ready for a night out.

After Cora and Nyle had left for home, we had a further week on this paradise isle.

One really enjoyable day, was when we were taken sight seeing and we ended up at Pearl Harbour. Everyone must have heard of one of the famous names of World War II, such as D. Day, Dunkirk, Dresden, Auschwitz, and Hiroshima, the place where thousands of lives were lost, as the Japanese made an unprovoked attack on America's pacific fleet. The USS Arizona memorial centre, pays homage to the lives lost on that terrible day. The area looked just as it was depicted in films about the event.

Zeni and I also booked a couple of tours. The first one

being an Hawaiian waterfall hiking adventure. We walked around the Ko'olau mountains, taking in a cascading waterfall, the rain forest and jungle, as well as the sights and sounds of the local birds. The plants with their different coloured blossoms and scents transported us to a different type of world. The mosquitoes were about though, and several people, including the two of us, were bitten. We are not keen on mosquitoes, even though they seem to love us!

The other trip involved a flight to the Big Island, the island of Hawaii. Our flight, on Aloha airlines flight AQ 82 took us to the very small international airport at Kona.

From here, we set out on a circular tour of the island. We were told that, Hawaii experiences most of the different climates of the world, from snow to desert temperatures, from rain forest to a temperate zone. After a short drive, we stopped and looked over Kealakekua Bay, at the white monument to Captain Cook. Clearly visible at the water's edge, in the middle of the coastline making up the bay. The Kona coffee plantation, with the bushes set in rows, behind the coffee beans, which were drying out, in the long, covered barn like building. I remembered that Mum and Dad, used to have Kona coffee in the café they had many years ago. Following the coastal road, we eventually came to Punalu'u beach. Evidently, it is famous for its black sand and green turtles that nest on the beach. We managed to see one swimming in the water not far out to sea. It must have seen me though, as it had no intention of coming ashore. Spectacular waterfalls and goodness knows how many different types of palm trees were scattered around the island.

As we followed the coast, the scenery made another dramatic change. This time though, it was slightly eerie. We were entering the volcanic area. There was a golf course and large hotel complex by the water, but up on the hill, where the main road ran, are mountains of lava. Solid from the cooling process, but not there long enough, for vegetation to start growing on it. The dark brown and black substance is so rough, that walking on the uneven surface would be very difficult.

Our next stop was in the Volcanoes National Park. We drove through banks of old lava, pushed up at either side with a bulldozer whilst still warm enough to do so. The rest area in the centre overlooked a huge crater. The sulphur was clearly visible all around the edge of the big basin. It was very noticeable, as all around was barren.

Steam was forcing itself from the earth below. One place was so pungent that the coach driver refused to let us out of the coach. A danger sign, outside the coach advised that volcanic fumes are hazardous and could be life threatening. What an interesting drive. The area of the most recent lava flows cut a near straight line through the established vegetation. Unfortunately, we didn't have time to see the active volcano, but we could see the plumes of smoke as we passed the end of the road leading to it. Out of the park, we stopped off at a lava tube. The lava set in such a way, that we were able to walk through it to the other side. All the area is now incorporated in rain forest or jungle.

Finally, we stopped off at an orchid nursery. The perfume from the flowers lingered outside. There were flowers all over. There was every shape and size of orchid you had ever seen, and more besides. The colourful wax like petals were in dozens of different colours and shades. Variations were immense as the pale pinks turned to pale purple before turning into a colourful yellow in the centre, purple with orange centres, orange with purple centres, orange and purple mix, whites, reds, and all shades in between.

It was strange, entering such a small international airport for our return flight. The security was there as always, but in such a small area it is hard to imagine, especially after going through large transit areas in London, New York, Los Angeles and Vancouver.

The Polynesian Cultural Centre, at the tip of the windward side of the island, has exhibits of seven pacific cultures, on its 42 acre site. Our first stop was Samoa, followed by New Zealand (Aotearoa), then Fiji. We managed to pop into Tonga and Tahiti, but ran out of time before visiting Marquesas, Hawaii, and a special exhibit on Easter Island. Each of the exhibits, portray life on the island. From climbing coconut trees in Samoa, to the dancing in Tahiti, the drumming in Tonga and the war clubs displayed in Fiji. The colourful canoe pageant represented all the islands, the traditional costumed natives, dancing, playing music, and performing their war dances, from twin hulled canoes, with a small stage on top. It was very good indeed, and the war dances looked quite frightening. The young ladies, performing their dances are very graceful. The evening show "Horizons" held in the Pacific Theatre was a spectacular event. All the performers were in national costumes, assisted by waterfalls, fountains, fire and a volcanic eruption. If ever you are fortunate enough, to visit Hawaii, do not miss this colourful spectacle.

An evening cruise on board the Navatek, provided us with excellent food and entertainment. On return, passing Diamond Head, the sun started to set. The pale yellow sky, on the watery horizon, reached up to the evening clouds. The white, bright, rays of the sun lit up the upper blue sky. The yellow sky was now turning orange, with the blue sky getting darker. Finally, and all in a matter of minutes, the whole sky turns orange, the colour spilling over into the darkening sea. Then the darkness spread quickly, from the sky above to the sea below, overtaking all. A magical sight!

Whenever there was spare time, Annie and her husband would be there ensuring we didn't miss anything, from the Pali lookout to the Luana Hills country club, and its breathtaking golf course. Marriott's new beach club, Ko Olina, with its magnificent beach, (and pool side bar) to the world famous Dole pineapple plantation (and pineapple ice cream). We visited North Shore with the surfing beaches and quiet coves, and the Shrimp Shack providing excellent food, rain forest, mountains, valleys, and the famous sandy beaches. We were at the end of our holiday and it had exceeded Zeni's dreams and my expectations.

MAHALO.

We wouldn't pass through Los Angeles, without seeing Zeni's relatives. Mary Jane picked us up at the airport and we stayed with her and Zeni's mum, then Cora and Nyle for two days. Of course, we were taken out. This time around the Long Beach area as well as Costa Mesa. Everyone looked after us as they normally do. Words cannot explain how wonderful, caring and generous, all of Zeni's relatives are. One evening, talk turned to Zeni's green card application for immigration into the U.S.A. It had been approved a few years earlier, but had not been taken up due to Giles and Craig's education. A few weeks earlier, she had written regarding it and we were waiting for a reply.

Whilst in North America, we had decided to visit Vancouver to make sure the apartment construction was on schedule. A bank account had to be opened. This is when we met Raymundo Lino, another Filipino. He has become a very good friend, and we always look forward to seeing him and his wife Liza, whenever we return.

Time was spent getting everything in place. Checking out different management companies, to look after our investment and ensure it is always occupied, when we are not there. There were appointments and meetings. We had to choose a Notary Public. We opted for Catherine Yong, who has an office just off Cambie Street, a short bus ride away.

A sail to Bowen Island sounded like a good idea. We left at 09.30am, from the Harbour Cruises jetty, in Coal Harbour, next to Stanley Park.

It was a lovely one and a half hour sail through Vancouver Harbour, under Lions Gate Bridge, towards Howe Sound. Passing all the expensive properties, along the shore of North and West Vancouver, there were small islands with only one or two homes on them. Trees covered most of the rocky areas. All shades of green, from the top of hills and mountains and stretching down to the sea. There are long trees, short trees, fat trees, thin trees, all reaching up for as much light as possible. In Howe Sound reaching past Bowen Island and Gambier Island, the wide expanse of water, narrows off at Squamish to become a river, its origin high up in the mountains.

Snug Cove welcomed us onto the island. There were sheltered bays for swimming and fishing, as well as the Killarney Lake, 13,000 acres of forest to explore, and also Crippen Regional Park. Unfortunately we didn't have enough time for everything. So it was a quick walk to the lake, taking in all the sights and sounds on the way. Looking down the hill from the tree lined picnic area, the parched grass, light brown in colour and crispy to walk on, went as far as the tree lined bay. All the different sizes of yacht masts hid the boat we had arrived on. The calm waters of Howe Sound were met by the trees reaching down from the mountains behind. Their wide white scars of the mountains showing where the mass of ice and snow start their downward journey into the narrowing gullies. Their fingers pointing to the watery highway, thousands of feet below.

Our return trip takes us past yachts racing to their home port. We see canoeists, paddling across from the mainland to the island we had just left, the lighthouse ready to issue its warning to ferries and other craft negotiating the night waters. Before entering the harbour in Vancouver, we had to wait for a float plane to take off. As we passed by the mountain of Sulphur, waiting to be exported, the boat came to a halt by one of the rafts of logs that had floated down river to the mill. Sea lions lay on top of the wood, basking in the sunshine.

Our room at the Holiday Inn in Downtown Vancouver, overlooked the apartment block where we had our investment. The large crane, pointed towards the building, which was the resting place for dozens of birds, as they fly backwards and forwards, checking on how the work is progressing.

An afternoon walk, took us along Davie Street and down to English Bay. Beach Avenue, the road leading from opposite Granville Island into Stanley Park, had been closed off. A procession of Hari Krishna followers, men, women, and children preceded the arches of multi-coloured balloons. The flower draped, red, yellow, and blue, painted carts, were flying more balloons. The carts carried yellow, blue, and taller red altar like structures. All except one of the carts were being pulled by two or three dozen people. The last cart seemed to be the lightest. It did not hold a structure, only the hoops of the old wagon draped in greenery, with garlands of flowers and yet more balloons. This was drawn by a hefty looking, dark brown bullock, with a white face. It was striding majestically in the middle of the entourage, towards the green spaces of the park. It was a really colour-ful sight.

The evening sky, overlooking English Bay and Burrard Inlet can produce sunsets similar to those in Hawaii. Truly magnificent! They say Canada is a cosmopolitan coun-try. If the remainder is anything like Vancouver is, then it certainly is. Apart from Canadian friends we have, Ray and Liza from the Philippines, Phil, Jane and Sam Baker from Sheffield, England, acquaintances from China, Iran, Malaysia, Japan, America, and Europe, all living together in peace and harmony. A testimony to the world.

In case there were any problems whilst away, we trav-elled with information on our house sale in Kidlington, furniture removal, purchase of the properties in Vancouver and El Gouna. We had also contacted someone in Cyprus, to see if we may like to buy property there. Everyday we were checking our e-mail, and were on the internet looking at properties in Malta and Italy.

Everything being in place for our future purchase, we head back home to sort out the rest of our lives.

11

THE Thames Valley, Chiltern Hills and the Cotswolds is a beautiful area, and Oxford, is a very historic city. Records show it has been in existence since 912, but was probably there 200 years earlier. The castle was built in the 11th century for William the Conqueror and in 1155, Oxford gained its royal charter. The city has been a seat of learning for centuries, since about 1096. The first University, Merton, being established in 1264, to become the oldest English speaking University in the world. Sir Christopher Wren, who studied at Christ Church, left his mark on the city with the Sheldonian Theatre. In 1542, Oxford got its own bishop and during the civil war, King Charles set up his headquarters in Christ Church. The Ashmolean museum and the botanical gardens are the oldest in Britain. Around the world we see jars of Frank Coopers marmalade which has been made here since 1874. In 1912, William Morris started producing his cars here, after having a bike shop and studying at Exeter College. As I said quite a historic place, and let's not forget Sir Roger Bannister's 4 minute mile, whilst also studying at Exeter. It is so interesting

DAVID & ZENI TARLING

seeing all the old architecture. I am so pleased that it is not being overtaken by modernity. Of course it has its shopping centres. The old castle, which later also incorporated a prison, now houses a hotel and several restaurants, and the Oxford Story is a ride through the city's past.

Walking down High Street, you will find some of the colleges, Queens, University, Oriel, Brasenose and Magdalen. St. Mary's church and All Saints Church amongst some old timber framed buildings. Lanes and passage ways lead off, one to the Chequers Inn which was built in 15th century, another leading to the covered market with its wonderful meat and produce stalls. The Mitre, dating back to 1600, was once an old coaching inn, now owned by a large chain. We often eat here.

Broad Street, with Blackwell's bookshop. Cornmarket and along the Thames from Folly Bridge and looking across to Christ Church College, one of the largest and founded by Cardinal Wolsey, on the site of 9th century St Frideswides monastery. It has its own cathedral, (Which other college has that?) and the Big Tom tower, housing the Great Tom bell. Further down St. Aldates, there is the Alice in Wonderland shop, selling items referring to the famous story by Lewis Carroll, who studied at the university as did fourteen Prime Ministers. Thirty nine colleges make up the University. So many famous people have attended. A few in addition to those already mentioned are, T.E.Lawrence (of Arabia), Richard Burton, Edmund Halley (comet), J.R.R.Tolkein (Lord of the Rings), Albert Einstein, Margaret Thatcher, Harold Wilson, Sir Walter Raleigh, Robert Peel (police force), John Paul Getty, David Cameron and Michael Palin.

In addition to the colleges, Oxford has a lot of private schools in and around the city.

A few are New College School, St Edwards, Dragon School and Magdalen College School. Most have had distinguished pupils. The Group Captains Douglas Bader and Leonard Cheshire, Sir John Betjeman, Tim Henman, Cardinal Wolsey, Ivor Novello and the award winning producer Sam Mendes are a few of the notables that attended them.

Climbing Carfax tower and the view overlooks the city of dreaming spires. We would wander down the old side streets, stopping for a cup of tea and a cake. The imposing Radcliffe Infirmary. Meander along St. Giles, where the annual fair is held in September, passing the Eagle and Child, a drinking establishment since 1650. St. Johns College, Tony Blair studied there, as did Jethro Tull the agriculture reformist. The martyrs memorial, sits across from the Randolph Hotel where Zeni and I first met.

The shopping areas around the High Street, Cornmarket, Westgate, Queens Street, the Clarendon Centre and Magdalen Street, with Borders book shop, where Zeni saw Hilary Clinton and got a signed copy of her book.

Walks can be taken along the river, to as far as Abingdon, around Folly Bridge or Port Meadows in Wolvercote, providing varying scenery. The sculling enthusiasts to the ordinary rowers, to those in punts or Kayaks, the swans or other waterfowl running across the top of the water before taking off for an unknown destination. The cattle can also be seen, chewing cud or wandering to the waters edge for a drink, disturbing the wildlife along the bank. The ponies graze or those being ridden, gallop along open spaces showing off their paces. You will see people walking the dogs close at hand or the children flying their kites.

We will cherish all the thoughts of such a lovely city, the surrounding towns, villages, and countryside.

Yarnton, with all its memories and the site of the civil war. Its church dates back to the 13th century and the manor house was built in the 1600's. There is also a great Post Office and marvellous people in the village!!!

Kidlington, was Zeni's home for so many years. She will certainly miss walking down to the shops and calling in at her friends, Esther and Roland. No more going to The Wise Alderman or Jolly Boatman for a meal, or attending the Annual Garden Open Day at Sir Richard Branson's house, which is just down the road and in aid of the Red Cross. Woodstock, a royal town from years past, has the historic Bear Hotel built in 1237, where we have been on a number of occasions. After the First Duke of Marlborough won the Battle of Blenheim in 1704, Queen Anne was so pleased she gave him the Manor at Woodstock and a grant for £240,000. Blenheim Palace was built between 1705 and 1722. Sir Winston Churchill was born there in 1874 and over 100 years later, it became a world heritage site.

North Leigh, has one of the best Roman villa remains in the country, and the Rollright Stones, to the north of Chipping Norton, date back to around 2,000 B.C. Long Hanborough, where we used to hold Sub Postmaster meetings. Bladon, which has the grave of Sir Winston Churchill. Eynsham and Witney, Banbury with its cross and famous cakes, as well as the well known nursery rhyme. Further afield we have Aylesbury and Warwick. All these places and many more besides, leaving us with tales to tell to those who will listen.

Wherever you go in the world, people have heard of Oxford. Go into a large bookshop and you will quite likely see a version of the Oxford English Dictionary. This is published and is part of the Oxford University Press, the largest university press in the world. It was started in 1478 and publishes 4,500 new titles every year.

12

I T is three years, since Zeni and I met. Years ago I would never have dreamed of leaving Britain. The present government and events they have brought about have now made us both think differently.

Who would have thought there could have been such a turn around in our lives?

Who would have thought we would be able to buy apartments in Canada and Egypt?

Who would have thought we would be wondering where to live?

Naturally at times, doubt creeps in. Was it right to sell the Post Office? Should we have carried on living in the same house?

It will be strange leaving Oxford, although we intend to return every few months, to see the family.

I had never been in a place for such a long time, fourteen years. From Lancashire to Surrey, Sussex to Yorkshire, Merseyside to Oxfordshire, altogether I have moved home 15 times, excluding my period at agricultural college, and three different lodgings in Northallerton, whilst working for the Milk Marketing Board.

Zeni had only lived in two places in Kidlington, whilst in England, apart from the nurses' homes.

Now though, the ultimate question was, "Where next?"

Rosemarie, Zeni's sister in Italy, 'phoned and asked us to live near her. When in America, we were asked if we would buy over there, and stay for 6 months every year.

So to sum up, we could occasionally live in our apartments in Canada, or Egypt. Try again for Dubai, or live near Rosemarie in Italy. Not forgetting Malta, Cyprus and now the United States. Why not in more than one place? Just think of the other countries in the world we can visit from any of our new homes!

That's it. We have made our minds up, and book a night stay at the Holiday Inn in Heathrow.

Zeni's sons, had bought a house in Bicester. The town we had got married in two and a half years earlier. The 2 bedroom home, will give them the stability we wanted them all to have before we left the country.

Sarah, had opted for a bed sit in one of our friends houses. The room had been emptied, thoroughly cleaned and painted. Sarah had also decided to have a wooden floor installed. There is a small bathroom downstairs, which she could use, as well as the bathroom upstairs. The kitchen would be shared. She assured us that she was quite happy, and we were not to worry. Needless to say, we did.

Lefkara

13

ON Saturday, the 28th August, 2004, our flight took off and we headed for Cyprus. Although we had never been to the island, we had been talking and finding out about it all the time we were in Hawaii and Vancouver. It is situated in the Eastern part of the Mediterranean only 47 miles from Turkey to the north, with Syria 60 miles away, Lebanon to the east and Egypt 200 miles to the South. The Greek island of Rhodes, which is the nearest point to Greece, is also 200 miles away. As you can now see, Cyprus is at the crossroads to three continents. The island is only 3,572 square miles, and has a population of around 820,000. It joined the European Union on May 1st 2004. The majority of the population can speak English as a second language, to Greek, which is the primary one. It has a temperate climate. So it is nice and warm, in the summer like Dubai and California. It gets a little cooler in the winter, and snow falls in the mountain areas. With only a four and a half hour flight to England, it didn't seem too far away. There is so much history on the island dating back over 9,000 years that it can only be recorded as we find out about it. If for some reason, we don't like the country, then we can move somewhere else after a couple of years.

Before the British Airways flight landed at Larnaca airport, our necks were straining to see the island and the place we may call home through the windows. Why didn't we buy shares in B.A? We have certainly helped to keep them going. Finding our cases on the carousel, was great fun, as the new machinery had broken down, and the baggage from three flights were all coming along the same conveyor belt.

We went outside to find a taxi to take us to our final destination, Limassol. As we drove the 70 Km, it was an opportunity to see the scenery and vegetation. The land looked very arid, with low bushes and olive trees, reminding me of the inside of the smaller biome, depicting the Mediterranean climate at The Eden Project in Cornwall we had visited 2 years earlier.

We were staying at the Demero Beach apartments, which is along the main road in the Germasogeas area. Our apartment was at the front of the building overlooking Desoudi Beach. Every evening, we could hear the tree crickets across the road. Even when the traffic was non stop outside, about 10.00pm, the crickets made themselves heard above the car and motor bike engines.

We had contacted Peter Stephenson whilst in Hawaii. It later transpired that I had been in touch with two different Peters whilst on the internet, arranging viewings with prospective sellers. It was decided that we would meet Peter Stephenson and his wife Avghi, on Monday.

The Sunday was spent walking around Limassol. Zeni soon found some shops and we wandered in and out of them, finding out what was different from what we had back in England. It is surprising, no matter where you go in the world, you see similar items. The biggest difference in Cyprus being, there are fewer of the designer clothes shops. Cyprus has an abundance of fresh fruit especially citrus. Some local grown vegetables and huge, pork chops were bought and we made a meal in the apartment, before wandering to the beach across the street. The holiday makers were there, letting the sun soak into their lightly clad bodies. Sun cream was applied liberally, after emerging from the calm blue warm water which looked so inviting and a relief from the heat and warm rays descending through the cloudless blue sky. Bodies of varying shades of white, red and brown occasionally left their small piece of paradise to walk a few yards for a nice cold drink, at the Desoudi beach restaurant. Near to the apartment and across the road from the beach, is the Woodman sports bar and restaurant. It has a number of televisions, and sporting events mainly from Britain, are being screened at most times. The good food is home made and includes Cypriot, Greek, English and a continental menu, British beer and spirits, as well as international and local ones, are available. I particularly like KEO, the local beer. Wine has been produced on the island from 2,000 years B.C., and Cyprus is one of the oldest wine producing countries in the world.

On Monday 30th August, Peter and Avghi picked us up from outside our rented apartment and we headed towards the Troodos range of mountains. Our first day included visiting houses in Pano Lefkara, Kalavasos, and two in Monogroulli, all very old villages, and about half way between Limassol and Larnaca.

When travelling back to Limassol we stopped off in the village of Parakklisia, for a drink. The waiter asked us what we wanted, Zeni asked for her usual diet Coke or Pepsi and when I asked for coffee, the reply was which type; Nescafe or the local coffee. I opted for the Nescafe. As the four of us talked we got to know more about Peter, whom was from Wales and became a qualified Charted Surveyor. He moved to Cyprus after meeting Avghi, who is a Greek Cypriot, and was living in England at the time. Avghi had previously married, but was like Peter divorced. When they got married they moved to Cyprus and set up an estate agency business in Limassol. Peter is the only foreign licensed estate agent on the island. Both are very kind and helpful, and told us about the island, the different areas, and gave us some very useful information about each area we visited. We knew that it was necessary, since the Turkish invasion, to ensure that the title deeds for the house were available. Peter and Avghi assured us that they did not deal with any property without the necessary and correct documentation.

After a full day looking at different properties, it was agreed we would meet them again the following day to see a further batch. This time we visited properties higher up in the Troodos range nearer Limassol. Vasa,Platres, and Trimikini. It was another opportunity to see more of the island. The more we saw, the more we liked it.

Now, it was just a matter of which house and where. Did we like any of the properties or should we start afresh? We had chosen older buildings that required some renovation, as well as some that were ready to move into. Our decision to live in the mountain area away from the coast could also be reviewed. It was agreed that we would be in touch with Peter and Avghi as soon as we had decided.

The following day we 'phoned Peter and told him we would like to see the very first property we viewed, the one in Pano Lefkara. It is a two bedroom house at the end of a small cul-de -sac. We could live in the house straight away. The small shower downstairs would serve us until we got a new bathroom upstairs. The kitchen and dining room needed to be completely renovated and it would be strange, going out of the downstairs part of the house and using the outside steps to get to the bedrooms. These just needed a good paint to get them looking better. We walked to the centre of the village, had a drink and something to eat, whilst talking more about the property and the village.

Pano Lefkara is a large tourist village which has all the necessary amenities; a health centre, doctors, a dentist, an ambulance and fire station as well as a Police Station, two schools, a church, food shops, a news agent, a Post Office with a friendly postmaster, and a butcher. It has been a dwelling place since at least the 12th century, and in the 16th century was the largest town on the island. There are innumerable souvenir shops, restaurants, tavernas and a couple of hotels. It is situated 8 km up the mountains, after leaving the main Limassol to Larnaca road. At 730 m. above sea level, it is higher than the main towns, of Limasssol and Larnaca, and also a little cooler, which can be a blessing in the hot summers. The very narrow streets, wind in between the rows of old houses and ruins, which are set on the side of the hill. The ladies of the village sit outside their shops or homes making lace items. Men can be found in the workshops, delicately making silver ware.

By the time we had finished eating, both Zeni and I were fairly certain that this was where we would live. Zeni fell in love with the place because of the magical atmosphere that surrounds it. On the way down the hill, we made our minds up and decided to buy the house and make Pano Lefkara on the island of Cyprus our home.

The second most important decision since Zeni and I had got married had been made. The first was deciding whether or not, to break up the family home, and let the children, make their own way in the world. As I said before, this was a really hard decision. With the decision of buying our home sorted out, it was time to look around the area.

We had received an e-mail from Egypt regarding our property there. A further document needed signatures, and had to be returned immediately by Federal Express. After asking for the nearest office, we were advised it was in Nicosia. We later found out there was one a few miles away in Limassol.

There are no trains on the island and buses only operate within the large town areas.

Apparently a taxi ride was necessary. The Cyprus government gives taxi firms different licences according to where they operate from and to. The intercity taxis operate between the major towns only and run every hour, within stated times. Service taxis operate between certain towns only and urban taxis operate at all times within the main towns. Services are also supplied from villages. We booked a taxi with the help of the owner of the apartment block to the island's capital. After eventually finding the office, and sending the documents, we went back into Nicosia for the taxi back home. Sightseeing unfortunately, would have to be for another day.

On September 4[th]we had booked a day sail on a catamaran which sailed around the bay of Limassol to Episkopi, which was near the sovereign base at Akrotiri. Both Zeni and I put on our best clothes. What a shame everyone else was casually dressed and some just in their swimwear. It transpired that we were to stop at Lady Mile Beach so everyone could go swimming off the catamaran. Yes, we looked like fish out of water. The captain/owner, did offer me some swimming shorts, but I declined. Despite that, we enjoyed ourselves, the food, the scenery and the sail. A lovely birthday celebration.

As we wanted to see more of the island we booked a couple of trips to different areas.

One was to Nicosia. There have been dwellings here for over 5,000 years and it has been the capital city for 1,000 years. The 4.5 metre thick walls were built by the Venetians after conquering the island in 1489. The new area of the city is built outside the walls, which house the old narrow streets. After the collapse of the Berlin Wall, Nicosia became and still is, the only divided capital in the world. It became so, when Turkey invaded the island on 20th July 1974, just after the country had stopped a coup by the Greek military government of the day. The Turkish Republic of Northern Cyprus is not recognised by any country in the world. Artefacts from the occupied area have turned up in auction houses in England, Netherlands, Germany and the United States. These have been plundered from museums, libraries, and even churches.

Talks were taking place at the United Nations regarding unification, but these broke down and the Status Quo currently exists. Our coach tour took us to one of the crossings along the green line, which is controlled by the United Nations. It reminded me how foolish it would be to buy property on the north of Island unless the political situation changes.

After being shown the Archbishopric, with its huge statue of archbishop Makarios, (the influential Archbishop took the island to independence from the British in 1960), we were taken to the war memorial, the House of Representatives, and shown different areas of the walls, before being given time to wander around the city. After having a lovely meal at a restaurant, we went right into Ledra main street and up some wooden steps onto a viewing platform, which enabled us to look over the wall into the Turkish side. It was difficult to judge what the other part of the city was like, as all we could see was ruins and narrow, dirty streets.

On our way back to Limassol we stopped at Lefkara, this time it was Kato Lefkara, or lower Lefkara. Pano Lefkara, the first village we visited is the Upper village. We wandered around the old narrow streets, looking at the hand made lace and bought some of the local honey. It was a good opportunity to have another look around the area.

Our second day out was to Pafos, on the western side of the island. Two thousand years before our visit, it was the capital of the island. The drive took us to Aphrodite's birth place, Petra Tou Romiou, where she rose from the waves. Lunch was taken at the restaurant overlooking the scenic area. Just before reaching Pafos we visited Geroskipou. Its 10th century church has five domes forming a cross.

In Pafos, we passed the site where St. Paul the apostle was chained to a small pillar of stone and lashed 39 times for preaching Christianity. He came over to Cyprus to introduce Christianity to the island and was joined by Barnabas who was a native of the island. Despite Paul's beatings, they succeeded in making Cyprus the first Christian state in the world.

The coach parked by the harbour, near to 12th century castle. Our tour to the UNESCO world heritage site, included a visit to see the mosaics dating from the early 4th century. To date, three or four villas have been excavated and work continues.

Inside the house of Dionysus, the mosaics depicted the God of Wine. The mosaics of marble and stone are truly remarkable. We followed up our visit with a quick meal and glass of red wine, before taking a walk round the harbour. Then off we went to see the Tomb of the Kings, just a short distance along the road. The site is nowhere near as impressive as the Valley of the Kings, we had seen in Egypt. It dates back to 300 years B.C. has large Doric Pillars, and is below ground level, making us believe it had some Egyptian influence. It is thought royalty had not been buried there, but ordinary men and women of that time.

On our drive back to Limassol we realised how the tour had given us a much greater insight into the island and its history.

Limassol hosts a wine festival, which takes place every year, since 1961. Naturally as it was on during our visit, we had to go. The best known wine of the island is Commandaria. It is a sweet wine and been produced for at least 2,000 years. We bought our entrance tickets and went into the Municipal Park. On each side of the wide pathway, the company stands displayed the different bottles and types of wine. Samples of any of the various types were flowing freely. On one stand it was possible to buy a small carafe for £2 cyp. We did this and went further along the path and found a stall giving away wine. Visitors had bottles, and carafes which were being filled from the huge vats. We took ours back to the apartment to enjoy with our next meal. Food stalls were very busy selling the barbecue chicken, filled pitas or souvlaki, (skewers of meat).

We both thoroughly enjoyed our first time on Cyprus, looking around the island, buying the house and enjoying the glorious weather.

On the 8th September we left for England, in order to get our finances in place and the relevant money sent to our newly opened bank account in Pano Lefkara.

Janet had decided to treat herself to a cruise down the Nile for her 60th birthday. So she was in Egypt when we were in England. We took her boys, Matthew and Neil out for a meal in Deddington and caught up with all the news, even though we had only been away for 2 weeks.

On the 20th of September, we headed to the airport, for one of our many British Airways flights, back to Cyprus, the Island of Love, The birthplace of Aphrodite, the Greek goddess of love. The island where we now live.

Sarah had come with us to make sure we got on the plane! We were very pleased she did. Zeni and I took our suitcases to the check-in. We had got used to the baggage allowance for transatlantic flights, and like a fool, I hadn't checked how much we were allowed. It was only one case each. We had two. Apart from that, they were overweight!

Sarah helped, as we transferred the important items of clothing etc., into the remaining cases. We got sorted out and our bags were finally accepted for the flight. I'll not make that mistake again.

It was 4.30 in the morning on the 21st September when the plane touched down. It was pitch black outside, except for the lights from the airport and those scattered around the hills. Zeni wanted to wait until it was lighter, so we wouldn't get lost and we could find our way, not only to Pano Lefkara, but also to our new house, down a small street, and along the cul-de-sac.

We collected the hire car at 05.00am, after enjoying a cup of coffee and cake from the coffee shop in the check-in area. Despite it still being dark, we set off for our new home. Yes, we made it without getting lost and pulled up along side the street, to a dog barking from deep inside the opposite house. We took our cases up the small incline and round the bend to our little house. We unlocked the metal door, leading into the courtyard, and then opened the door leading into the lounge area.

We just dropped our cases and went to park the car in the public car park, just down the road. The short walk back to the house saw the sun beginning to show its first sign of light across the mountains.

Before leaving the island we had booked a room in the local hotel, the Agora. It was just a few streets away. We decide to wait until a reasonable time to check in at the hotel, so we sat on the bed settee that we had bought from the previous owners. We were full of all sorts of emotions, tiredness, anxiety, sorrow, elation, and also a little trepidation. Tiredness, after the early start and late arrival, without any sleep. Anxiety, at leaving the "children". Sorrow at leaving not only the family, but friends as well. Elation, for the new life ahead, the two of us forging a new pathway in an unknown place, and trepidation, at what the future holds for us.

The one thing that stands out over everything is the love Zeni and I have for each other. I can honestly say that I have never been happier in my life.

We spent three nights at the hotel whilst we cleaned everything in sight at our new home. Each day we walked into the village, to get cleaning equipment, food and water. As there are a number of restaurants we visited different ones, as we tried to sort out our cooking arrangements at home.

Let Zeni take up the next part of our story.

14

WE checked out of the Agora hotel, and headed to the house we called our own. It was about 10.00 o'clock, and a bright sunny morning. As we entered, it felt so calm and quiet. Although the house is adjoined on both sides, the two dwellings are empty.

One is owned by a Cypriot now living in America, whom we have never seen, the other by an old lady who unfortunately now lives in a nursing home.

During the day, David and I finished the cleaning. As night approached I started to become frightened. The house is at least 200 years old, and I was petrified of the unknown. Similar to how I would have felt, if I had stayed at Rosemarie's friend and known about the ghost, before I slept there!

I became very restless. Poor David kept trying to re-assure me, saying that everything was fine and there was nothing to worry about.

We were going to sleep downstairs, on the old bed settee we had bought from the previous occupants, as I refused to sleep upstairs until the bathroom and toilet were installed.

Naturally, the thought of walking outside, down the steps, into the downstairs part of the house in the dark was scary. There was an old bed sheet left in the house. David put it up to cover the door and the surrounding parts of the French windows on either side. I told him that I didn't want to see any shadows or movement from outside. I was really scared because of the new area, and the security left behind in Kidlington. Also I missed the children very much. When we had made the bed, we snuggled up, talking about the day's events, and what we would do tomorrow. I told David how scared I was, and asked him if I could wake him up during the night, if I needed to go to the bathroom. He agreed and fell off to sleep. There were so many things worrying me, I couldn't sleep. The bed clothes were pulled over my head, and they stayed there, even though I was so hot I felt I could hardly breathe. My body was so tense that my legs were aching. I was listening out for any strange sound, but it was a long, silent and worrying night. I don't think I got any sleep at all. If I did, it wasn't much. When David woke up in the morning, he remarked that I looked very tired. I told him what a terrible night it had been. He put his arms around me, hugged me, comforted and talked to me. After breakfast we went into Nicosia, so we could buy some proper curtains for the house. As soon as we got back, David put them up across all the glass windows on a thin curtain wire. I felt a lot better then. The royal blue chiffon was big enough to double up and make the room feel more like home. I did sleep a bit that night, because I was so tired, and I only woke David up once, when I had to go to the bathroom.

The following day, I telephoned my sister in California. I told her about our new home and its age. Instead of encouraging me about everything, she actually made me more afraid. In the end I wish I hadn't phoned her. Being even more upset, I told David about the conversation. He is so patient and very reassuring. He always makes sure I am happy. He is very consoling and always by my side. When I went upstairs, David would have to come with me. I don't think I could ever live without him, as we do everything together.

One day, I was thinking that I couldn't live like this, as I was missing the children, I decided to give them a ring. I just wanted to burst into tears when I heard them. I felt so sorry for David, as he tried his best to assure me that our new life would be fine. I knew that I should be offering David reassurance, as he was going through the same transition as myself. All I could see when I looked at him was his smiling face offering his love and care. I knew I had agreed to the move, as the property was cheap and needed renovating, which was to be our project. So we could work and be together. Day by day things got better, as David's reassurance, attentiveness, caring and consoling attitude, made me look at the positive side of our life and what we had.

One day when I was cleaning the house, I saw a lizard on the wall, and two cockroaches that had just flown in. Naturally, I called David to get rid of them. David was moving quickly around, as the lizard ran round the walls before it left. The cockroaches were killed with a spray. It was the same type of spray that killed another cockroach. It was in the toilet in the middle of the night. David soon killed it, but it stopped me from getting to sleep again. One morning as David was making the bed, a cockroach was fast asleep between the sheets. That was it. David spent hours, finding out where they were coming from. The hole behind the water closet was filled in, as well as the cockroaches. We had no more!!

A lot of time, was spent going backwards and forwards, to the do-it-yourself shop in Limassol, as we were still waiting for our belongings to arrive from England. Tiles, paint, filler, hammer and nails, screws and screwdrivers were all bought.

We would call in at an internet café, whilst in Limassol, and see if anyone had sent us a note. The first time we did this, there was one from Sarah. It was the first she had sent, and it was from the airport just after we had gone through to departures. She wished us good luck and told us not to worry about anything. We still have the message on our computer.

When at home, I made sure David always had some good food and plenty of coffee to drink, when he had a break. I remember one day, when I was cooking a nice steak, the sweat was pouring off him, as he tried to get the tiles fitted on the wall in a straight line. It was so bad I felt like running over with the bucket, so the floor wouldn't get too wet! As time passed, I got to like the place and even got braver. I made sure I would try and please David and make him happy. I supported his decisions on the house projects, and our love for each other grew stronger, despite the creepy crawlies. I am now thoroughly enjoying our life in Cyprus, the village with its friendly and welcoming inhabitants, as well as the lifestyle and wonderful weather on this beautiful island.

Everything is going very well, as we meet new friends, including some English couples. We use our local supermarket, which is just like an old English village store. If you hunt hard enough, you will find what you want.

We are living in a beautiful village full of character, with the houses so close together. Many years ago, I had dreamed of such a place, over and over again, when I was by myself. It is lovely walking into the centre of the village every morning, being greeted by the locals with " Kalimera", (good morning), or "Yasas" (hello).

We always try to visit our friends, Harry and Maro Loizou, who own a lace shop. If we have any problems, or need any advice we know we can always go there for help. Thank you both very much. It's good to talk about what's going on, and David and Harry always catch up with the football news, especially anything to do with Liverpool. Harry used to play football for the Cyprus team of Alki, in a centre midfield role and played semi-pro in Liverpool before moving to the Island. Maro is a great cook. Her dolmades (stuffed vine leaves), beat any restaurants. We have been very fortunate to be invited to their house on a number of occasions for a meal. She always makes us feel at home. We have been introduced to their family and friends, making us feel even more settled in the village.

David found a good hairdresser called Peter. A Greek Cypriot who used to live and work in London. He also does ladies hair and he has looked after mine a number of times since living in Lefkara. Along the same street is the dentist, also very good, and for a short time there was a takeaway food shop called BJ's. Bill and Jan from England tried the venture and we became friendly with them.

Chris Komodromos is a lovely lady who also used to live in England. I get on very well with her. She is very kind-hearted, and like all Cypriots very proud of their family. We call and see her in her alley shop two or three times a week. Jan and Steve live just outside the village with their dogs and cats. We heard that an English couple had taken over the Lefkara Village Hotel, and hoped to open it up early next year.

The culture of the Cypriots is very similar to the culture back home in the Philippines. People are kind, caring and very religious. David says Filipinos are probably the nicest race on earth. I feel so proud when he tells people this.

Lefkara is the home of "Lefkaritika. This is hand made type of lace-like embroidery, the art of which has been handed down through the centuries. Leonardo da Vinci, apparently bought some here in 1481, and gave it to Milan Cathedral for an altar cloth. This encouraged the men folk of the village to travel abroad selling the product, which has since become known all around the world. The Second World War saw a drastic decrease in lace/embroidered products. It only increased again when tourism became an important part of the islands economy, in the late 1970s.

David prefers the silverware, especially the filigree work in broaches, earrings and other jewellery, ornaments depicting trains, horses, coaches, musical instruments. In fact I am sure that whatever you want they will make. I love the silver trays and goblets as well as all the jewellery. David has kindly bought me a number of items from Harry.

When we go round the village, it is nice to see the older men sitting in their chairs, drinking coffee and playing backgammon or just catching up with all the news.

The Church of the Holy Cross dates back to the 14th century. It is said that a fragment of the original cross, on which Jesus died, is embedded into the church's silver cross and is venerated by many. Documents state that St. Helena, visited the monastery at Stavaravouni and left part of the original cross there. The monastery can be seen from the village. It is also believed that St. Helena distributed parts of the cross to cities around Europe. St. Helena was the mother of Constantine the Great, the first Roman Emperor to embrace Christianity.

From outside the church you can see for miles, the sea in the distance, enticing us to leave the work and head for the beach.

Now I have got used to the village, I can say that it is a lovely place. It is magical, calm, peaceful, and serene. It is a place where you can forget all your worries. In fact, it is Home.

15

WE headed back to England in the middle of December. The renovation was well under way. The dining room was nearly tiled, after the original wall covering had to be removed in places. The two foot thick stone walls caused a problem when trying to put pictures and mirrors up.

Unfortunately the kitchen had not yet been fitted out, but the upstairs bathroom had been completed and the tiling finished just before leaving. The furniture and belongings from England had been delayed a bit, and wouldn't you believe it; delivery had now been scheduled for the day after we had left for Oxford, so they would have to be stored until our return.

Even so, we had managed quite well under the circumstances. The downstairs shower was a bit awkward, and the wash basin very small, but it was home.

During the short time we had been on Cyprus, we had spent most of the time in the house, or going to do-it-yourself shops. Time was found to go to the beach, visit Limassol, Nicosia, and a few trips into Larnaca.

We had managed to visit one historical site, that of Tenta in Kalavasos, only a few miles away. Down the hill to the main road, then head towards Limassol. The site dates back to around 7,000 years B.C. The area of the settlement is easily seen, with the rooms set out in the circular huts. Walls were plastered, and there was evidence of wall paintings on them, one depicting two humans. It is believed, they were set out at the bottom of the hill in a circle for security reasons. The varying rock and soil samples, show, that it is possible, they were never cut off from the mainland. The dead were buried beneath the floors and in between the open spaces of the domestic buildings. In the storage and production area, it showed that olive oil was produced there. The site was excavated between 1976 and 1984, but was originally excavated in 1947. As early as 1897 a team from the British museum thought of it as a place of interest.

It is well worth a visit and makes you think what may have been going on there so many years ago. It is not known what made civilisation disappear from the site and from Cyprus for about 1,500 years.

It is marvellous living in such a lovely country. The majority of the time the sun shines from the perfectly blue sky. If there are any clouds, they gradually disappear, whilst we looked up at them, from our small courtyard, as the heat from the plains met the cooler air that had just crossed the mountain range. When the rains come, there is no doubt what is happening. It is a bit different from back home in England. The heavens open and the deluge of water pours down. It makes you wonder how much rain could fall in such a short time. We soon found out one day when getting a newspaper. The dark clouds opened, the rains started, and the water began running down the street. Within a few minutes the water was as high as the 3" step. Foolhardy as we are, we left the dry sanctuary and headed off to see Harry and Maro. That was easier said than done. After deciding that the water running down one street was too fast and deep to cross safely, we headed along the higher street and managed to get within a few feet of the shop. Fortunately the rain was easing and the wooden palate that Harry had put in front of his steps had just stopped from floating down the hill. It was certainly a good introduction to what happens on the few days of the year, when the blue sky gets covered with the dark black clouds and the arid land cries out to the heavens for the life giving moisture. What a shock the ground must get! So dry that it cannot easily absorb the heavy drops, only to see it rush down to the lowest point and be gathered in the lake or reservoir. Dry river beds become torrents, before soon drying up, to await the next onslaught, be it the next day, week or year.

Every morning as Zeni comes down the outside steps, she will look at the walls of the house next door. On a number of occasions she will see the lizards, lying absolutely still, before a sudden movement sends them scurrying to their sanctuary, behind the shutters of the windows.

Rumour has it that Saint Helena introduced cats to the island in order to get rid of the snakes. It may sound appealing and practical but the animals were on Cyprus long before that. Whether they remained is another matter. The oldest pet cat in the world, so far, was found buried on Cyprus, in the village of Shillourokambos, just a few miles east of Limassol. It was found along with its owner in a grave dating back 9,500 years. It is thought the Egyptians bred cats as pets, from the 20th or 19th century B.C.

Most mornings, the local green grocer can be heard, as he pips the horn of his mobile shop, when at the end of the cul de sac. Very handy if we have forgotten to buy something the day before! The ladies from nearby houses will go and buy their requirements for the day. The older ones dressed in black dresses, often covered with a black shawl. The fresh fruit and vegetables looked so appetising that something has to be bought. After 20 minutes or so, with everyone being satisfied, the older gentleman will set off with the vehicle and visit another part of the village to look after the inhabitants who cannot get to the shops easily.

Sarah flew out to stay with us before we left. It was the opportunity for a break and days out to Larnaca, Limassol, and Pafos. We had a meal in one of the restaurants alongside Pafos harbour. The wind was cold as we looked at the castle and ate our meal.

We had never been to Agia Napa, on the South East side of the island. It is a favourite tourist area for the young British holidaymaker. We took the A5 road towards Larnaca, then onto the A3 at the airport junction. Arriving in Agia Napa we drove through the town to the car park overlooking the sea. Keeping our coats on as we walked nearby, we watched as the waves crashed onto the rocks and broke into innumerable droplets forming spray which glinted in the weak sunshine. We passed the harbour and carried on along the now quiet sandy beaches.

The drive to Protares took us along the beautiful coastline of Cape Greko, with its beaches and rocky coves.

The first few flakes of snow, advertised that winter had arrived on this sunshine island in the Eastern Mediterranean.

There was still a lot to do in the house, but family come first, especially at Christmas. We would not be back in Pano Lefkara until the end of February, so on our return we would be very busy getting our house in better shape. Even so, we still had a few ideas about places to visit during the course of the year.

16

THIS Christmas was to be special though. The family, Giles, Craig, Sarah, Zeni and I, were to spend Christmas in Vancouver at our new apartment. Just before leaving Cyprus we received an email from the agents in Vancouver, to say completion was now likely just after Christmas. It was already four months late.

On arrival in Vancouver we had to sort out accommodation and find somewhere for a Christmas Day meal. After searching through the yellow pages and an hour or two pounding the streets of Vancouver we walked into "The Sunset Inn", which is situated just off Davie Street in the downtown area of the city, and booked an apartment for 4 weeks.

We managed to book a Christmas Day meal at the Holiday Inn Downtown, which is half way between our rented room and out new apartment.

The next day we had arranged to visit the new apartment to check for any faults or unfinished work. It was finished extremely well and only a few minor items required attention. What a shame we wouldn't be able to take it over, because some further safety work had to be carried out in another part of the building.

The family were due to land on the evening of the 23rd .Unfortunately bad snow storms had hit the Eastern side of the continent and was spreading over to the west.

A phone call from Craig in Chicago advised us of their predicament. There was a plane to either Seattle or Minnesota with a connecting flight to Vancouver. A few frantic phone calls and an hour or so later, we phoned Craig to be told they were actually running for a connecting flight to Vancouver. Amid deep breaths he advised us that they were in Minnesota and they would be with us soon. We both breathed a sigh of relief. I expect they all did as well when they got their breath back!

They arrived on the 24th, around 12 hours late. Still one more problem awaited. Craig's suitcase was one of 12,000 pieces of luggage that were missing due to the adverse weather conditions By now the snow had arrived in Vancouver, with a covering over the streets and more over the mountains.

I had already decided to treat us to a late lunch at Altitudes Restaurant at the top of Grouse Mountain, which is only a ten minute drive from the city centre.

The cable car deposited all its occupants at the Peak of Vancouver, ready for skiing snowboarding, or like us, just visiting. Following the meal we walked out onto the inner balcony of the area. The carol singers below were just ending their rendition of "O Come all ye faithful", near the log fire. Its red and yellow flames reaching into the chimney, before a log rolled over sending sparks, of various colours around the fire. The flickering flames then re-started their upward journey into the dark chimney breast. A huge Christmas tree was on the opposite side of the area. Its lights and baubles bringing colour to the green branches reaching up to the wooden ceiling.

As we followed the winter sports enthusiasts outside, we negotiated the skis and snowboards of those within. Directly opposite the main building, the log fire in front of the skating area, was keeping warm those huddled around it. The children and parents were enjoying the skating, whilst we took in a truly magical postcard scene. To the left of the rink the reindeers waiting for people to stroke them. Unfortunately there was not enough snow for a sleigh ride. To the right, of where we were standing the large wooden figures, made by the lumberjacks wielding their chainsaws, looked down on the visitors. The white blanket of snow getting deeper as it reached further up the mountain. Dark green fir trees appeared to get smaller, as they climb the rocky, white hillside until at the summit they resemble black matchsticks piercing a white cloth. From within the chalet, to the outside scenery, it all resembled a Christmas card. Never before had we experienced such a happy, magical and magnificent seasonal sight. This alone was worth the flight from England.

It was starting to get dark as we made our way back into Vancouver after a truly magnificent time.

The Christmas Day meal was excellent and we were looked after very well. It was the first time Sarah and I had been away from home for Christmas.

Other families had decided to save their wives or mothers cooking, and the first sitting was completely full. Laughing and talking until we left more than 2 hours later.

The family decided they wanted to try snowboarding, so on the 27th December we experienced another trip to the top of Grouse Mountain.

Zeni and I decided to go snowshoeing. We walked past the huge natural enclosure, which allows injured bears to be viewed until they are released again into the wild. At the base of the rocks leading to the summit, we turned left along a pathway and were soon in a world of our own. The solitude, as the voices of those enjoying themselves around the main area, disappeared into the cool mountain air. The snowy path was showing signs of those who had already experienced the beauty of the white surroundings. Before turning back we stopped to look at the blue sky above as it cast its colour into the snow below. The rays of light, shining past the trees, boughs and branches above to the white, powdery floor, covering any vestige of plant life and undergrowth, many inches below.

Craig and Sarah were just finishing their snowboarding class on our return. They then decided to head for the downward slope. It looked daunting for me, let alone for them as they attempted to stand up, whoops, then slither their way down the mountain side. It didn't seem very long before they reappeared at our sides ready to set off again on their downward travels.

A trip on the 29th December to Squamish, a town on the sea to sky highway, ended at Brackendale. This is reputed to be the bald eagle capital of the world. Every winter thousands of the birds gather in the trees surrounding the river as they wait to feed on the salmon in the clear, fast flowing water. Every year in a given area, the number of eagles are counted. The record is 3,766 in 1994. Walking along the river bank it was possible to see the birds waiting patiently in the trees, or flying off to what they thought would be a better fishing place. An ornithologist had a telescope trained on one on the opposite bank and he kindly let us look at the bird of prey. It was then you realise how large they are and how powerful their beaks and talons are.

On 30 December as we walked by the shore along English Bay, Giles, Craig and Sarah wanted to have a look inside the aquarium. Zeni and I had been there on a previous occasion, but it was well worth another visit. From the beluga whale to the piranha, the small turtle to the alligator, all available to see in lovely surroundings. We noticed that it was possible to spend a night there over New Years Eve. We decided against it and would go downtown where there were further celebrations taking place.

The following day we wandered into and around Gastown having a meal at "The Spaghetti Factory". We then walked along by the bay and past Coal Harbour, before arriving at Stanley Park. By now it was dark and perfect to view the one million "Bright Lights", which have been lit for the past 20 years at Christmas and transform the central area of the park.

One of the New Years Eve celebrations was being held around the Vancouver Library and opposite the television station. By the time midnight arrived the pavements and roads were full of people, watching the clock ticking the seconds off until the uproar of voices wishing their loved ones, and those nearby "A Happy New Year".

New Year's Day was spent just wandering around the city. An early lunch, or rather late breakfast was enjoyed in "Denny's" along Davie Street. Just round the corner of where we were staying. The evening meal had to be at Cloud 9, on the 42nd floor of the Landmark Hotel, along Robson Street, which we first visited in July 2002. We enjoy looking down at Vancouver, with the mountains, ocean, and buildings. It reminds me of "Gulliver's Travels". The vehicles and people below gave the impression of being in Lilliput. All in the restaurant being of normal size and all below being mere miniature toys, moving, walking ,talking, shopping, or just strolling hand in hand along Vancouver's most prestigious shopping area. The revolving restaurant, takes in views all around the city, during its slow circuit allowing us all to experience the magnificent scenery, when not talking!

No matter where we go for a meal, Craig and Sarah, love the deserts. In fact I think at times they prefer them to the main meal. They did themselves proud on this occasion. We merely had fresh fruit salad, ice creams OR a sumptuous gateau. At 8.20 pm the toffee fondue arrived at the table, then skewers of fruit salad, portions of gateau, as well as ice cream. Seeing both their faces as it arrived was worth every penny of the meal. The smiles and pictures of pleasure they exuded, lasted until we arrived back at the apartment.

Guess what!! The next day Craig's luggage arrived. Great! Just like Christmas all over again as we opened our presents and Craig must have thought it was his birthday, as he could decide which clothes to wear, instead of having to wash the others all the time. Mind you, he had taken it all in his stride and was just enjoying his holiday, like us all.

The 3rd January was the next snowboarding excursion, this time to Cypress Mountain, and before long they were all setting off up the slopes.

Zeni and I decided on something a little more sedate. We went snowshoeing again. We enjoyed it so much the first time. The snow was still clean and pristine as if it had just fallen. Small rivulets of water occasionally rippled into sight, trying to find a way through the fluffy white deposit that was forming a barrier to its passage. The only signs, being those of the smaller animals and birds in the area, or the footprints of the few people who had already made their way along the track, which was deep in snow. We carried on walking, higher than those on the ski slopes. Their small human forms speeding down the white slippery slope to the large assembly area below. The snow laden branches all around, occasionally dropping their burden to the ground as a bird decides to rest its weary body on the thin frail piece of twig extending from the main branch. Each turn of a corner gave a new scene of the mountains above or the valley way down below. Trees towering above or people walking around the buildings and slopes in the distance. We met a lady who had been snowshoeing for years. Unlike us she had ski poles in order to assist with the awkward terrain or help keep her balance negotiating the many lumps and bumps, cracks and crannies along the way. We must get some of those for our next outing!

By the time we returned to the bottom of the ski slope, the family had finished their session and we stopped at the restaurant for a bite to eat.

We then headed to Mount Seymour to see what facilities were offered. It was late afternoon on arrival at the ice covered car park. Some of the cars were sliding into parking spaces, or trying to get moving in order to make way for others. Gingerly we walked to the edge of a nearby slope, giving a view over the city across Burrard Inlet a few miles away. The family walked to the top of a nearby bank. As the sun set, an orange aura appeared from behind a chalet, giving the appearance of the sky being aglow with the heat from sun, then as it sank below the horizon, the chalet became invisible in the darkness now surrounding it.

Needless to say we were all exhausted when we got back to our comfy chairs and a nice cup of coffee with Christmas cake.

Craig suggested a visit to Vancouver Zoo, which the other two endorsed. It is sighted on the outskirts of Greater Vancouver in the Langley area.

The fifth of January was a very cold but clear day. We drove into the car park which had very few cars in the vast open space. It was so cold we decided to have a warming drink before setting off to view the animals, most of which were seeking shelter in their warmer sheds. We saw the tigers as they paced up and down along the side of their enclosure. The huge feet having made a noticeable path, as their all seeing eyes view the outside world and wonder what it would be like to be on the other side of the fence. Wallabies were hopping around, bison, elk and bear patrolling their own territories. As we approach the wolves in their light cream coats, they started howling for their lunch. First one and then another would echo forth their cry. The cacophony of their calls lasting until we were almost ready to leave, half an hour later. The zebra and ostriches were congregating together at the end of their field and in front of their warm wooden home. A few quick photo's of Sarah with a smiling camel, Craig with the colourful monkeys near the entrance, and Giles near the antelope, then back to the car. The heater full on to drive out the bitter cold that had penetrated our clothes.

On a visit to the Capilano Suspension Bridge, Giles decided that he would prefer to stay on firm ground, as the rest of us traversed over the swaying bridge above the fast flowing river below. Sarah bought me a hat for my Christmas present at the souvenir shop, and I must admit that it has travelled thousands of miles and through many countries with me since.

Zeni and I were really sad when on the 7th January the time came to say goodbye to our children at the airport. At 10.40 they walked into the U.S.A. departure area to start their journey home. Everyone's luggage arrived back with them! It was such a marvellous Christmas that we decided we would do it again in the next few years.

Within a few hours of arriving back from the airport, and after a meal in the apartment, we arranged to meet Ray and Liza. On getting out of the lift at "The Sunset Inn", we met another English couple with their son. Phil and Jane Baker had decided to try and emigrate to Vancouver with their son Sam. They too had got disillusioned with the present government in the United Kingdom and opted for a new life in Canada. We arranged to call and see them in their apartment later that evening. It was the start of another good friendship.

Zeni decided to phone Mary Jane in California and she came to visit us for a few days before our return to England, Of course the completion of the apartment was of our uppermost concern now. When will it be completed and how long is the furniture likely to be in storage? Well that's another story.

ISBN 142512046-6

9 781425 120467